IMAGES
of America

OLD TOWN TEMECULA

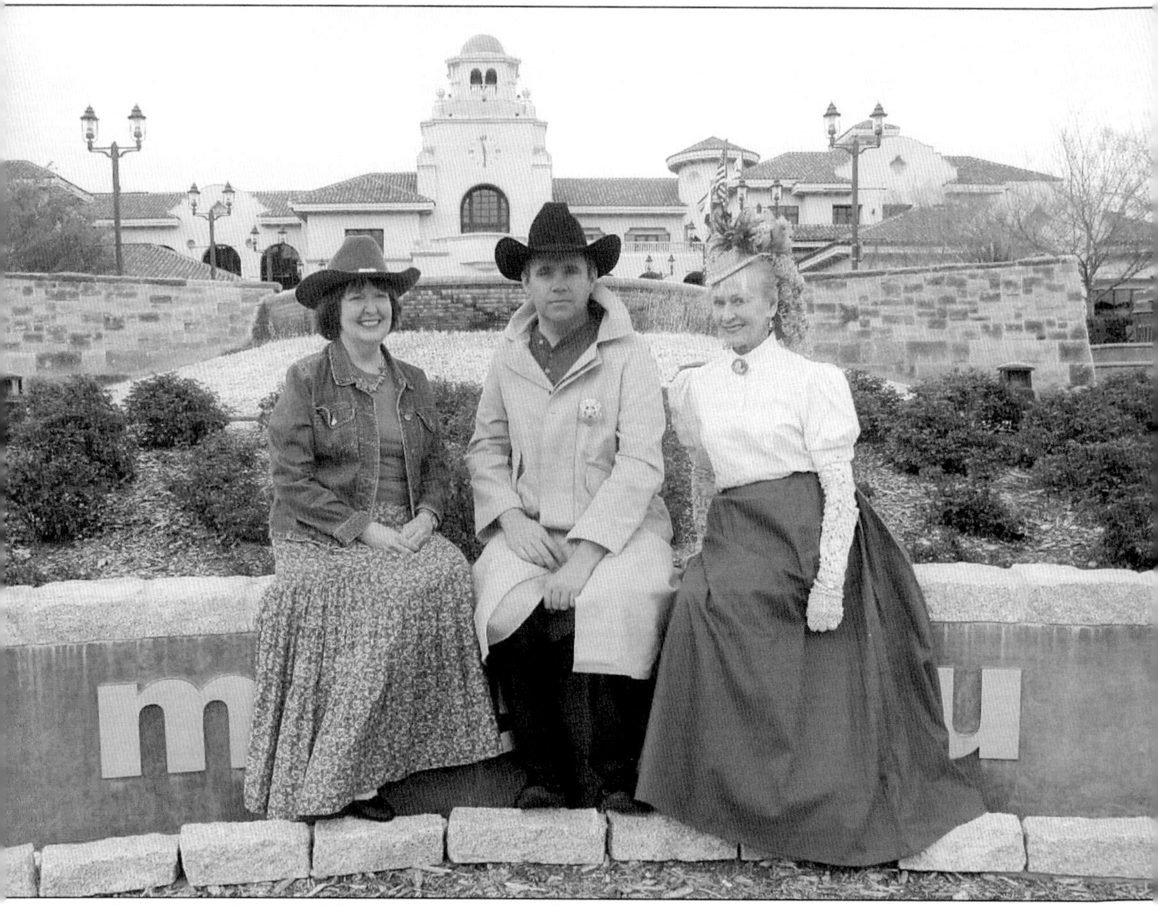

AUTHORS BY LUISEÑO BASKET FOUNTAIN. Rebecca Farnbach, Jeffery Harmon, and Loretta Barnett pose by the fountain at the Temecula Civic Center, which was inspired by a Luiseño Basket and designed by sculptor Christopher Pardell. The fountain and civic center symbolize the bridge of time between the first residents of the Old Town area to present day with a view toward the future. (Bonnie Martland.)

ON THE COVER: HISTORIC OLD TOWN. The blacksmith in his doorway, shaded from the heat of the day in the dusty little town at the end of the railroad tracks, did not dream of the bustling city of over 100,000 people that would be at his doorstep within 100 years. Likewise, it is not known what lays ahead for the historic Old Town, but one can hope there will always be remembrance of the past. (Temecula Valley Museum.)

IMAGES
of America

OLD TOWN TEMECULA

Loretta Barnett, Rebecca Farnbach,
and Jeffery Harmon
for the Vail Ranch Restoration Association

ARCADIA
PUBLISHING

ISBN 978-0-7385-9590-0

Published by Arcadia Publishing
Charleston, South Carolina

Printed in the United States of America

Library of Congress Control Number: 2012937256

For all general information, please contact Arcadia Publishing:
Telephone 843-853-2070
Fax 843-853-0044
E-mail sales@arcadiapublishing.com
For customer service and orders:
Toll-Free 1-888-313-2665

Visit us on the Internet at www.arcadiapublishing.com

To John Bianchi, Tommy Hotchkiss, Sam Hicks, Bob Morris, and others who, in 1977, envisioned and promoted the 1890s Western theme for Old Town Temecula

Contents

Acknowledgments

The Vail Ranch Restoration Association (VaRRA) and the authors Jeffery Harmon (JH), Rebecca Farnbach (RF), and Loretta Barnett (LB) thank the following people and organizations for their generous donations of time, images, and information.

We thank the Pechanga Cultural Resources Department (PCRD), Pechanga Tribal Chairman Mark Macarro, Lisa Woodward, PhD, and Teresa Lorden for providing information and images for Chapter One. We thank Raymond Basquez Sr. (RB) for supplying photographs from his personal collection. We thank the National Anthropological Archives, Smithsonian Institution (NAA), and National Archives (NA) for use of images in their collection. We also thank the Temecula Valley Museum (TVM), the San Diego History Center (SDHC), and Sherman Library (SL) for supplying images. Thank you John W. Robinson (JWR) for donating the photograph and research files on Horace Magee. We thank Dell Random House for permission to use McNeil photographs from the June 1949 edition of *Front Page Detective*.

Thank you Jack Roripaugh (JR), David Barnett (DB), Robert "Bob" Morris (RM), Gene and Barbara Tobin (GT), Marvin Curran (MC), Judy Knott (JK), Tony Guenther (TG), Otto and Nancy Baron (OB), Judy Otto Jones (JJ), Edward and Peggy Querry (EQ), Roger Honberger (RH), Jesus Gutierrez (JG), Marilyn Kitch Selover and Lori Selover Zaviski (MK/LZ), John Moramarco (JM), Judy Parker Hancock (JPH), Irene Hotchkiss (IH), Stephen Eldred Photography (SE), and Robert Motroni (ROM) for donating images and information for the book.

We thank Anne J. Miller, PhD, John Hunneman, and Dick Fox for supplying information and proofreading for accuracy. Thank you Robin Smith for sharing information on Temecula school history. Thanks to the Temecula Museum staff for help finding photographs. We thank Malcolm Barnett and Darell Farnbach (DF) for their assistance in compiling this book. Special thanks go to Bonnie Martland (BM), current president of the Temecula Valley Historical Society (TVHS), for taking some of the modern-day images.

We also want to acknowledge the diligent work and dedication of Sam Hicks, Horace Parker, Tom Hudson, Bill Cox, Bill Harker, and Phil Brigandi who researched and published stories about people and past events in Temecula Valley history. These chroniclers kept the spark alive that eventually lit the flame to honor the heritage of this historical area and left paper trails for us to follow.

INTRODUCTION

Everyone senses shadows of the past in the historic Old Town Temecula. Some traces are covered, while others, still present, capture our imagination. You may wonder which buildings in Old Town are authentic and which were designed to keep the spirit of this little Western town alive. In this book, we have attempted to present a faithful account of the buildings, events, and people who influenced the once fledgling village nestled along the hills and old railway.

What will you learn from this book? Let's start at the beginning with information given directly from the Pechanga Tribe. The Temecula Indians (Temecula Indians of the 1800s, because of the eviction of 1875, today exist under the identity of Pechanga), like many other groups in the area under the jurisdiction of the San Luis Rey Mission in Oceanside, are referred to as Luiseño. Temecula is a name of Native American derivation. Although popular local musical plays and publications romanticized the translation as "where the sun shines through the mist," that is not correct. The name is actually derived from two words, 'Exva Teméeku, which together represent to the Luiseño the place where all things—trees, rocks, plants, animals, and people—were created. *'Exva* is from the word *'éxla*, which means "sand," and *Teméeku* is from the word *temét*, which means "sun," so together *'éxva teméeku* means the "place of sand and sun" or where the earth came together with the sky. This location is named in Luiseño traditional songs and narratives as the place of creation.

The name is in reference to Túukumit Father Night Sky and to Tamáayawut Mother Day Earth of which all of the First People, the Káamalam, were born. When Temét, the sun, was born he was so bright that he hurt his siblings. So Tamáayawut put him away until he was ready to be cast into the sky from 'Exva Teméeku. The Luiseño language attaches the suffix "-nga" to indicate it is a place. When the Spanish missionaries arrived they probably heard the name 'Exva Teméekunga and not being able to pronounce it, they changed it to Temecula.

Local Luiseño people lived, loved, and played along the creeks and through the verdant lands of the Temecula Valley until the day their world was invaded by usurpers under the Spanish Crown and under the guise of the Catholic Church. Thereafter, the Luiseño Indians were enslaved as a convenient workforce for the mission. In his October 3, 1797, journal entry, Fr. Fermin Lasuen wrote that he and his companions climbed over the Santa Rosa Mountains and entered the Temecula Valley, calling the Indian village "Temaco."

Within a few years, every part of life in the valley changed. The Mission San Luis Rey de Francia, headquartered in present-day Oceanside, established an outpost on the high granite hill south of the village. Grapes, wheat, and corn were cultivated, and livestock was raised in the valley to benefit the mission.

In 1834, the Mexican government secularized California missions. Then, no longer owned or administered by the Roman Catholic Church and Spain, valuable mission lands became Mexican land grants made available to private owners.

In 1844, after heated competition with other notables including Gov. Pio Pico, a 26,000-acre Rancho Temecula was given to Mexican army officer Felix Valdez by the Mexican governor. The land spread roughly from today's Temecula Parkway to Clinton Keith Road, west to the Santa Rosa Mountains, and east approximately to Butterfield Stage Road. It included land that would later be the original townsites for Temecula and Murrieta.

In 1846, Jean Louis Vignes took ownership of the rancho. Vignes, a Frenchman and one of the first commercial winemakers in California, also owned the neighboring Rancho Pauba that spanned from the eastern border of Rancho Temecula to beyond today's Vail Lake and approximately from Temecula Parkway to Rancho California Road. Jacob Snyder, a signer of the California State Constitution, purchased both ranchos from Vignes in 1853. In 1873, Spaniards Domingo Pujol, Francisco Sanjurjo, and brothers Juan and Ezequiel Murrieta purchased Ranchos Temecula and Pauba, altogether 25,675 acres at $1.50 an acre for a total of $77,055.

The newcomers removed Native Americans from their lands, considering the earliest inhabitants squatters. They also disputed with the Indians regarding ownership of livestock. Indians were evicted at gunpoint from their self-sufficient homeland in Pauba Valley in 1875 and were dispossessed and homeless for eight years. This eventually led to the establishment of the Pechanga Reservation along the Pechanga Creek in 1882.

The name Pechanga (pronounced *pe-CHONG-ah*) means "where water is drips." From 1882 to the present, they have been known as the Pechanga Band of Luiseño Indians.

The commercial center of Temecula started at the Wolf Store adobe in the Little Temecula Rancho, near present-day Redhawk and Temecula Parkways. In 1882, the New Town of Temecula began when the California Southern Railroad constructed tracks along the western foothills. A new town was laid out around a train depot, starting what we now call Old Town.

In 1905, Walter Vail came to the valley and purchased parts of Ranchos Pauba, Little Temecula, Santa Rosa, and about half of Rancho Temecula, amassing an 87,500-acre cattle ranch. The little town of Temecula was surrounded by Vail land, stagnating growth. Like an old-time Western movie set, Temecula had Main Street saloons with hitching posts outside and gunfights between cowboys and Indians.

Times changed with the introduction of automobiles, telephones, electricity, and the paving of Highway 395 through the heart of town. In 1964, the Vail Ranch was sold to developer Kaiser-Aetna for $21 million, who designed a new planned community named Rancho California. New homes and industries popped up where cattle had grazed. By 1989, the little settlement of 2,000 people grew to 27,000, and the city of Temecula was born. When citizens voted for cityhood in 1989, they chose the name Temecula to honor the name of the original village.

Some have constructed buildings to resemble those of the past; others have started events to celebrate bygone days. At times, developers like Zev Buffman have proposed to turn Old Town into a music destination. Changes have come, and it is time to view the real Old Town as it was.

With several eras of historical significance for Old Town Temecula, we made a decision to consolidate some of the stories, so you may see the Machado Store, for example, on a two-page spread that spans 70 years of history, then turn the page to see the Escallier Pool Hall in the early 1900s. We determined that carrying through a story line would be better than to break it up into several sections in the book. Sometimes the photographs of one building were taken during different periods of time compared to the photographs of the building next to it, so readers need to adjust to a little back-and-forth time travel.

To organize chapter themes, we are beginning each with familiar emblems. Four chapters start with images of the bronze medallions embedded in the sidewalks at the corners of Main and Front Streets, one is a logo, and the final chapter opens with the image of one of the arches defining the historic district.

To gain a full perspective of the scope of Temecula history, we recommend using both this book and our Images of America: *Temecula*, available at the Little Temecula History Center, at local bookstores, and from online book retailers. For any duplication of photographs in the two books, we have told different facets of the story.

We apologize that we could not mention every important person, family, or event in this small volume. Perhaps, we did not have knowledge of them at the time of writing or we may not have had access to adequate resources to present the stories here. If you believe we have neglected to tell part of the Old Town Temecula story, we would like to invite you to contact us at info@vailranch.org. We will be pleased to present the stories in our quarterly newsletter.

One

Native American Origins

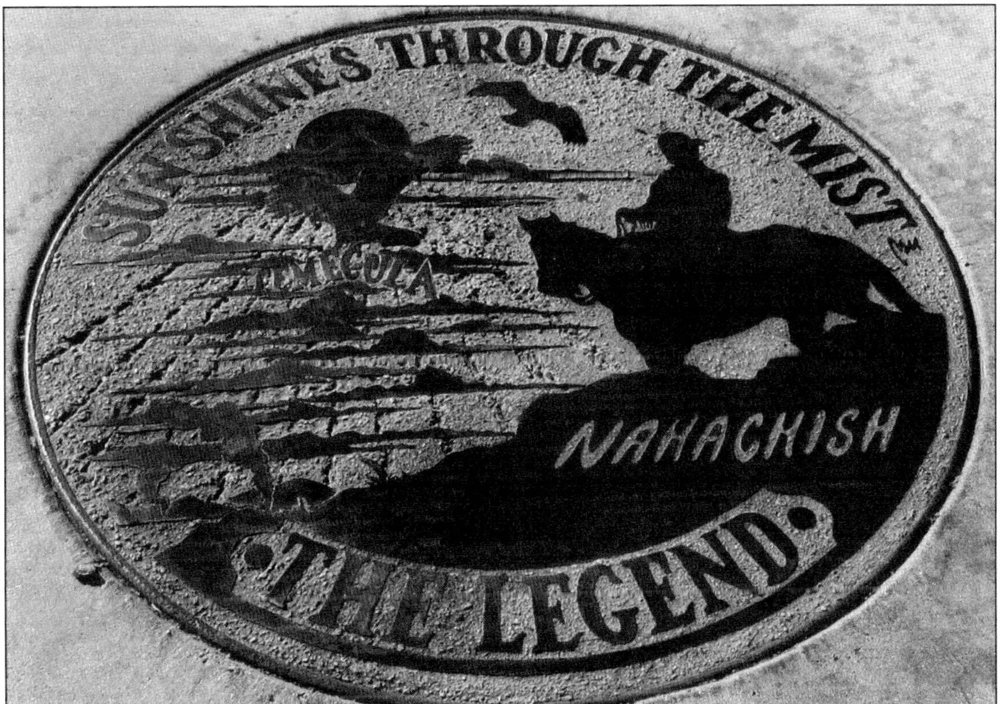

Naháchish Medallion. This medallion honors Naháchish, an ancient person a generation or two removed from the Káamalam, the First Children of the Creation, who named many of the places throughout the Luiseño ancestral territory. It is said that Naháchish was killed on the trail from Rainbow to Temecula, now known as Rainbow Canyon Road and turned into a rock that is on the east side of the highway, between the towns of Temecula and Rainbow. (BM.)

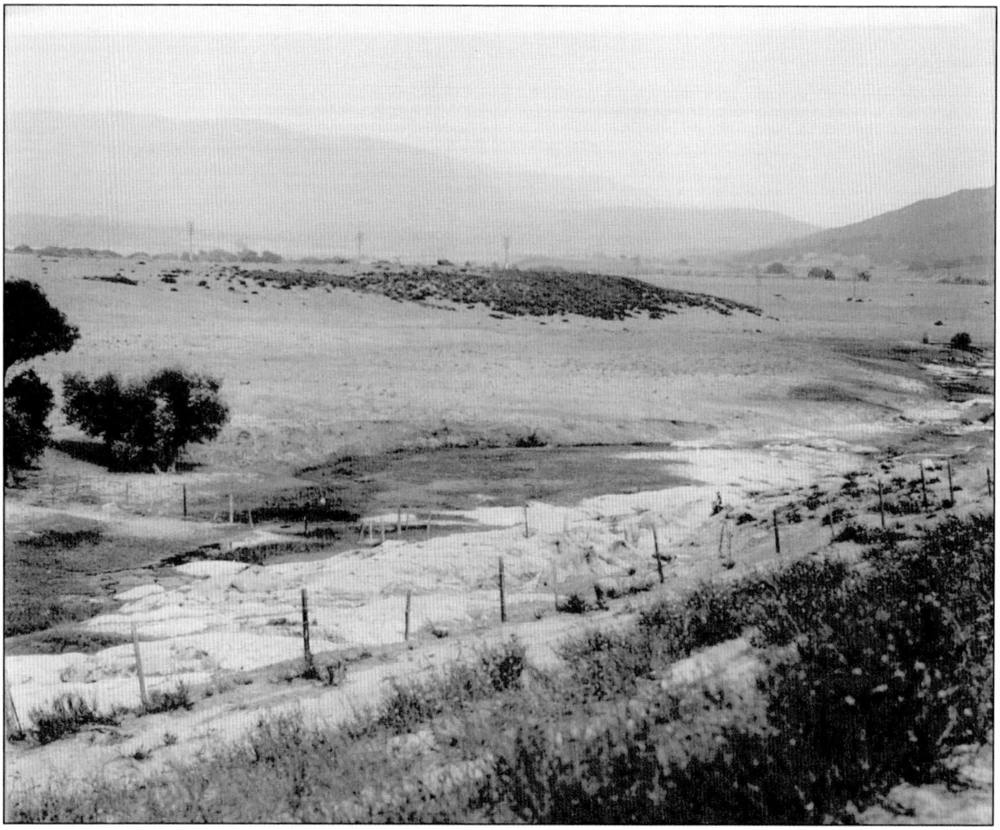

Murrieta Creek, Looking South. While visiting Temecula in 1932, linguist John P. Harrington took this photograph just south of Old Town. A few years earlier, cattle were driven through this area to be loaded onto the train. Notice the lack of vegetation in the photograph; it is a stark contrast to how the verdant creek looks today. (NAA.)

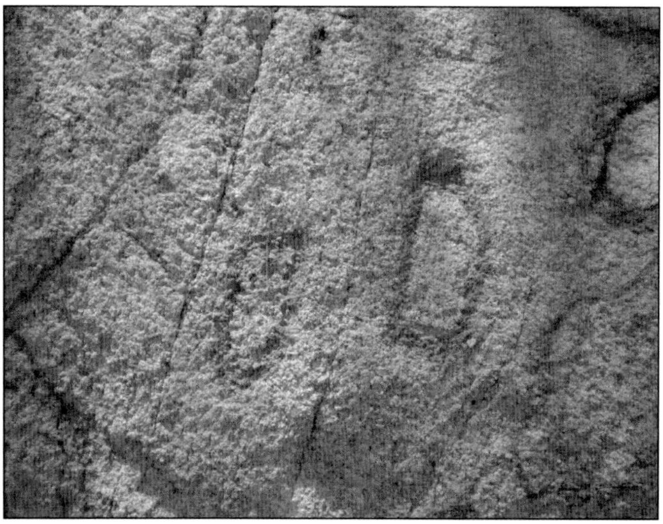

Footprint Stones. It is said that before the rocks became solid, the Káamalam, the First People, left their footprints in certain areas. These features are not common and are only found in a few places in Luiseño territory. Two sets of rocks with footprints are found along the bank of Murrieta Creek near the mouth of Temecula Canyon. Several of Harrington's Luiseño consultants commented on the presence and importance of these foot tracks. (PCRD.)

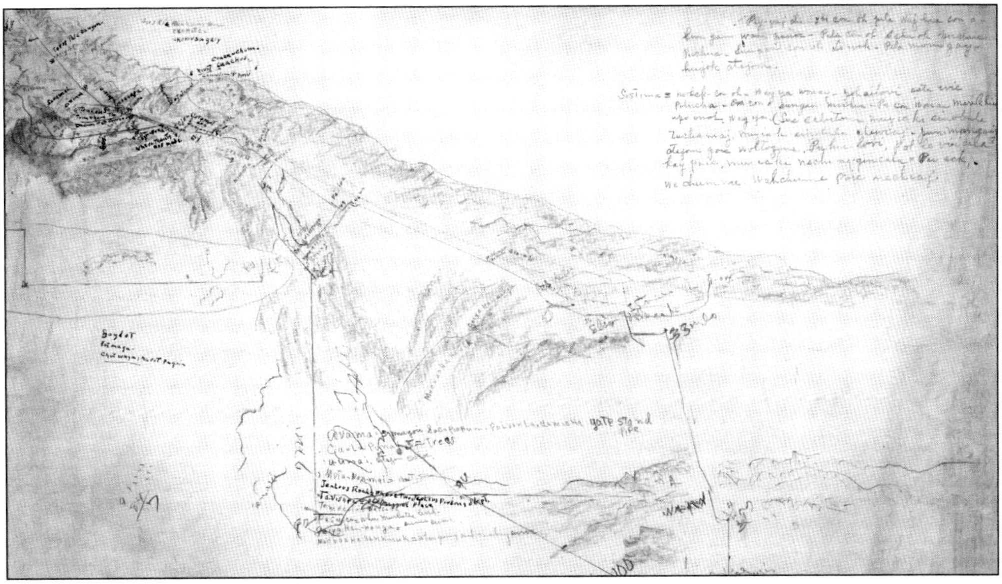

J.P. Harrington's Map. This map of the Temecula-Elsinore Valley contains the Luiseño names of places. Although the creator of the map is unknown, due to its extensive and detailed cultural information, it was most likely compiled by a person from the Pechanga Reservation for John P. Harrington, a linguist employed by the Bureau of American Ethnology, who visited the area in 1932–1933. (NAA.)

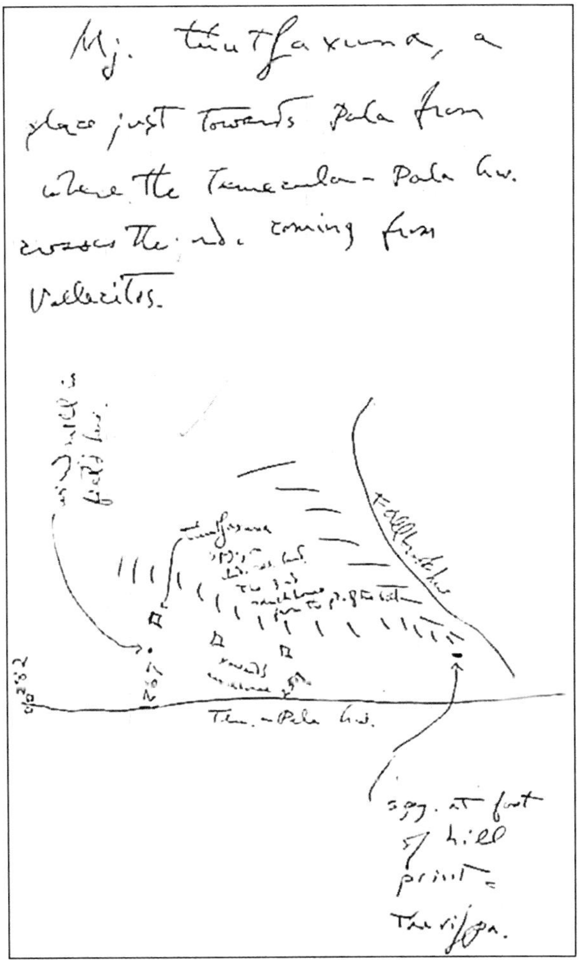

J.P. Harrington Text Description. John P. Harrington was a linguist and ethnographer employed by the Bureau of American Ethnology from 1915 to 1951. He dedicated the majority of his 40-year career to documenting the languages and cultures of the Native Peoples of California and the Southwest. In the early 1930s, he interviewed many Luiseño people residing on the Indian reservations in Riverside and San Diego Counties. (NAA.)

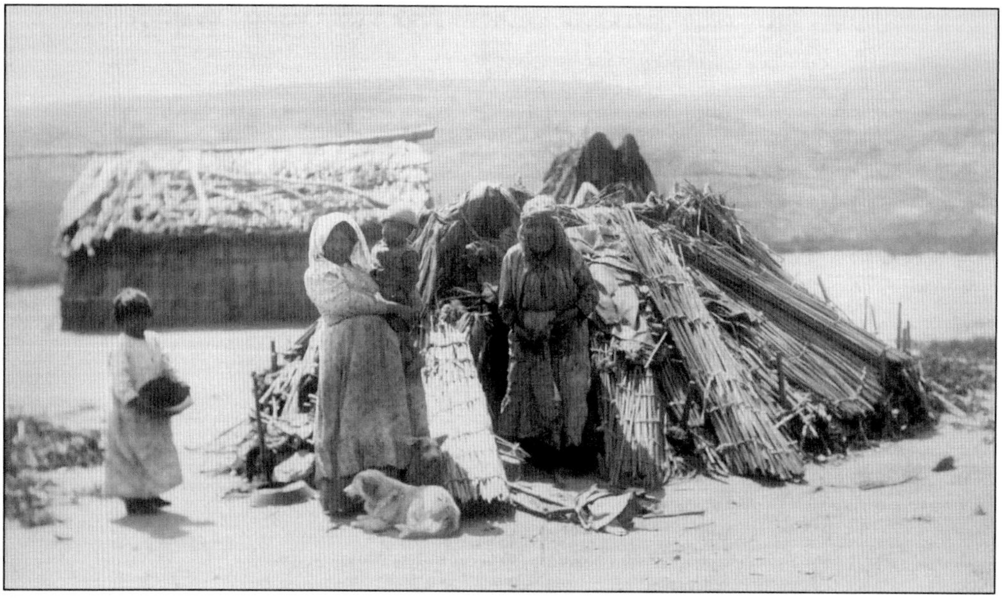

Old Woman at San Luis Rey Village. After the missions were secularized in 1834, the Luiseño people originally from that area remained in their village near the mission. This image shows both the traditional and Western styles of house construction. The house in the foreground is made of tule. The house in the background is made from willow and tule in the Western style. (NAA.)

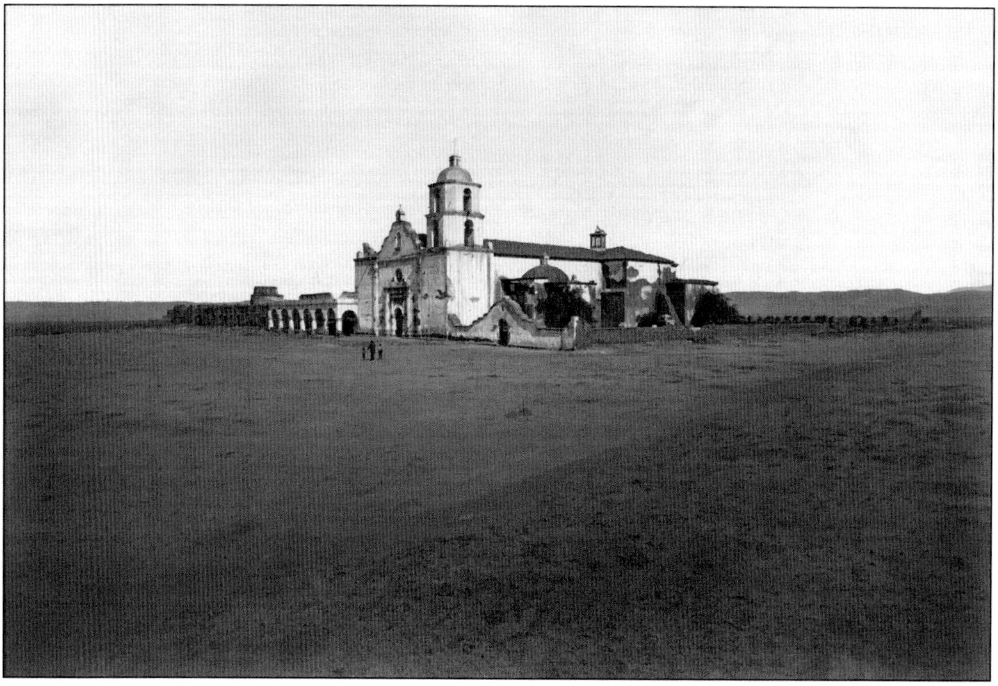

San Luis Rey. The mission, established in Oceanside in 1798, became known as the largest of all the California missions with 3,000 Indians under its rule. The tribe name Luiseño is derived from the name of this mission: San Luís Rey de Fráncia. A Luiseño or San Luiseño was an Indian under the control and jurisdiction of Mission San Luis Rey. The Temecula Valley mission outpost was on the hill south of the confluence of the creeks. (PCRD.)

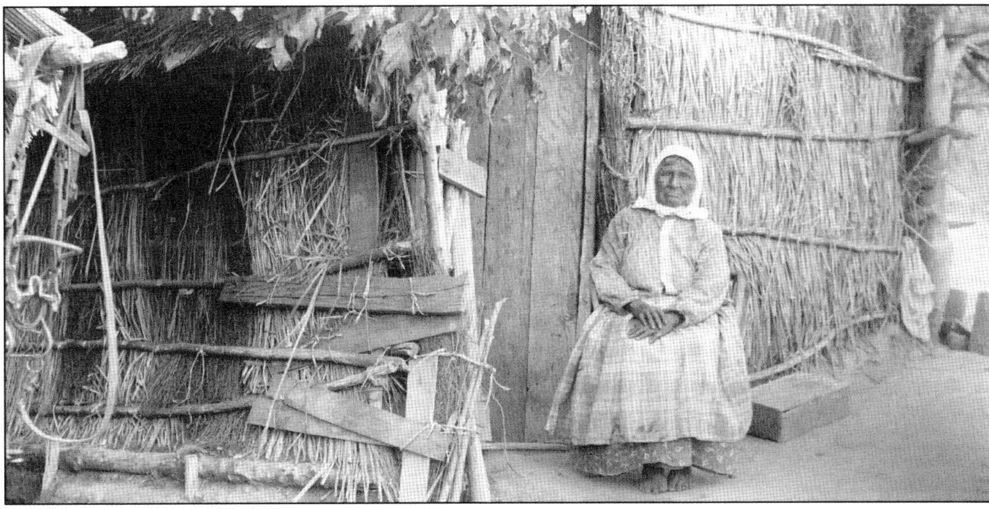

Grejovia Pa by Brush House. In 1894, Grejovia was the oldest resident of the Pechanga Reservation. Born the same year the Mission San Luis Rey was founded, she made adobe bricks for the Pala Mission as a child. While the older Indians were in chapel learning their catechism, the younger children were punished if they failed to make their daily quota of bricks. (NAA.)

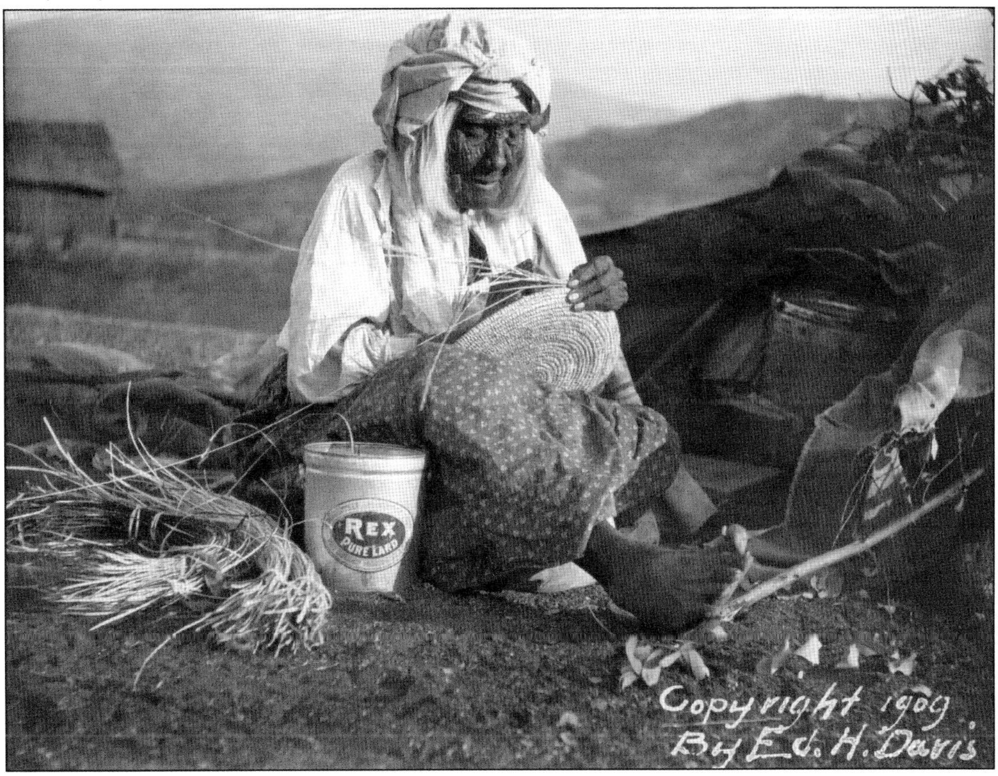

Leona Kengish Weaving, 1909. According to Leona's obituary in 1915, she was the oldest woman in Riverside County, who passed at the age of 113 while sitting in her jacal, weaving a basket. It also stated that, though deaf and nearly blind for 20 years, Leona sat daily in the open with boughs at her back, the traditional, untethered windbreak, described as the only habitation of many of the Indians. There, she sat and wove baskets. (SDHC.)

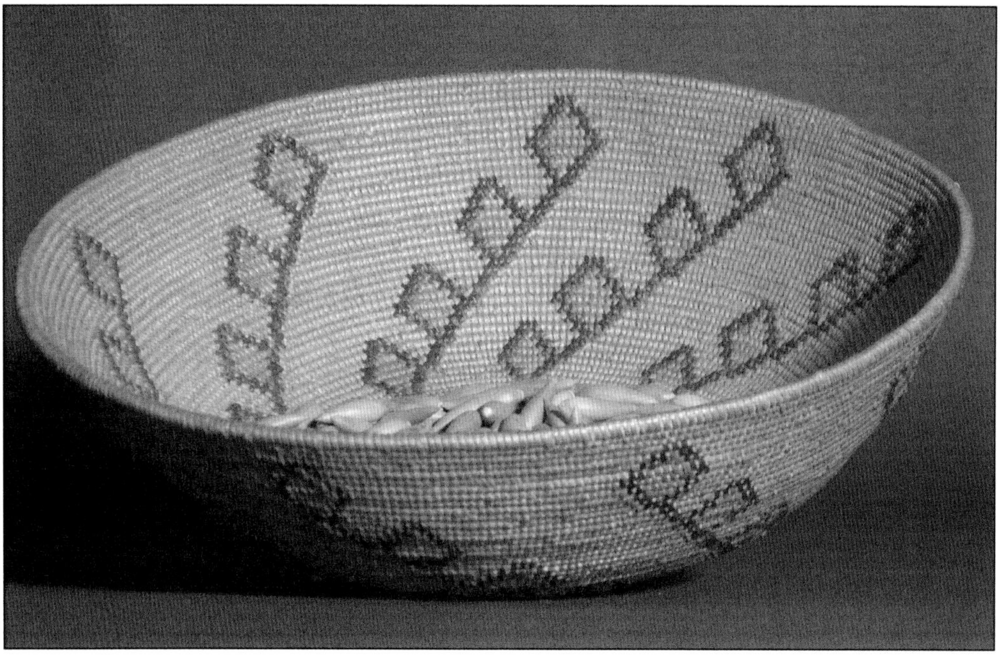

Luiseno Basket with Acorns. Acorns were an important food to the Luiseño and many other tribes throughout California. Large acorns, called *kwiila*, found at higher elevations, were preferred. Families camped on Palomar Mountain in the fall to harvest *kwiila*. They stored acorns in a woven granary. This basket shows a typical Luiseño pattern. Some of the Luiseño baskets were woven tightly enough to hold water. (PCRD.)

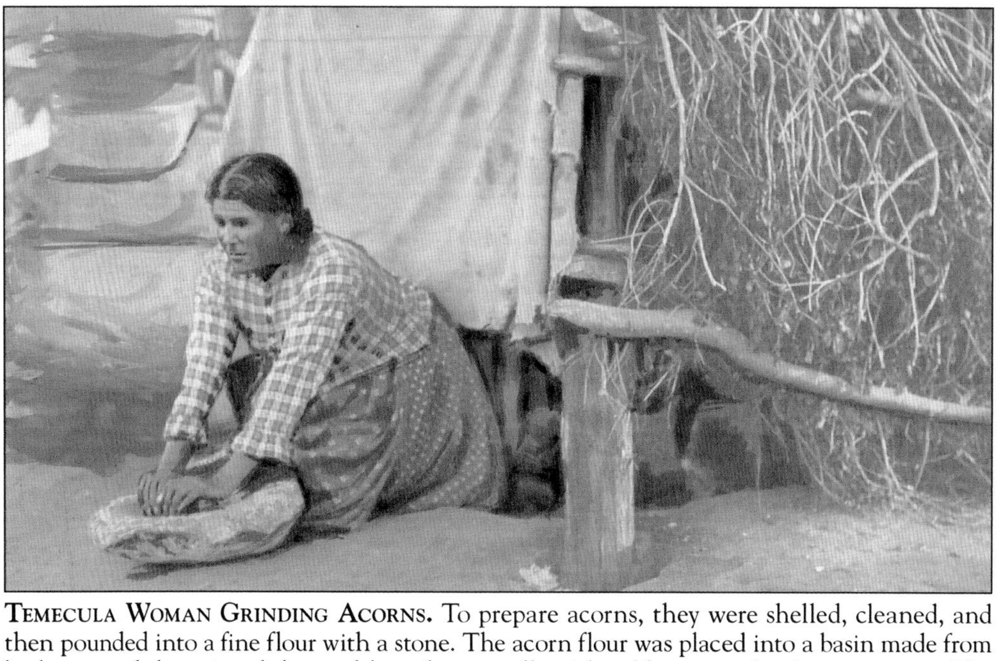

Temecula Woman Grinding Acorns. To prepare acorns, they were shelled, cleaned, and then pounded into a fine flour with a stone. The acorn flour was placed into a basin made from basketry, and then rinsed thoroughly and repeatedly with cold water to leach out tannins. The acorn flour was combined with water in a watertight basket and then cooked like gravy over low heat while stirring constantly. (PCRD.)

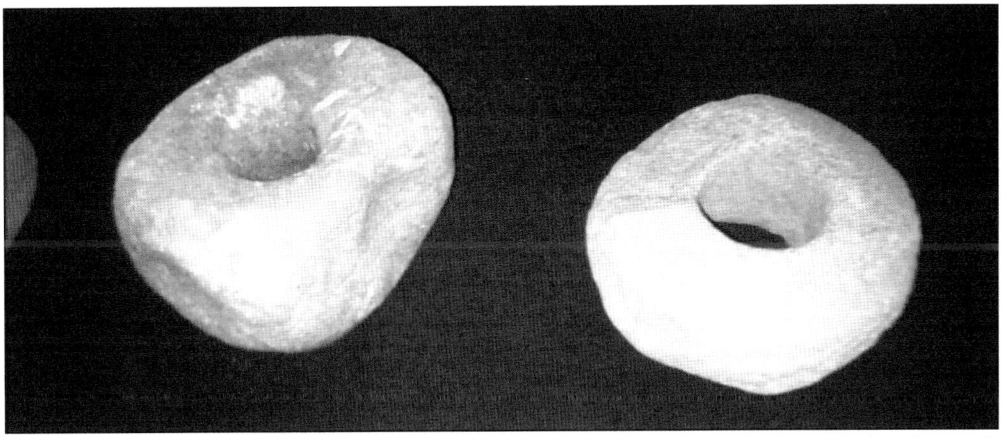

Cooking Stones. Hot rocks from the fire were added to a basket to cook acorn mush. The mush was included as a starchy but highly nutritious part of every meal, in the same way potatoes, rice, wheat, or corn products are used. Sometimes bits of meat were added to flavor the mush. The prepared acorn is called *wíiwish* in Luiseño. The rocks measure about four inches across. (RF.)

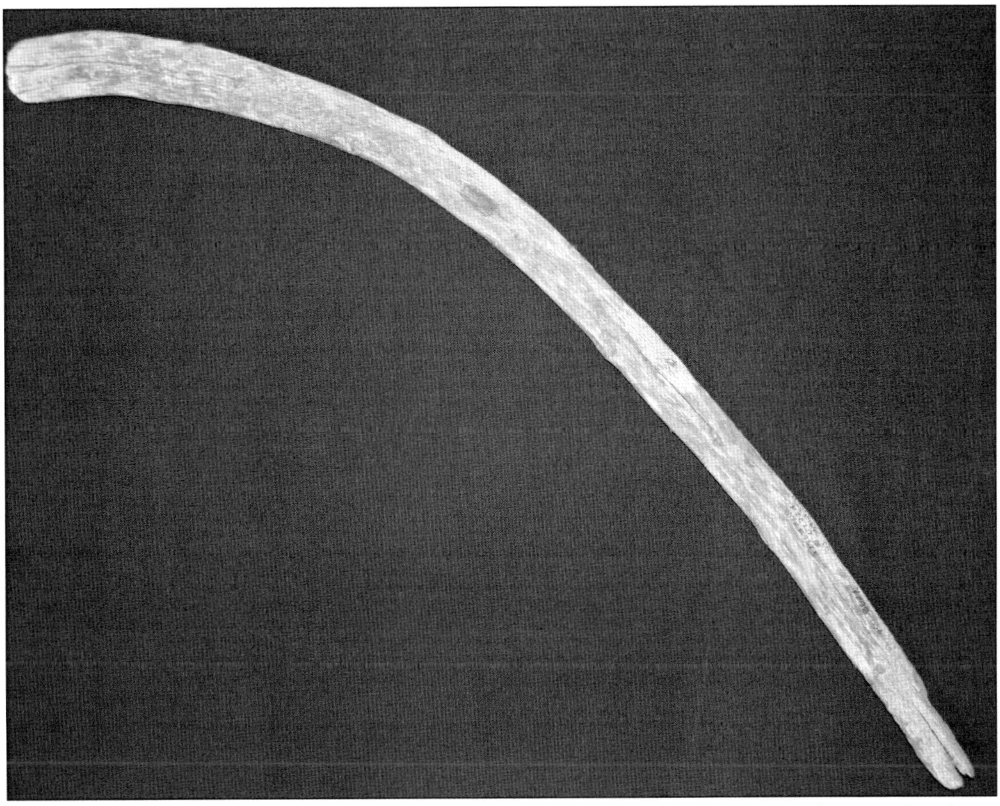

Throwing Stick. This hunting tool, called *wáakat* in Luiseño, was most often used to hunt rabbits. It resembles the Australian boomerang but does not return to the person when thrown. It was easiest to catch rabbits in the early morning or evening. A hunt leader and a small group of men conducted the rabbit hunt. Since rabbits could be found year-round, it was a staple food. (PCRD.)

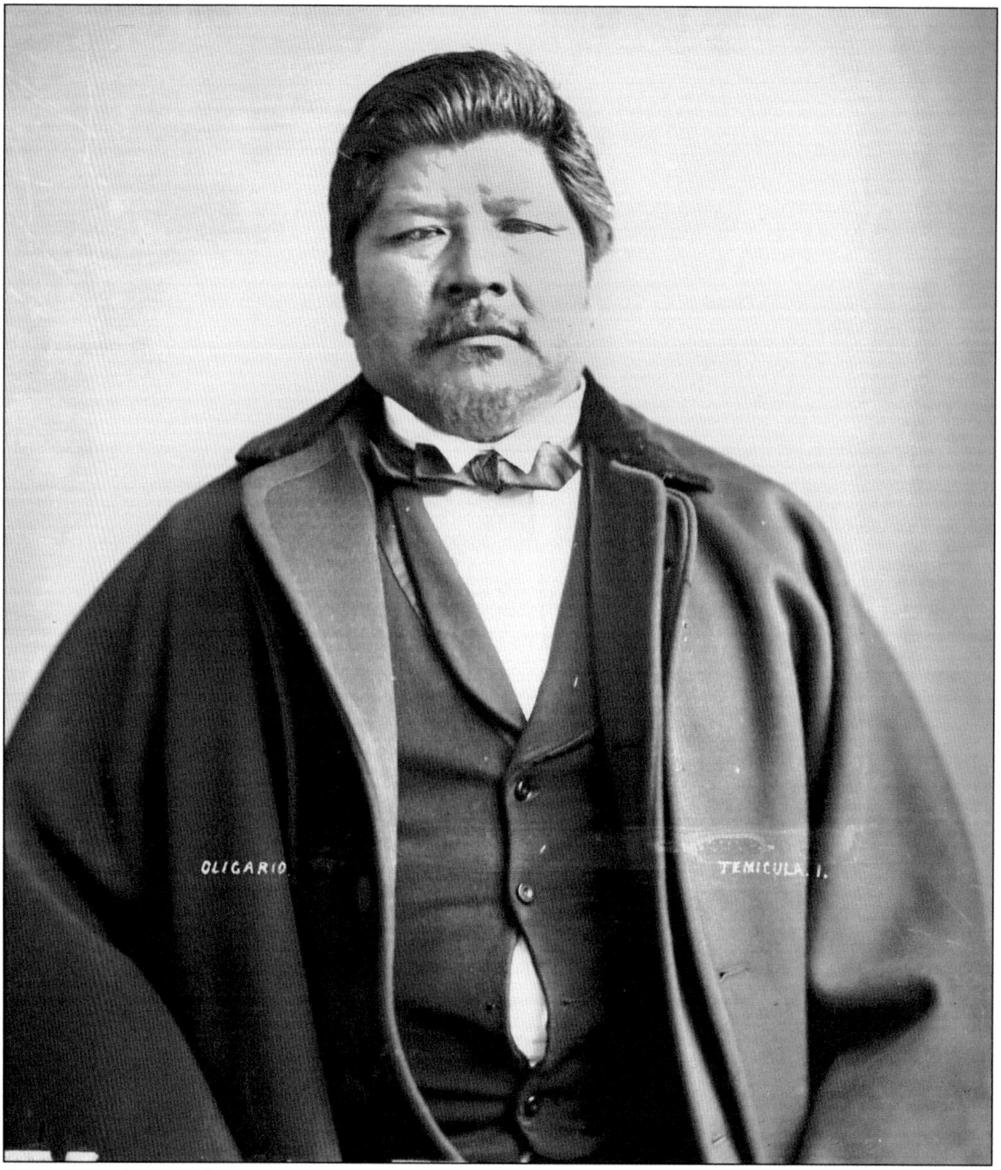

Olegario Calac. Beginning on September 20, 1875, between 200 to 300 Temecula Indians were evicted over three days' time by San Diego sheriff Nicholas Hunsaker and 20 armed men. The Indians did not fight back because they would be shot. They protested by sitting down and refusing to move any of their belongings. They were forced to abandon crops and livestock and to leave the village following wagons filled with their belongings. Once they were off their homeland village, the eviction posse threw all their possessions onto the ground, smashing pottery that contained food and belongings. Under the Ejection Decree, confiscation of the Indians' property was permitted to recoup the costs incurred. Some of the livestock the Indians took with them wandered back to the ranch. The ranch owner corralled them and requested compensation. The original Indian owners were accused of rustling the livestock. In most cases, the Indians did not have the funds to reclaim their livestock, and the animals were sold for profit. After the eviction, Olegario Calac traveled to Washington, DC, as part of a delegation to inquire about their rights. (PCRD.)

SALVADOR QUILIQ. Salvador was born in 1834 and raised in the Aguanga area as a young child. His son Merchol attended Sherman Indian School and became a carpenter; his skills were known on most reservations in Southern California. He built a "modern" home for his parents in 1915. He also constructed the pews for the Pechanga Church, which are still in use. Merchol also served on the Pechanga Tribal Council. (RB.)

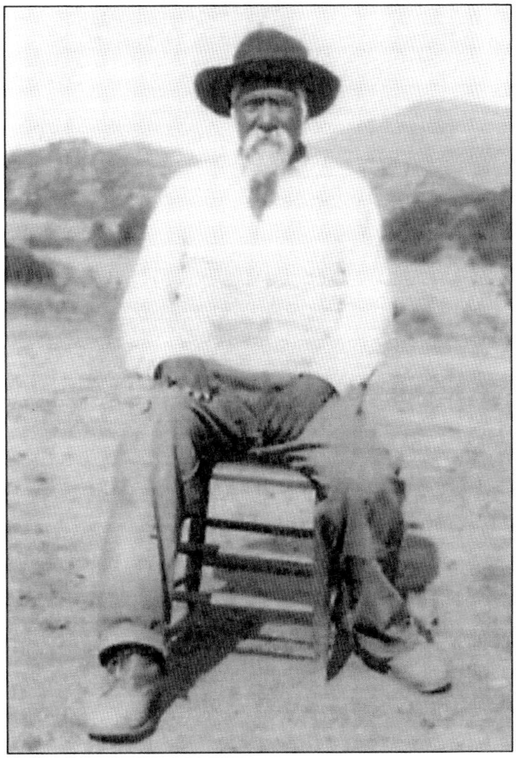

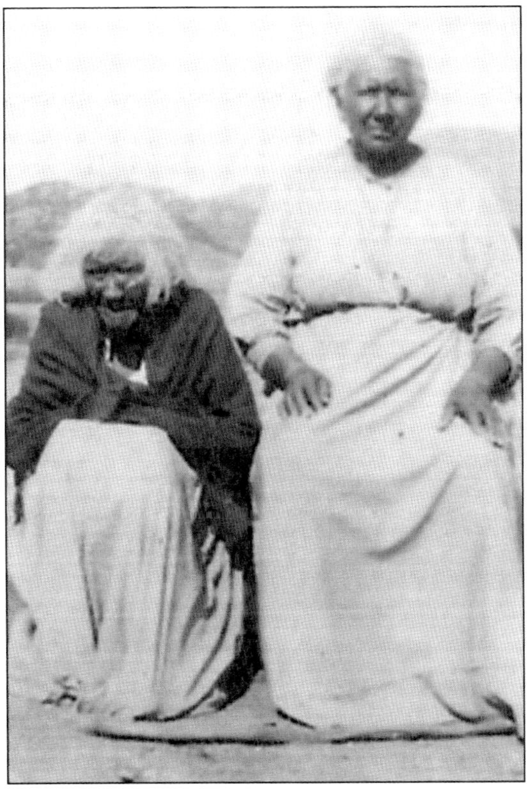

LEONA KENGISH AND MICAELA QUILIQ. Born around 1845 in Temecula, Micaela (right) was the daughter of Leona (left) and the wife of Salvador Quiliq. Micaela and Salvador were well respected in the Pechanga community and they often aided other tribal members. Leona was a renowned basket weaver, and one of her baskets is in the Southwest Museum's collection. Kengish is shown weaving a basket in the bottom image on page 13. (RB.)

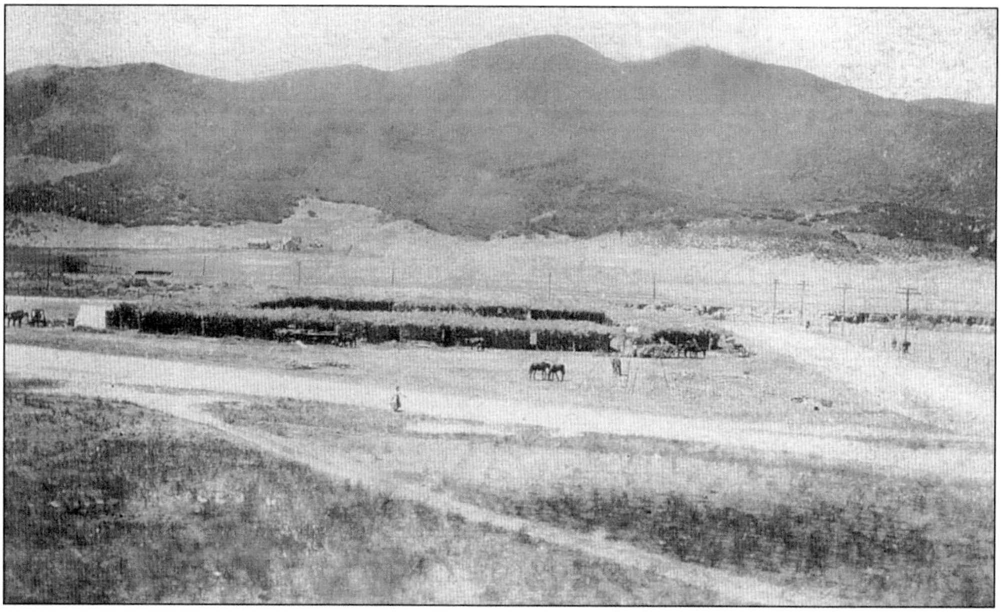

Temecula Fiesta Grounds. This place called *Kutúumut Hánganqat* in Luiseño, which means the "flag flying place," was a social gathering area. The image shows the fiesta held on the property owned by a Native American family that is located across from today's Dan's Feed and Seed, adjacent to First Street Bridge. (LB.)

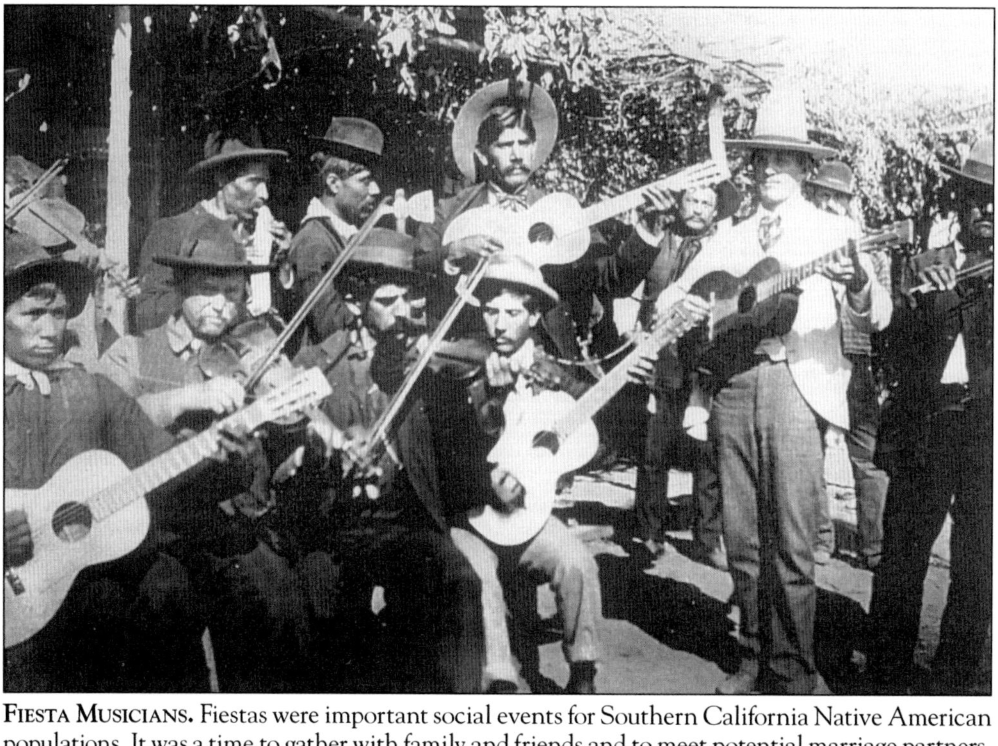

Fiesta Musicians. Fiestas were important social events for Southern California Native American populations. It was a time to gather with family and friends and to meet potential marriage partners. Entertainment included music, dancing, and playing *téeponish/pión*, a traditional gambling strategy game. Participants competed in horseback riding and other athletic events. (LB.)

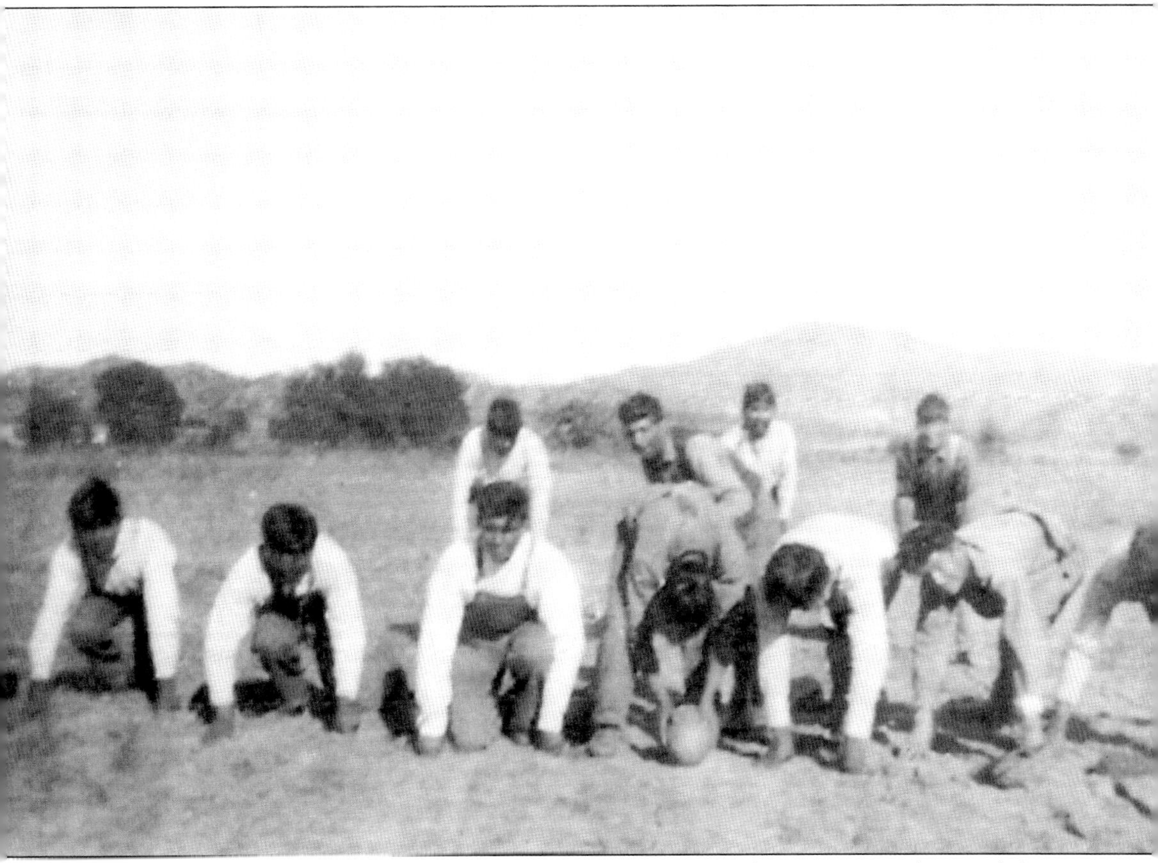

Pechanga Football Team, 1905. A note says "Pichanga Foot Ball team, 1905. Who met defeat at the hands of Temecula team after a hard struggle. The score standing 5 to 0 in favor of the giants." Native American students were introduced to sports when they were forced to attend boarding schools such as Sherman Indian School in Riverside and Carlisle in the East. This team was made up of some of these students who brought football back to the reservation. They often played local non-Indian teams. Dan Magee, a brother of Horace Magee, was a star football player for the Sherman Indians. Pete Calac and Reginald Attache played with the Oorang Indians in 1922 with Jim Thorpe, the football legend. (RB.)

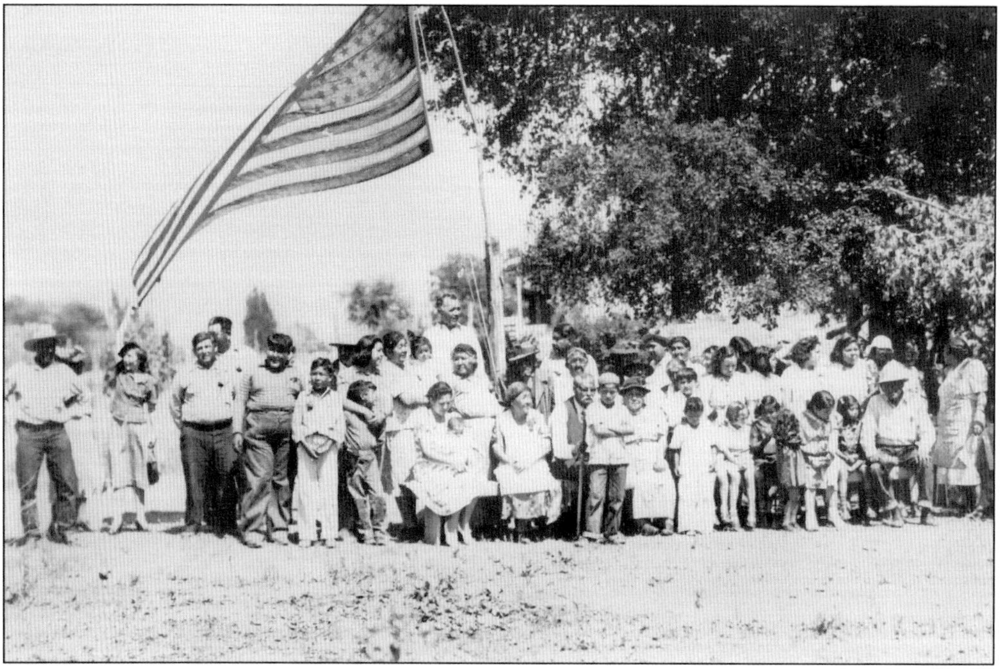

Mother's Day at Pechanga, 1940. A census taker learned while visiting Erle Stanley Gardner's ranch that several Pechanga families had four generations living at the same time. Gardner arranged for his photographer to capture the families together in one photograph. The census taker was able to document the large number of families that had multiple generations alive in 1940. (RB.)

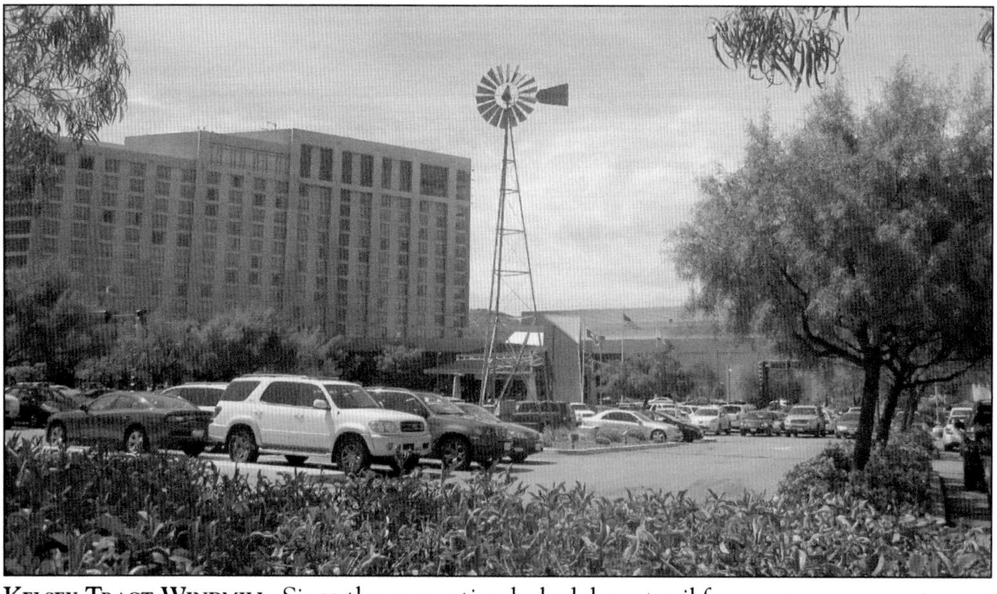

Kelsey Tract Windmill. Since the reservation lacked decent soil for crops, government agent Charles E. Kelsey negotiated the purchase of additional land for the tribe in 1907. Heads of households were assigned plots to farm. This 1930s windmill is located in the same spot as the original, which is now in the Pechanga Casino parking lot. The Pechanga people see the windmill as a link to a perspective of their historical past. (BM.)

Two

ARRIVAL OF OTHERS

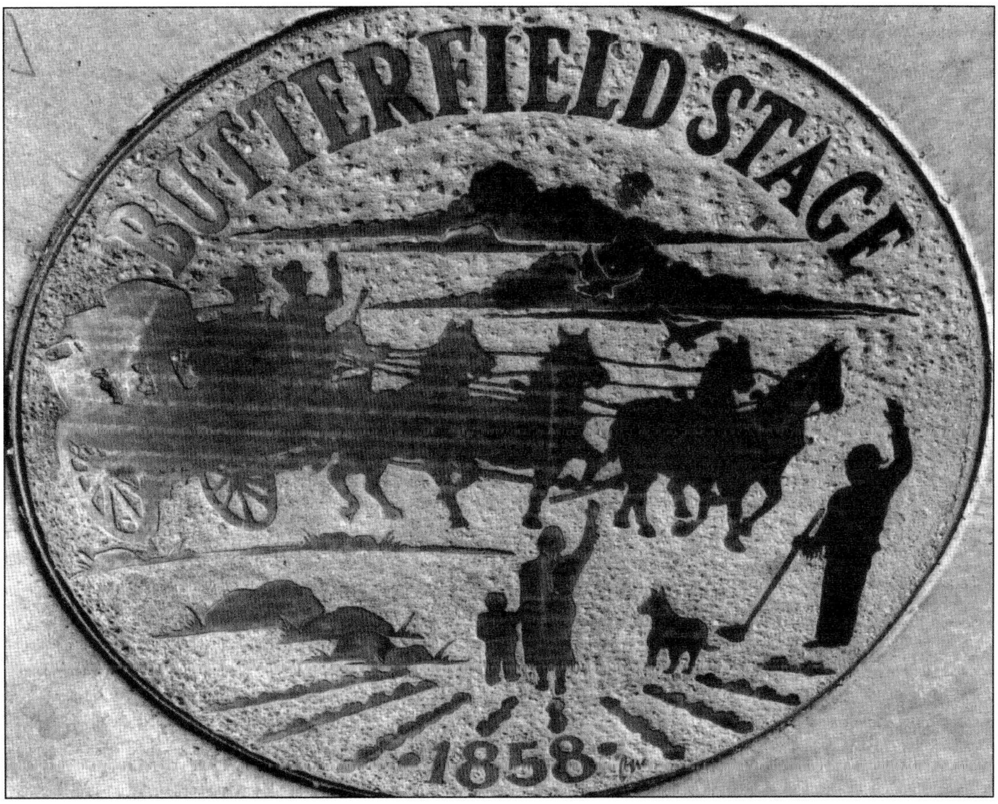

BUTTERFIELD STAGE MEDALLION. First used as an Indian footpath, the Southern Emigrant Trail, later utilized by the Butterfield Overland Mail, was the only year-round route to California. This well-worn route eventually brought thousands of people, horses, and wagons into Southern California. The trail passed through the Old Town area, following the foothills of the Santa Rosa Mountains. (BM.)

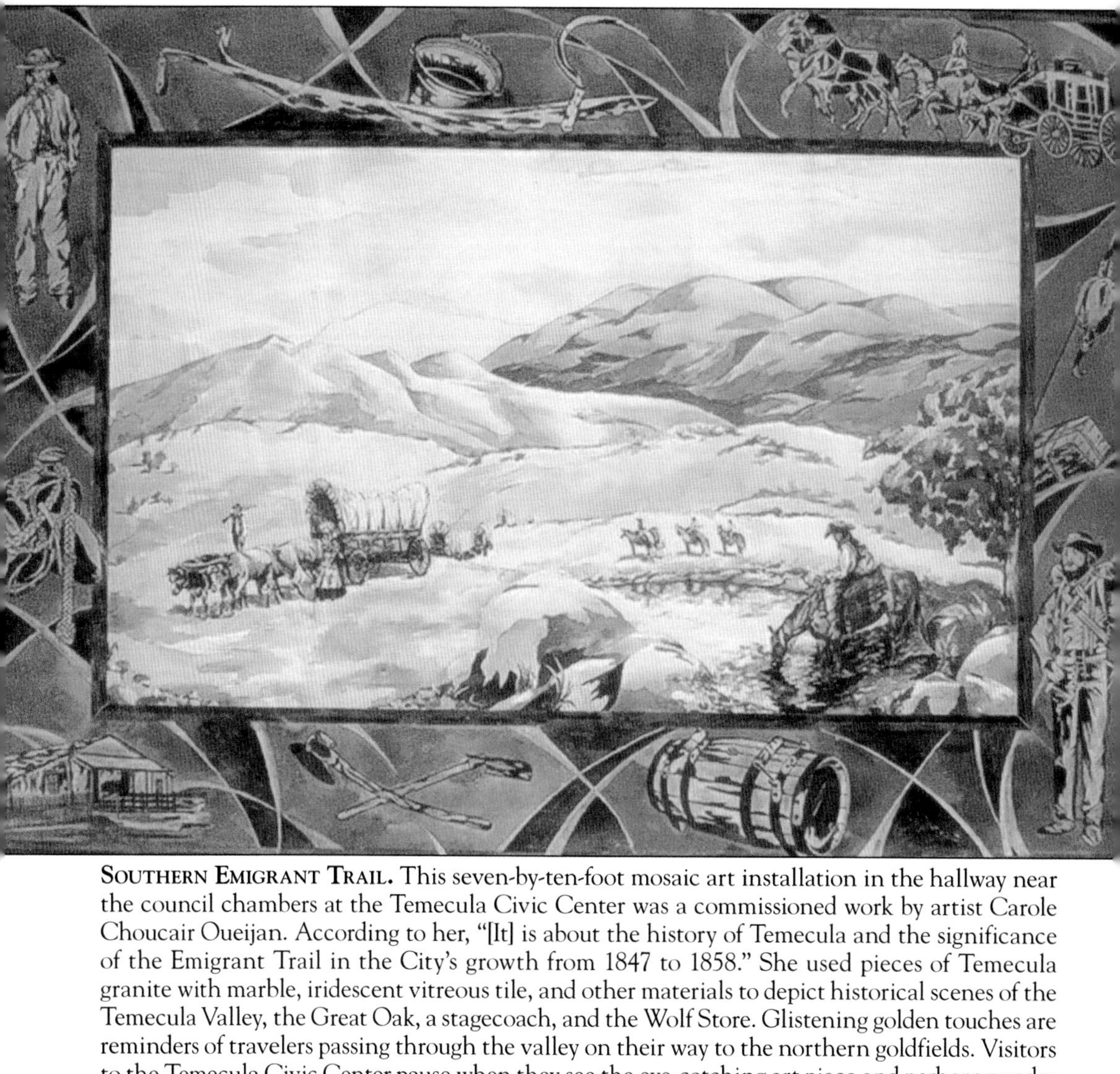

Southern Emigrant Trail. This seven-by-ten-foot mosaic art installation in the hallway near the council chambers at the Temecula Civic Center was a commissioned work by artist Carole Choucair Oueijan. According to her, "[It] is about the history of Temecula and the significance of the Emigrant Trail in the City's growth from 1847 to 1858." She used pieces of Temecula granite with marble, iridescent vitreous tile, and other materials to depict historical scenes of the Temecula Valley, the Great Oak, a stagecoach, and the Wolf Store. Glistening golden touches are reminders of travelers passing through the valley on their way to the northern goldfields. Visitors to the Temecula Civic Center pause when they see the eye-catching art piece and perhaps ponder about the people who lived in the times the scenes depict. (DF.)

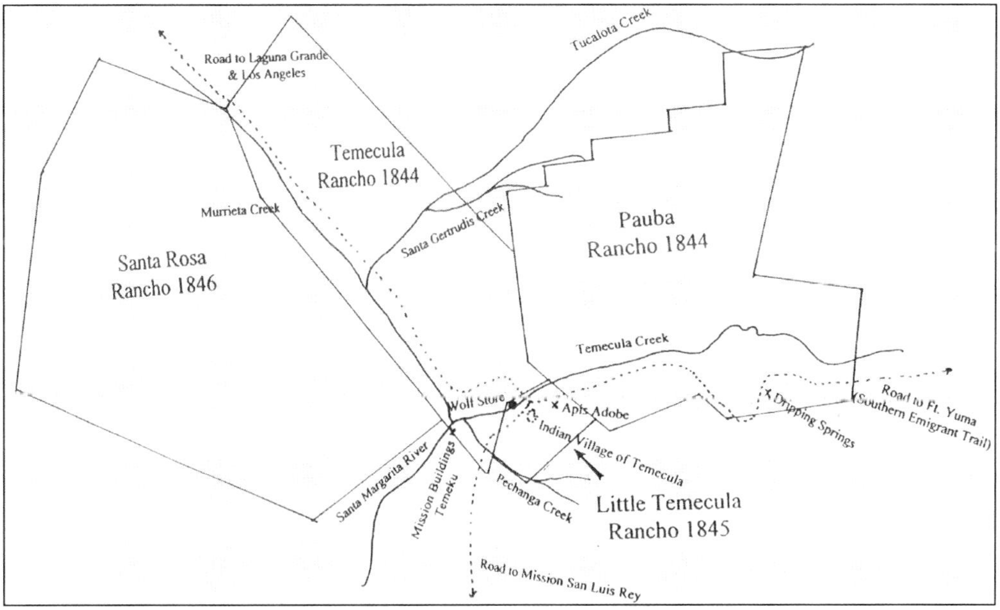

Ranchos of Temecula Valley. By 1845, the valley was settled by newcomers who eventually displaced native inhabitants onto government reservations. The lands formerly owned by Spain as mission holdings became available for private ownership under Mexican rule. The valley was divided into four ranchos, most of which were purchased by Walter Vail in 1905. Old Town is located in the former Temecula Rancho. (DF.)

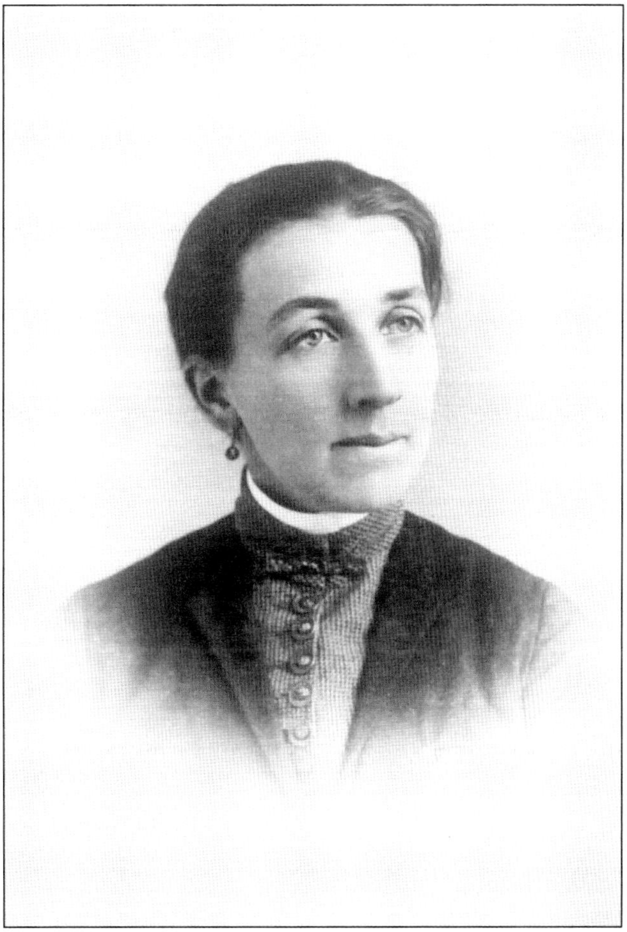

Mercedes Pujol. A group of Spanish investors—Domingo Pujol, Francisco Sanjurjo, and Juan and Ezequiel Murrieta—purchased parts of the Temecula and Pauba Ranchos in 1873. When they disbanded their partnership in 1876, Pujol received title to about half of the Temecula Rancho. Pujol returned to Spain, and his widow, Mercedes, returned in 1881 to settle his estate, which included much of Old Town. (TVM.)

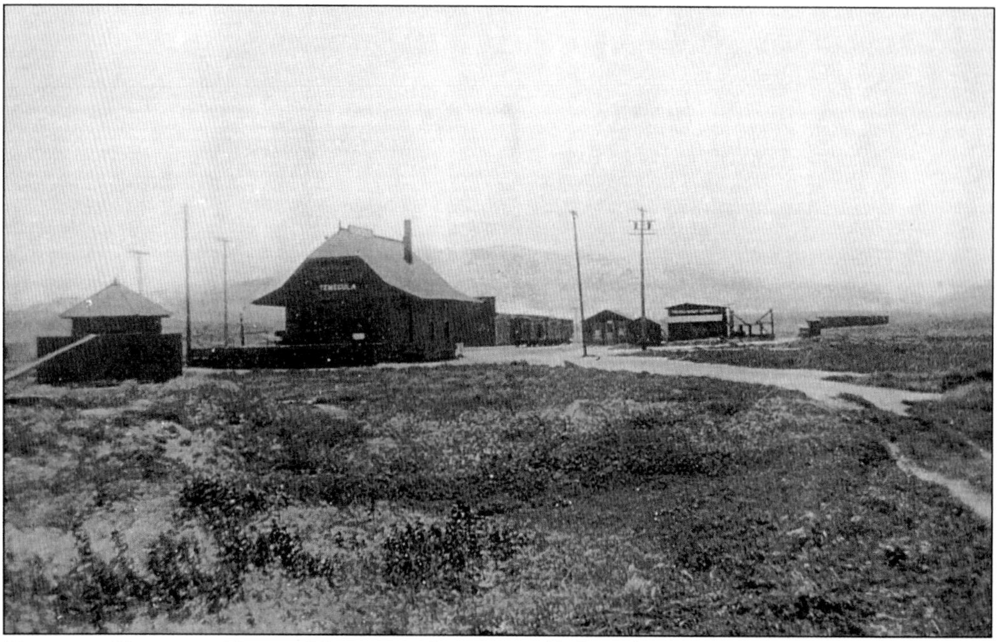

Temecula Railroad Depot. The original station, called Linda Rosa, stood near today's Diaz and Winchester Roads and was moved in the mid-1890s to the location pictured, now an empty lot between the creek and today's Pujol Street, north of Main Street. The station was remodeled in 1898. On the right are the Vail Company warehouse and the Temecula lumberyard. (TVM.)

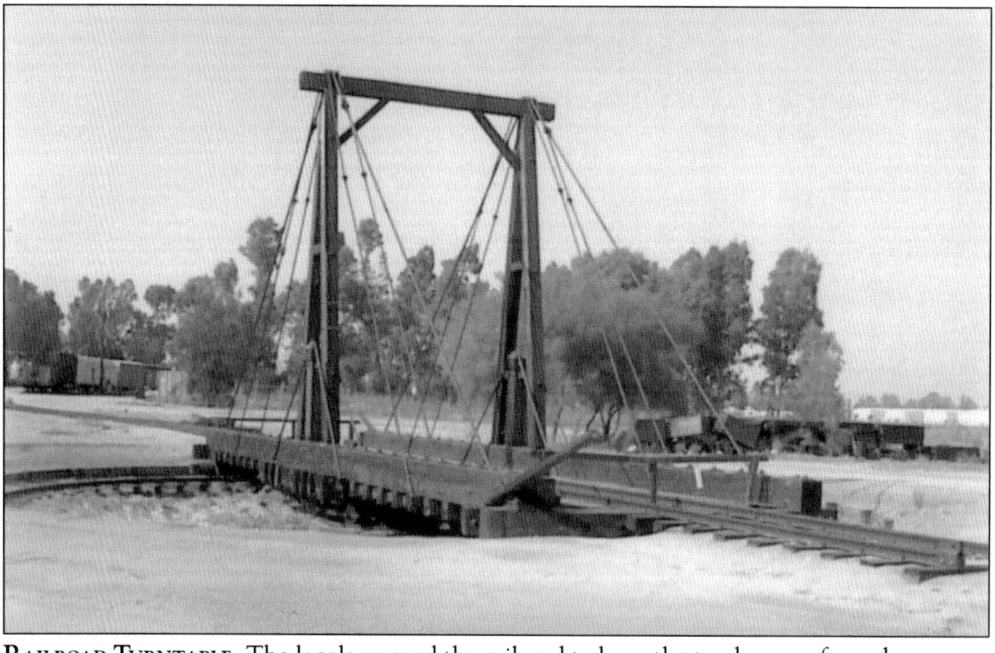

Railroad Turntable. The locals warned the railroad to keep the tracks away from the canyon floor. It was in 1891, after the third washout, when the canyon route was abandoned, and Temecula became the end of the line. A turntable like this one would turn the engine around after arriving in Temecula. An old handwritten map showed it between the depot house and the depot. No sign of it remains. (DF.)

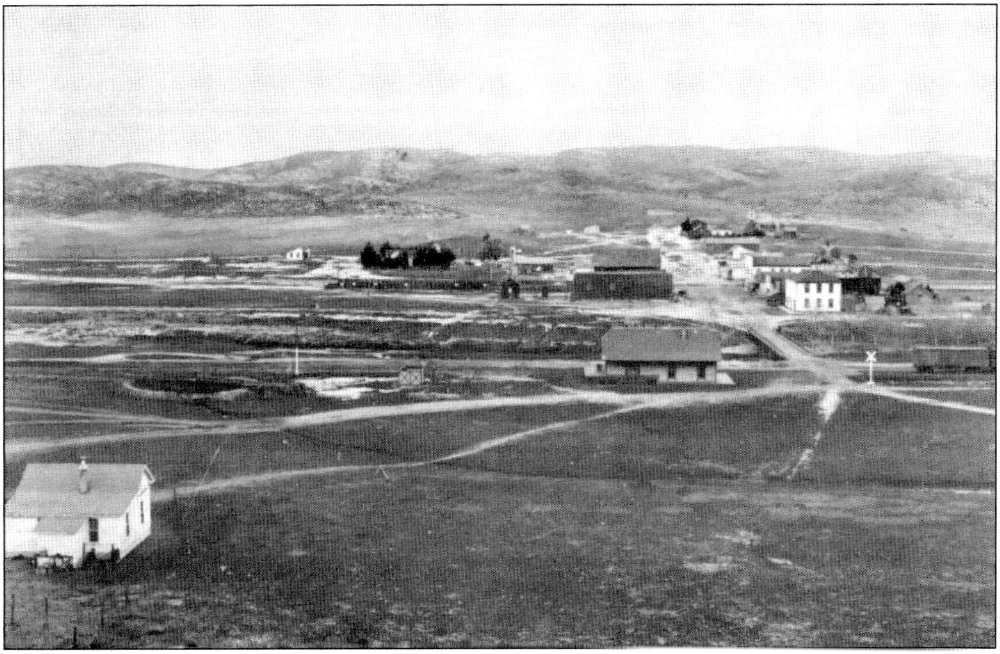

LOOKING EASTWARD INTO TOWN, 1906. Few buildings dotted the open land between the western foothills and across to where the Temecula Town Center shopping center is now on the east side of Interstate 15. Comparing photographs like this one to maps and deeds helps historians piece together the story of Old Town Temecula. (LB.)

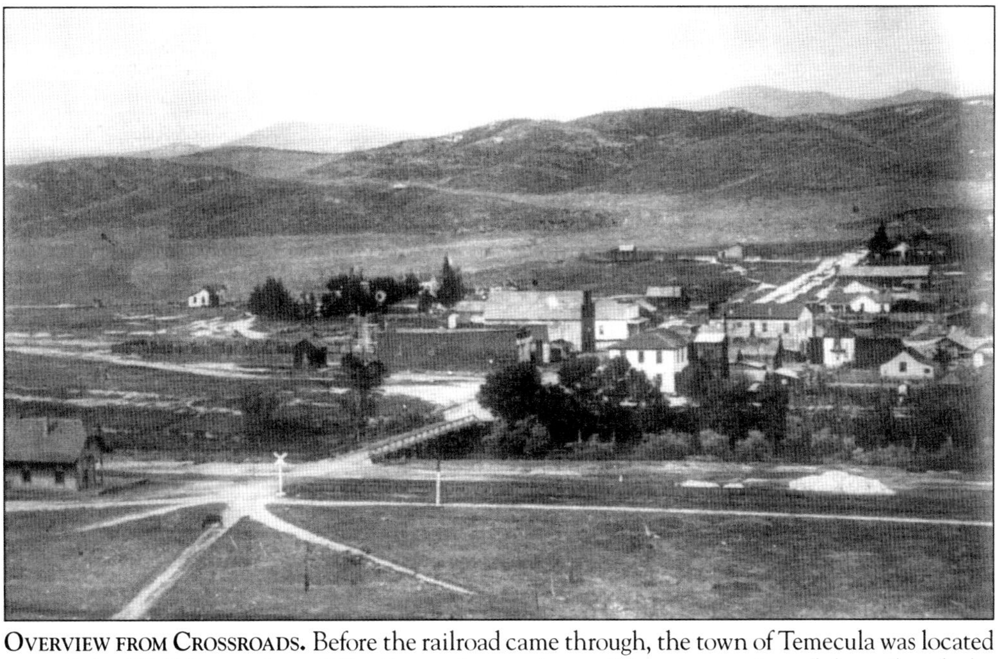

OVERVIEW FROM CROSSROADS. Before the railroad came through, the town of Temecula was located around the Wolf Store, about 2.5 miles to the southeast. With the coming of the railroad, the New Town of Temecula was built, and Main Street was an important access to the train depot. When the rail line was disbanded in 1935, Front Street became more important as motorists passed through on US Highway 395. (GT.)

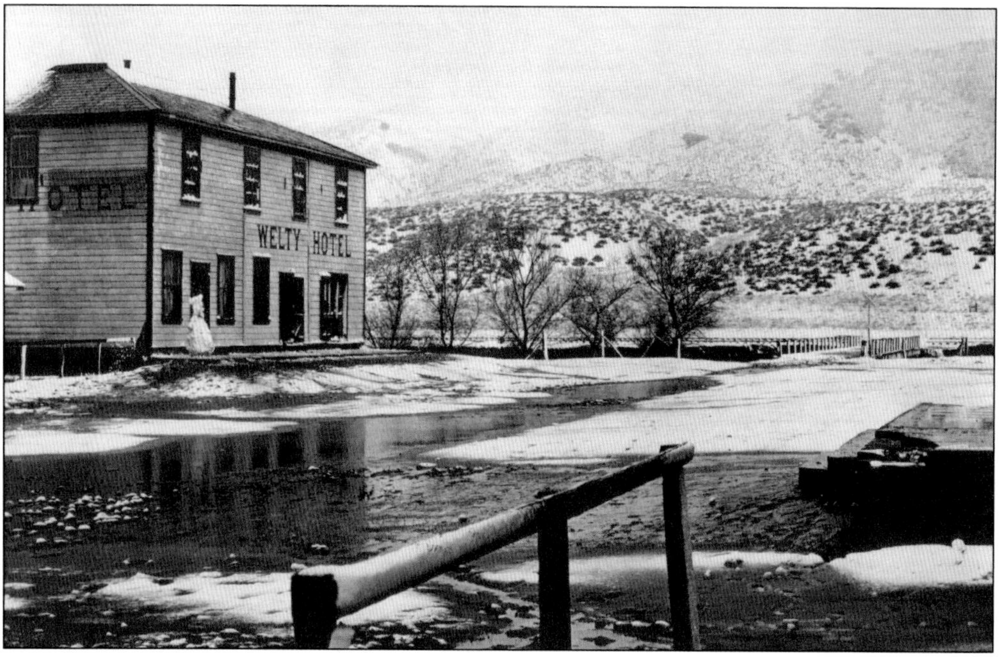

WELTY HOTEL AFTER SNOWFALL. In the foreground is a hitching rail, once commonplace in Old Town. Opened as a railroad hotel, the Welty Hotel also served as a boardinghouse to local workers. John and Mary Jane Welty built the first hotel in 1886. After it burned down in 1891, they rebuilt and added to it in 1904. It was renamed the Temecula Hotel when Grace LeClare bought it in 1925. (GT.)

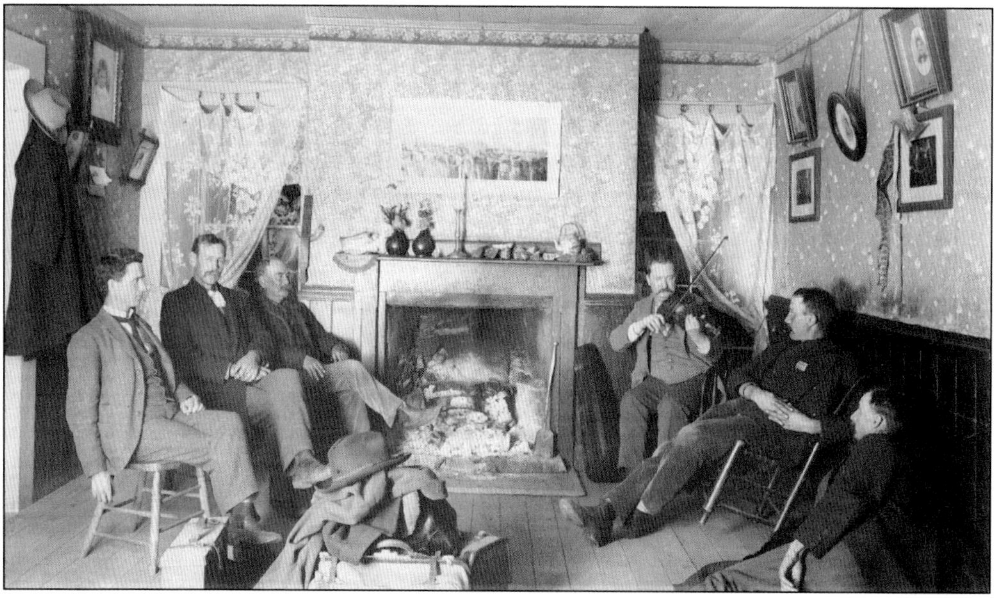

WAITING FOR THE OAK GROVE STAGE. The Butterfield Overland Mail stage line operated only from 1858 until 1862, when it was disrupted by the Civil War. Other local stage lines continued regional service. Before the train came to Temecula, people depended on stage lines for transportation and deliveries. The Oak Grove Station, an original Butterfield Station on the route between Warner Springs and Temecula, is still standing. (TVM.)

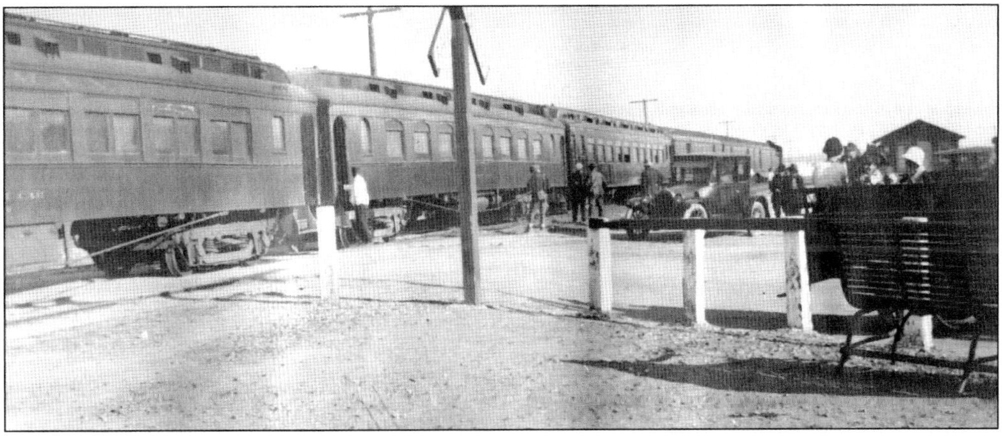

Train at Temecula Station. California Southern carried passengers and goods between Colton and National City starting in 1882. They sold to the Atchison, Topeka & Santa Fe in 1906. Temecula received lumber and other goods and shipped out cattle, granite, and produce. When the Temecula Station closed in 1935, Elsinore was the end of the line. (TVM.)

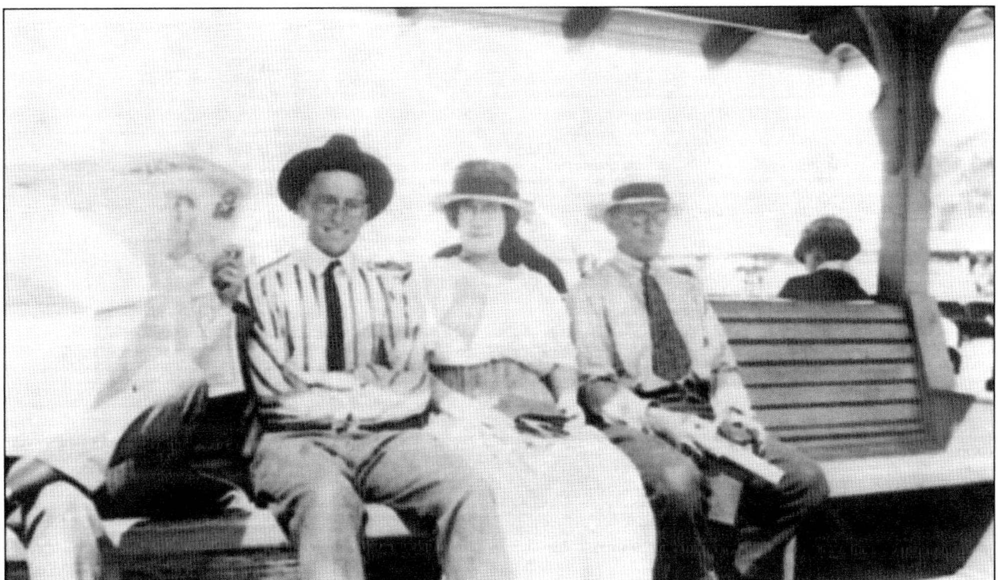

Waiting at the Station. From left to right, Joe Cantarini, Lillian Taylor, and Will Friedemann waited for the train at the Temecula Station. The depot was the center of activity—a place where people would watch to see who came into town, wait for mail and merchandise, and listen for news from surrounding areas. (TVM.)

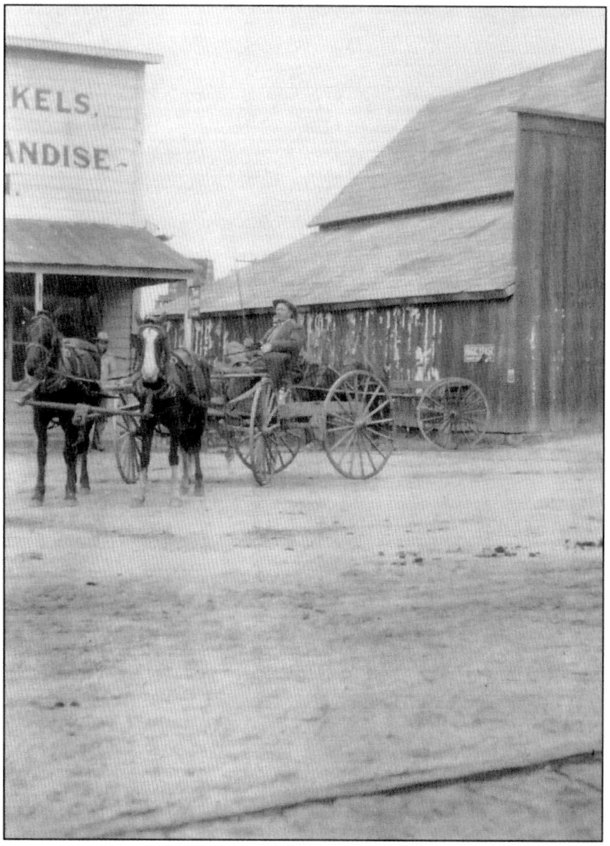

Joe Winkels's Store. Hugh McConville hired Winkels through a Los Angeles employment agency to work at the livery stable. Within five years, Winkels opened his store between the livery stable and mercantile store on Main Street. He also operated a "blind pig" saloon, the Ramona Inn, across the street in what is now known as the Welty Building. The Ramona Inn attracted Hollywood stars and other notables during Prohibition. (GT.)

Horses and Wagons by Train. Before motorized trucks, farmers depended on their horses and wagons to haul livestock or produce to the station to ship it out to buyers. The McSweenys had a warehouse near the station where they stored potatoes for shipping. They also grew carrots and sold carrot seeds. A newspaper notice mentioned a shipment of roses received by Alice Machado. (TVM.)

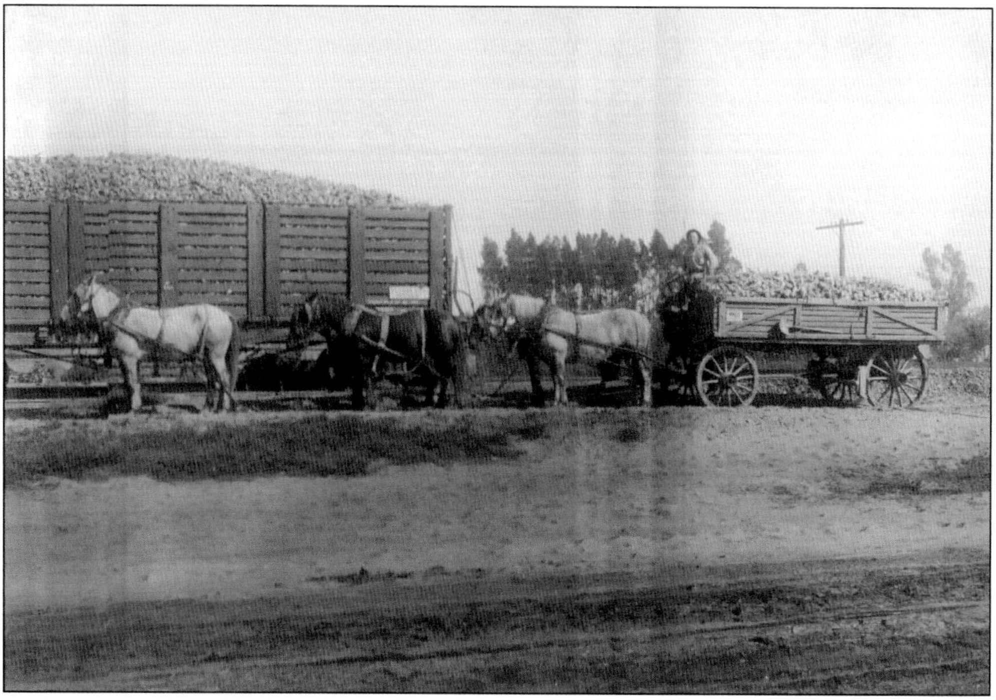

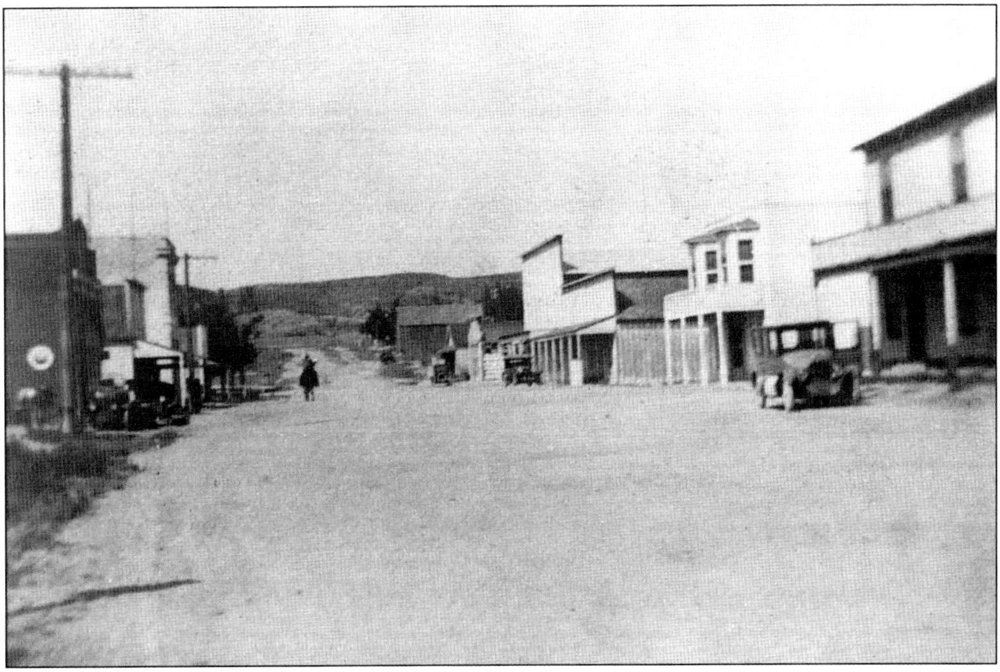

HORSE AND AUTOMOBILE ON MAIN STREET. This photograph demonstrates the transition from horses to motorized vehicles. Front Street was paved in 1918. From the right are the Welty Hotel with a porch, the meat market, and the Ramona Inn. Telephones came to Temecula prior to 1917. The telephone office was at the livery stable where the Bank of Mexican Food is today. Electricity was brought to town in 1922. (TVM.)

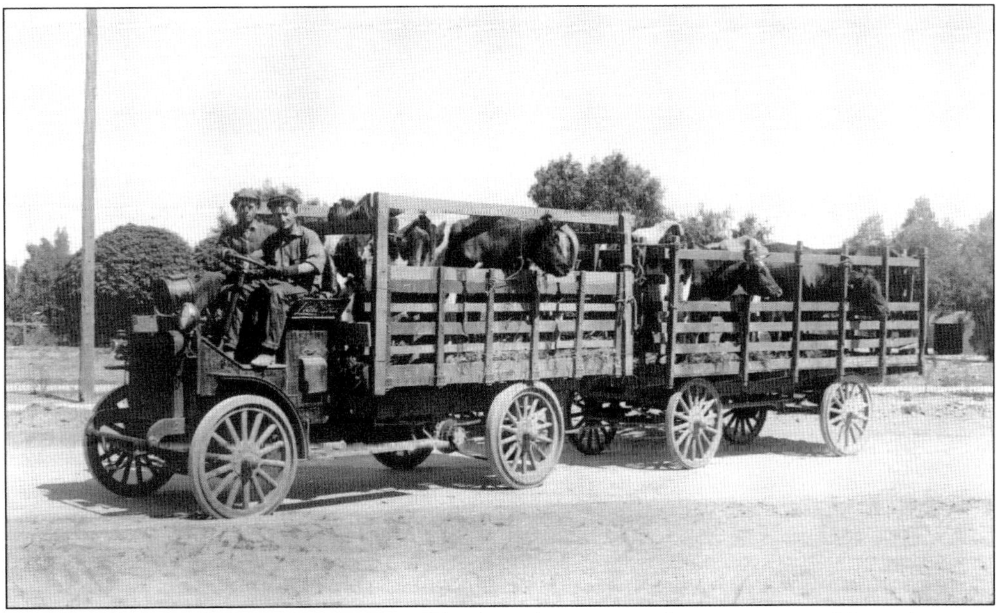

LIVESTOCK IN MOTORIZED TRUCK. By 1935, when the train tracks were removed from this area, the Vails and other ranchers trucked their livestock. Although some meat was processed at the slaughterhouse on Pujol Street, the bulk of the beef was shipped to packing plants in the Los Angeles area. (JR.)

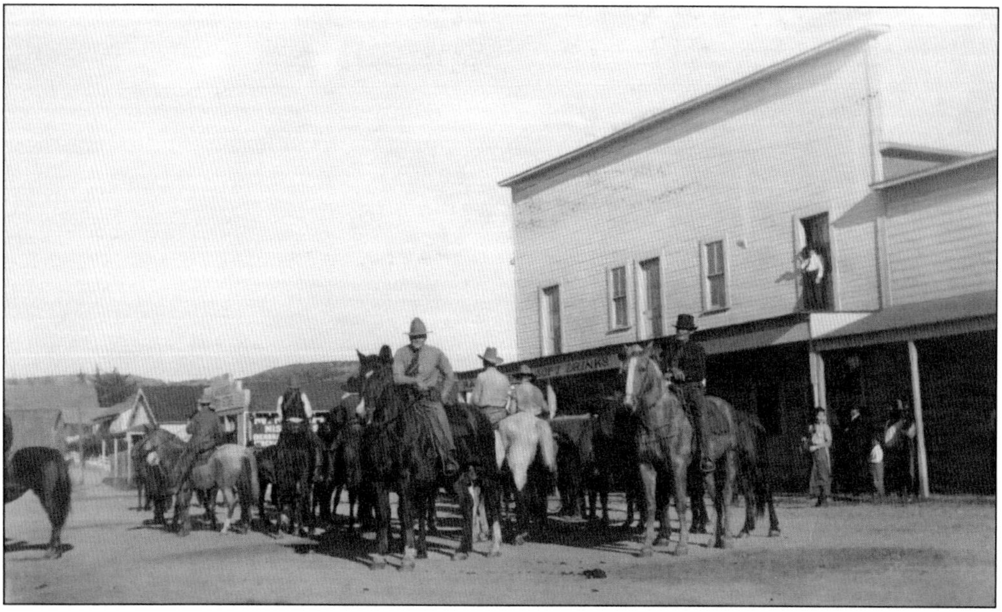

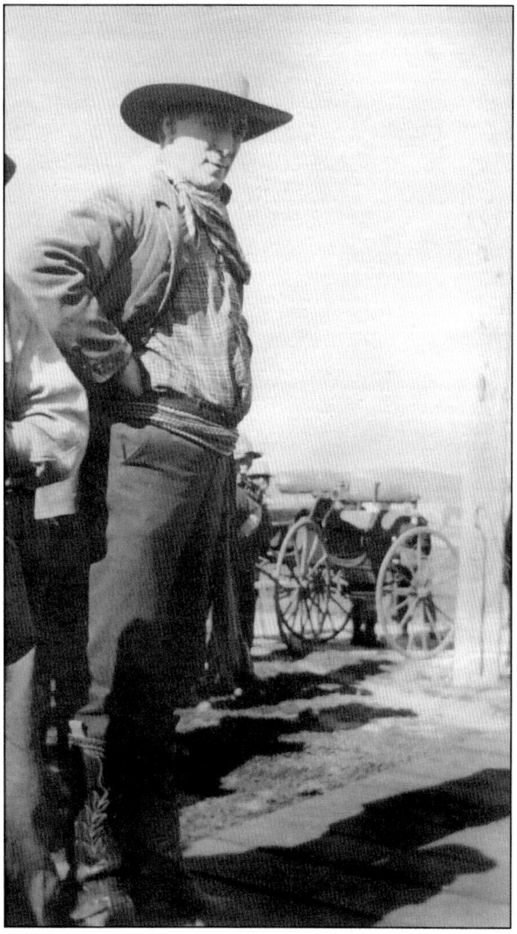

FILMING ON MAIN STREET. Because of its genuine Old West charm, Temecula was a valuable filming location in the 1920s and later. All the elements of the Wild West were found in Temecula. The close proximity to Hollywood and convenient train connection and hotel accommodations made it an ideal place for filming. Joe Winkels also made sure the movie crowd felt welcome in his saloon. (TVM.)

WILLIAM S. HART. Actor Hart starred in *Three Word Brand*, a movie filmed on location in 1921 on Main and Pujol Streets. *Cross Trails* was filmed in Old Town in 1923. From 1995 to 2011, Temecula hosted an annual Fall International Film Festival to debut new talent and honor contributors to the fine art of films and to provide instructional workshops. (TVM.)

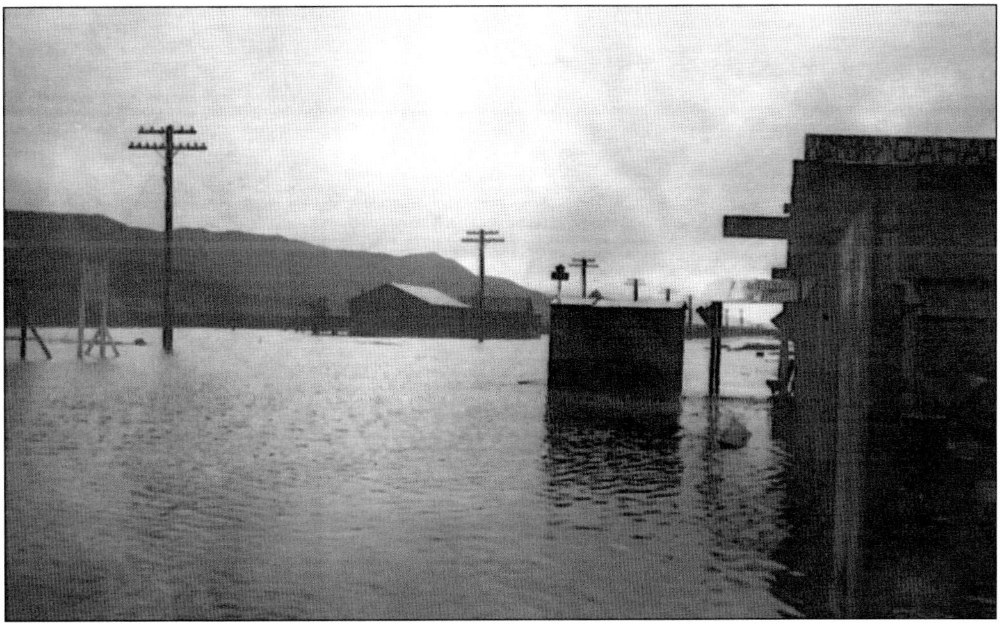

Old Town Flood. The Murrieta Creek used to flow year-round and sometimes overflowed with heavy rain. In 1916, when a storm flooded most of Southern California, two feet of water covered Front Street. In 1938, the Main Street Bridge washed out. More recently, Old Town flooded in 1992, resulting in heavy property losses. Since then, a creek bed maintenance program prevents flooding. (TVM.)

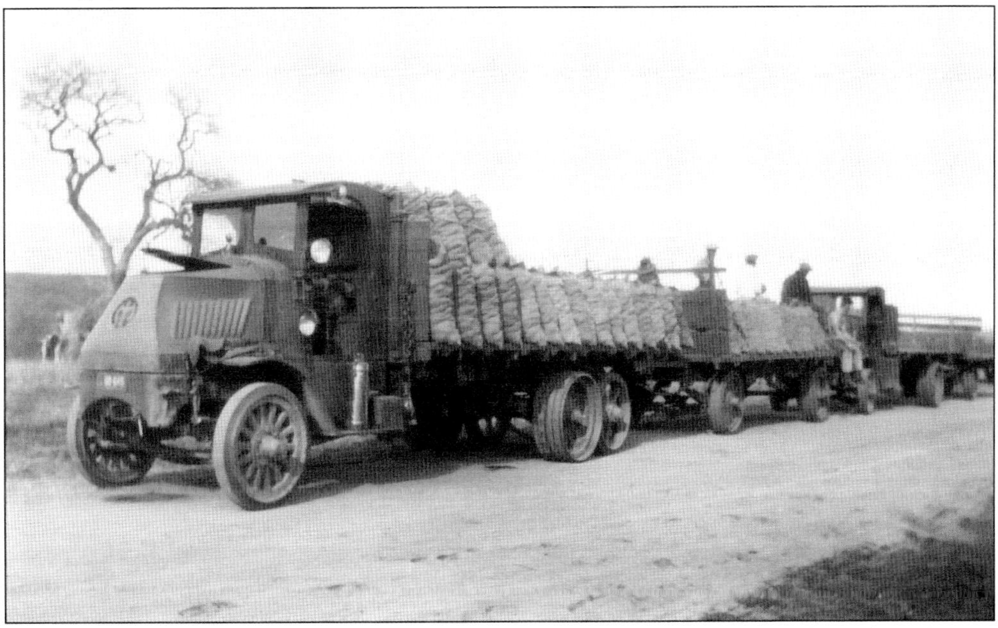

Potato Truck. The McSweenys and Yoders had thriving potato yields and hired truckers to haul the produce to market, either for shipment by rail or truck. The McSweenys farmed Lower Camp along today's Pechanga Parkway. Yoder Camp was at the present Maurice Car'rie Winery location. The area around today's Promenade Mall produced tons of potatoes that were shipped out of the area. (JR.)

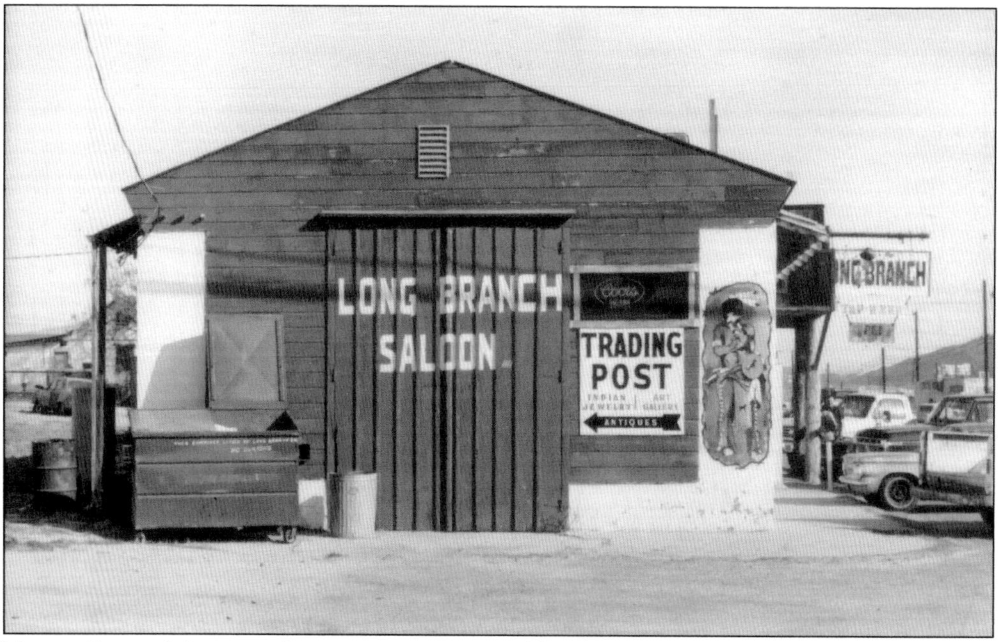

North End of Machado Store, 1974. Louis Wolf and Macedonia "Mac" Machado purchased a store in this location from Simon Mundt in the mid-1880s. After Wolf died, Machado ran the general store until it burned in 1888. He set up in the Welty Hotel until it burned in 1891. In 1910, he constructed the stucco-covered, terra-cotta, brick building that is still standing. (VaRRA.)

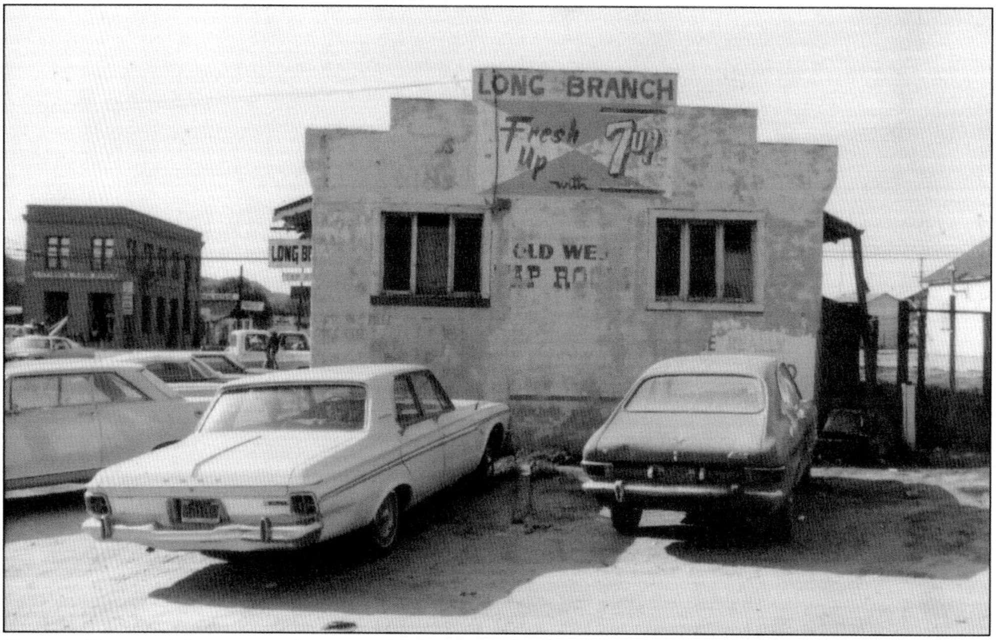

South End of Machado Store, 1974. The rebuilt store was sometimes called the Mission Store because of Machado's extensive Indian basket collection. Machado sold real estate in Old Town, and his signature is seen on many of the existing deeds. He also provided banking services, according to his ledger book. The Vail Company bought the building in the 1930s and used it as a warehouse. (VaRRA)

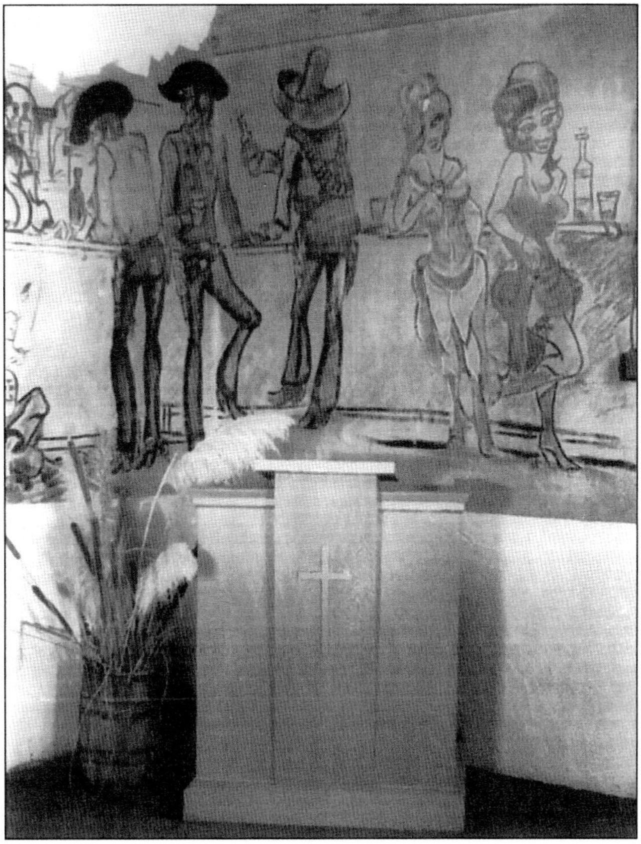

Pulpit inside Long Branch Saloon, 1984. The former store eventually became a bar. As the population grew, new churches sprang up and needed meeting places. In 1979, after the saloon closed, Hope Lutheran rented the facility for a year. One can imagine how distracting the bawdy paintings behind the preacher would be while listening to a sermon. (TVM.)

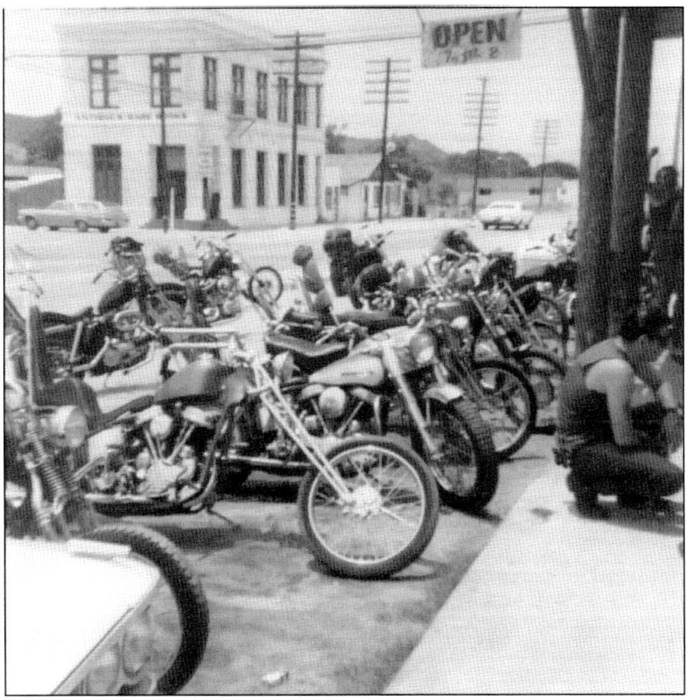

Motorcycles at the Long Branch Saloon. The saloon, sometimes called the Indian Bar, attracted a tough element and was frequently the scene of bar brawls and shootings. People who remember the saloon say it was a dangerous place where no respectable woman would step inside. Since the days of the saloon, the building has been an antique store and a clothing boutique and is presently for sale. (TVM.)

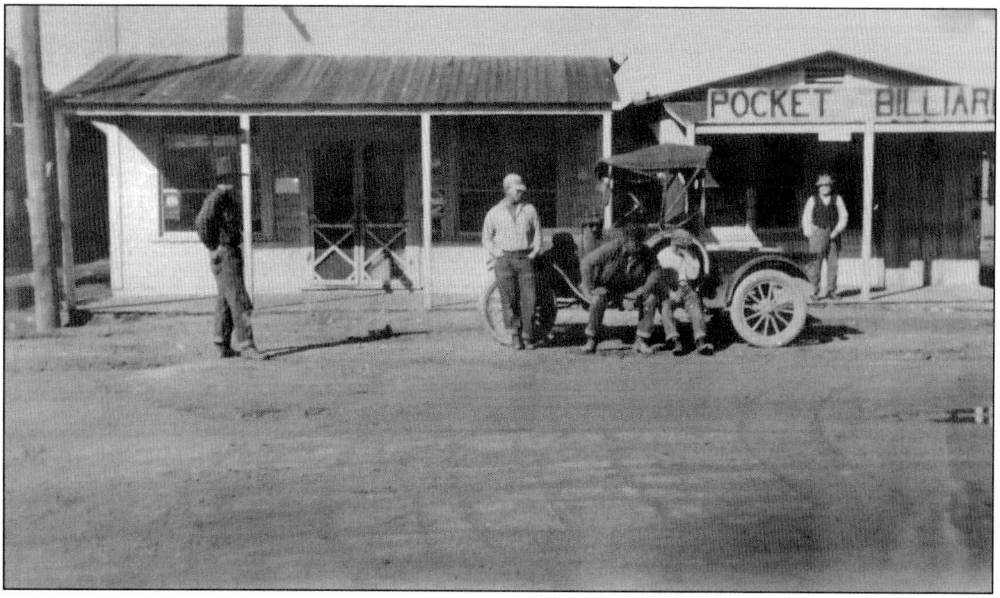

Escallier Pool Hall. This was one of the first buildings in Old Town and holds the title of many firsts, including the first hotel and theater. It also served as a billiard hall, rooming house, barbershop, and drinking establishment. The proprietors showed movies on Friday evenings. The building was located where Rosa's Cantina is today. (GT.)

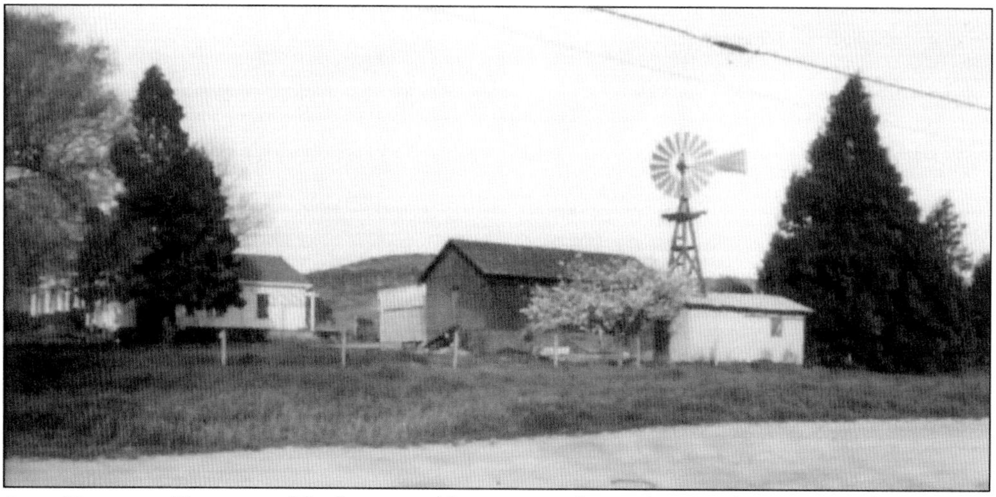

Alex Escallier Property. The house and barn were relocated to Pujol Street to make room for the Temecula Civic Center and donated by the city for use by the Temecula Community Pantry. The barn is believed to be the first wine-making and storage facility in Temecula. Some of the local granite at the base of the barn was used around the Temecula Civic Center Luiseno basket fountain. (DF.)

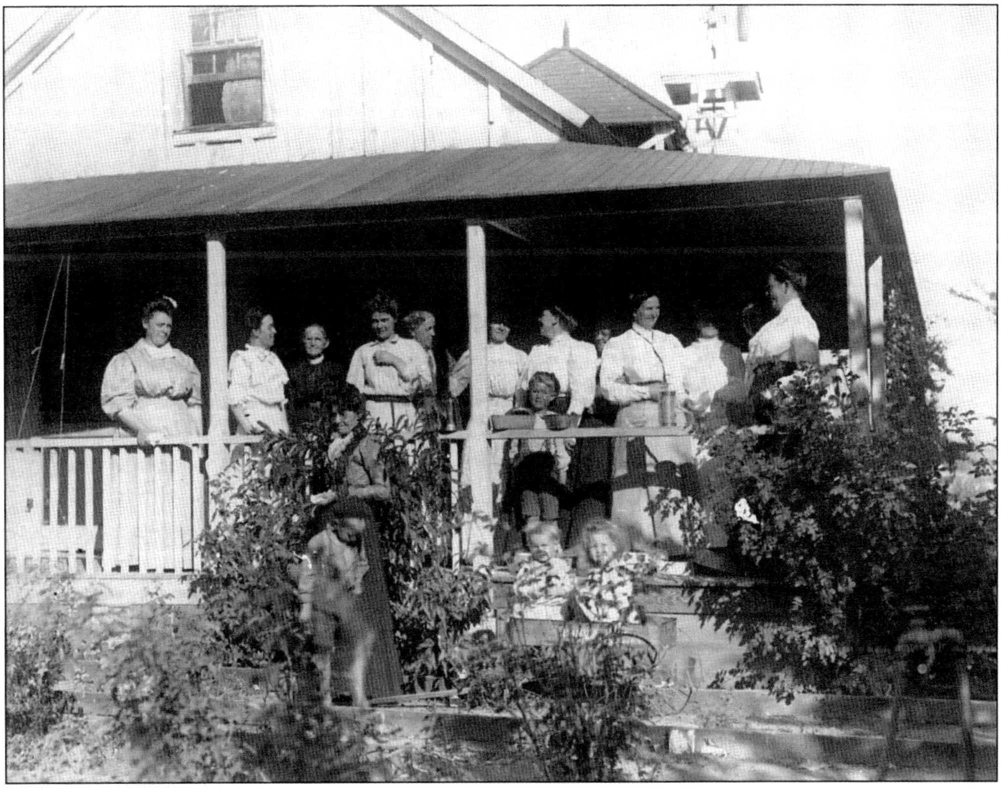

Women at Fernald House, Early 1900s. One wonders what event brought together all the notable women of Temecula: a bridal shower, an Eastern Star meeting, or a whist game? From left to right on the porch are Gertrude Hadsell, Ysabel "Bessie" Barnett, Mary Jane Welty, Trixie Fernald, Grace Gonzales, Sarah Burnham, Laura McConville, four unidentified women, and Alice Machado. In front are, from left to right, Loren, Neil, Bert, and Dolly Fernald. (TVM.)

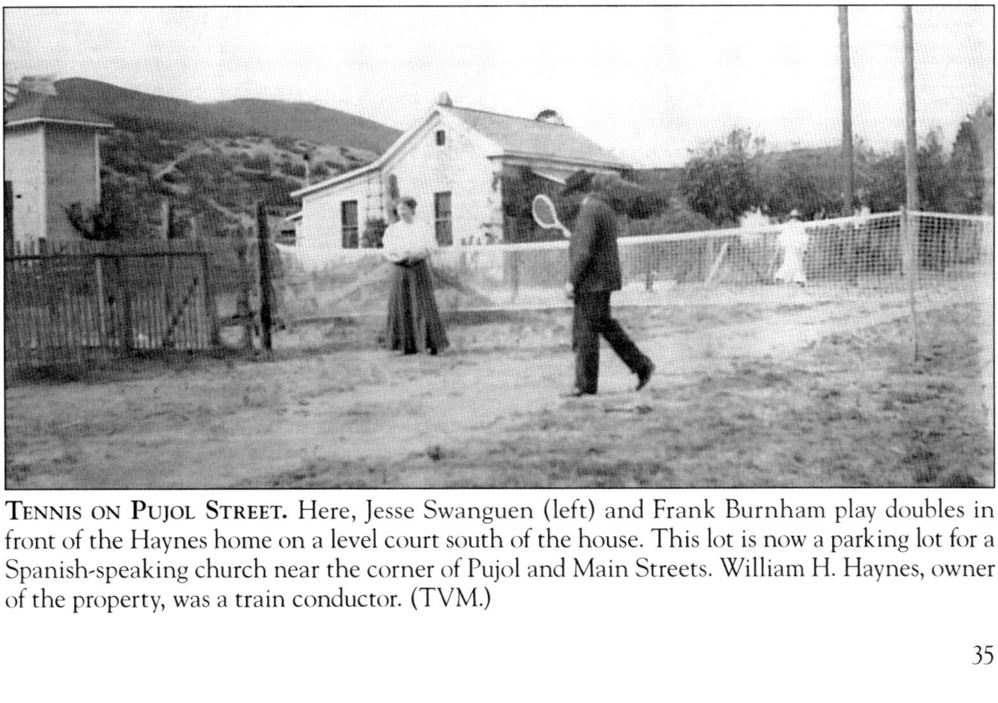

Tennis on Pujol Street. Here, Jesse Swanguen (left) and Frank Burnham play doubles in front of the Haynes home on a level court south of the house. This lot is now a parking lot for a Spanish-speaking church near the corner of Pujol and Main Streets. William H. Haynes, owner of the property, was a train conductor. (TVM.)

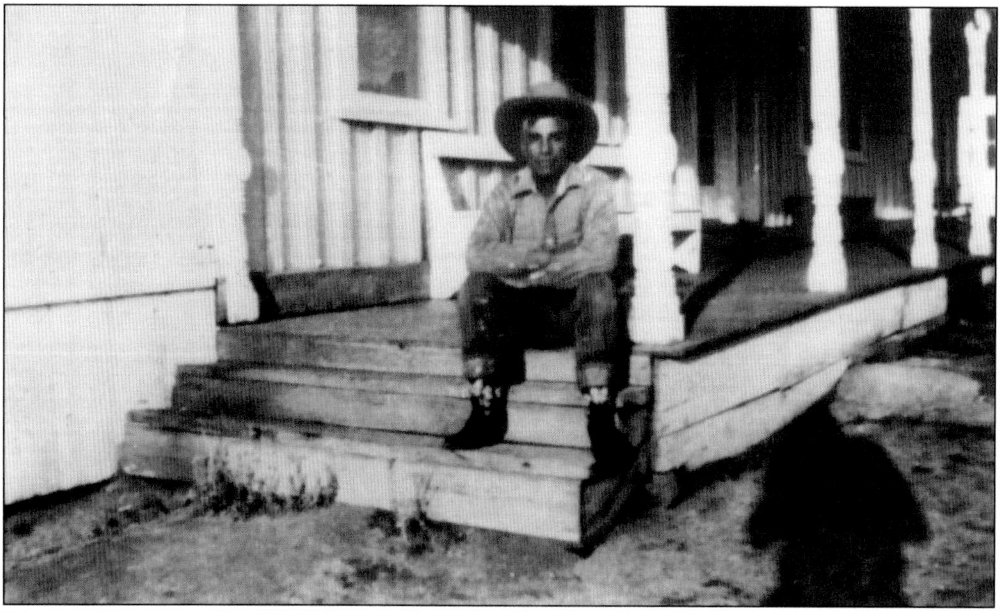

Horace Magee in Garner Valley. On December 24, 1907, Horace, the son of Judge John Magee, and Louis Escallier got into an argument at Escallier Pool Hall. After Escallier burned Magee with a cigar, Magee became enraged and went to Frank Fernald's store on Main Street and bought a gun. He returned to the pool hall and started shooting. When Constable Preston Swanguen and Escallier approached, Magee killed them. (JWR.)

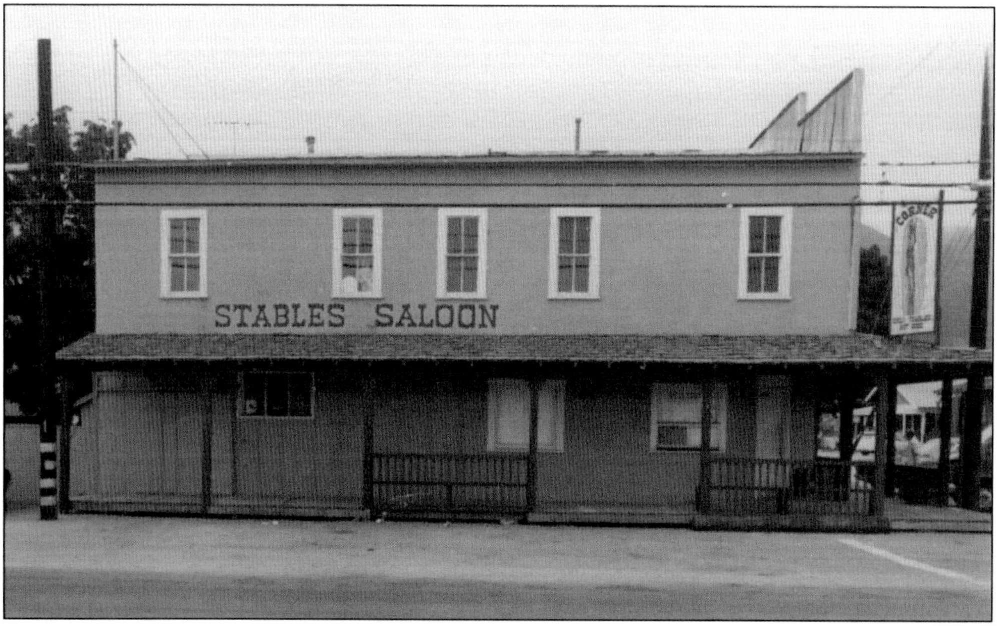

Stables Saloon. Magee had been drinking at Winkels's Ramona Inn, later named the Stables, just before going to the Escallier Pool Hall. After Magee killed Escallier and Swanguen, John Jackson, the Santa Fe brakeman, struck Magee with a billiard cue. Magee was bound and thrown into a stall at the McConville livery stable. Early Christmas morning, Deputy Sheriff Hugh McConville escorted Magee to the Riverside jail to avoid a lynching. (TVM.)

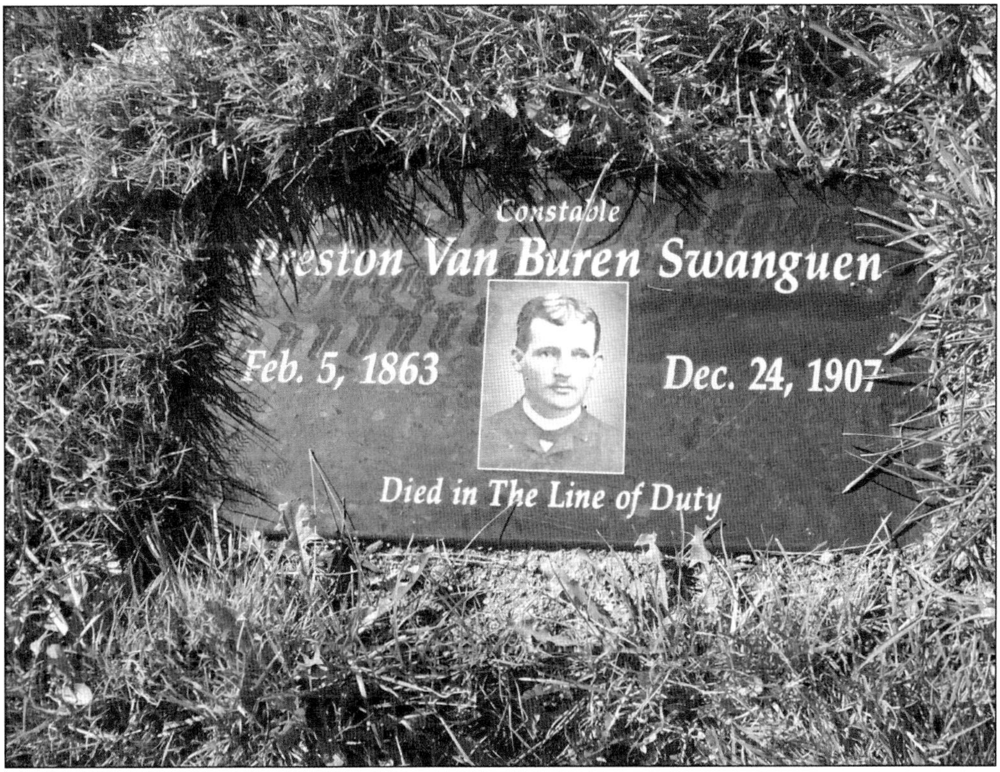

PRESTON SWANGUEN'S GRAVE MARKER. Constable Swanguen was enjoying a holiday meal with friends when he received the message of a disturbance at Escallier Pool Hall. Confident he could calm Magee down, Swanguen headed to the bar without his firearm. When he entered the pool hall, Magee shot and killed the constable. In 2010, this grave marker was placed to honor Swanguen's sacrifice in the line of duty.

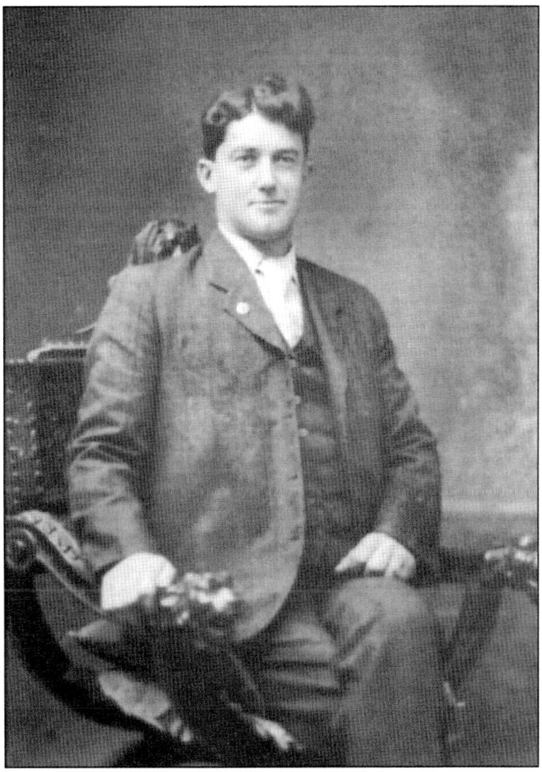

JOE WINKELS. Winkels was the proprietor of the Ramona Inn, where Hollywood producers and journalists from Los Angeles knew they could get a drink. Winkels was known as a hardworking man but also as a practical joker. He left town for a few months after the double murder and was later arrested for illegally selling liquor. Boxing legends Jack Dempsey, Jack Sharkey, and Fatty Arbuckle frequented the Ramona Inn. (TVM.)

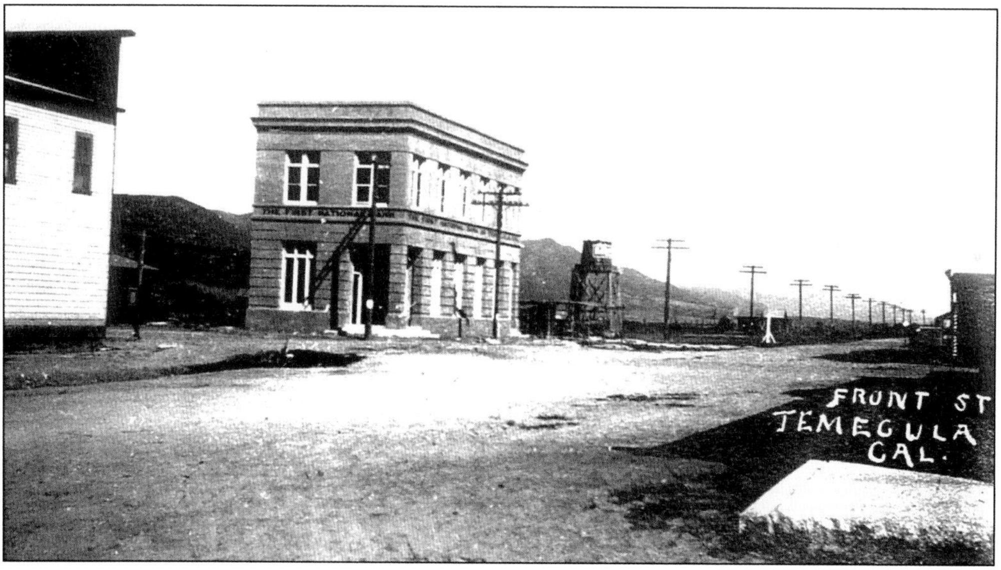

The Bank. On August 13, 1930, Miguel Diaz, a ranch hand on the Vail Ranch, entered the First National Bank and pointed his revolver at teller Agnes Freeman and banker John W. Chisholm and demanded cash. He locked the two in the vault and left, unaware that Chisholm had jammed a screwdriver in the vault door, which prevented it from locking. Diaz drove away in a stolen Ford. (GT.)

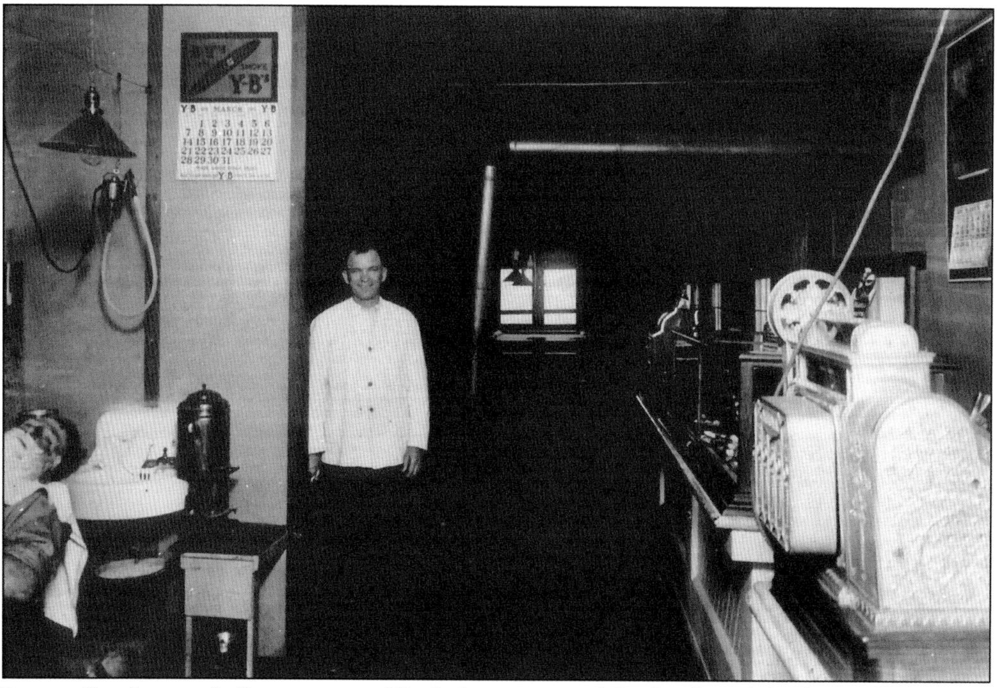

Inside Ole Larson's Barbershop. Chisholm ran out of the bank and fired two shots at the fleeing suspect. John McSweeny, who was getting a shave at the barbershop next door, like the man pictured, heard the noise and ran outside to investigate. McSweeny jumped into his Buick, Chisholm jumped on the running board, and the duo sped off after Diaz. After bullets struck his windshield, Diaz surrendered. (LB.)

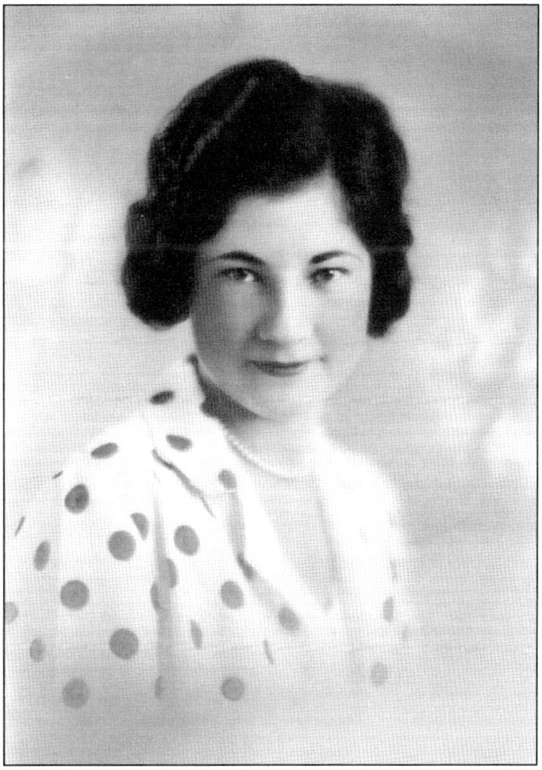

AGNES FREEMAN, 1930. Agnes knew Miguel Diaz because he worked for her father, James Freeman, who was the foreman of the Vail Ranch. Diaz later said he wanted the money so he could enroll in a flight school. Agnes later married Roger Honberger, a Perris businessman, and raised their son Roger. (RH.)

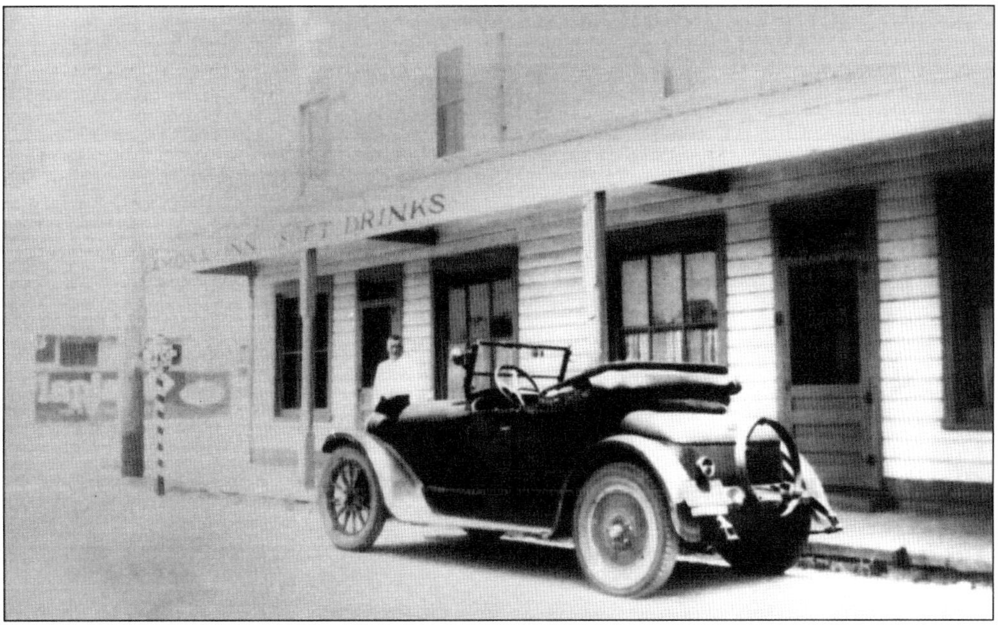

CAR OUTSIDE WELTY BUILDING. Some reports indicated an accomplice waited in the Ford coupe, while Diaz went into the bank. McSweeny's Buick outran the Ford after a five-mile chase. Diaz surrendered after two bullets from Chisholm's pistol pierced the windshield. Instead of taking flight training, Diaz spent three years in prison. The Temecula Olive Oil Company is in this building today. (TVM.)

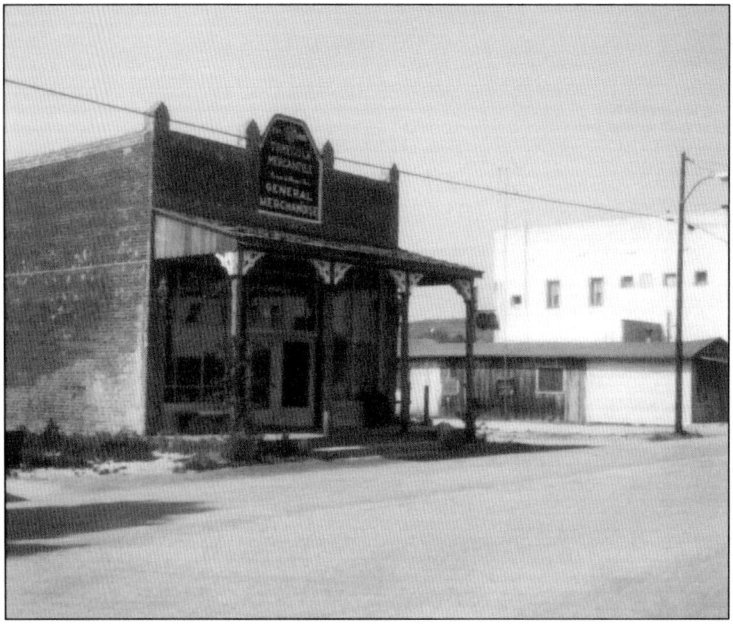

MERCANTILE STORE, 1973. In the late 1870s, a brickyard was started in Wolf Valley, anticipating a need for bricks after the railroad was to be constructed there. When the tracks were put into Santa Margarita Canyon instead, the brickyard was abandoned. In 1889, after Philip Pohlman won a lottery for Lot 12 on Main Street, he hauled away some of the bricks and built the store, which is still standing. (GT.)

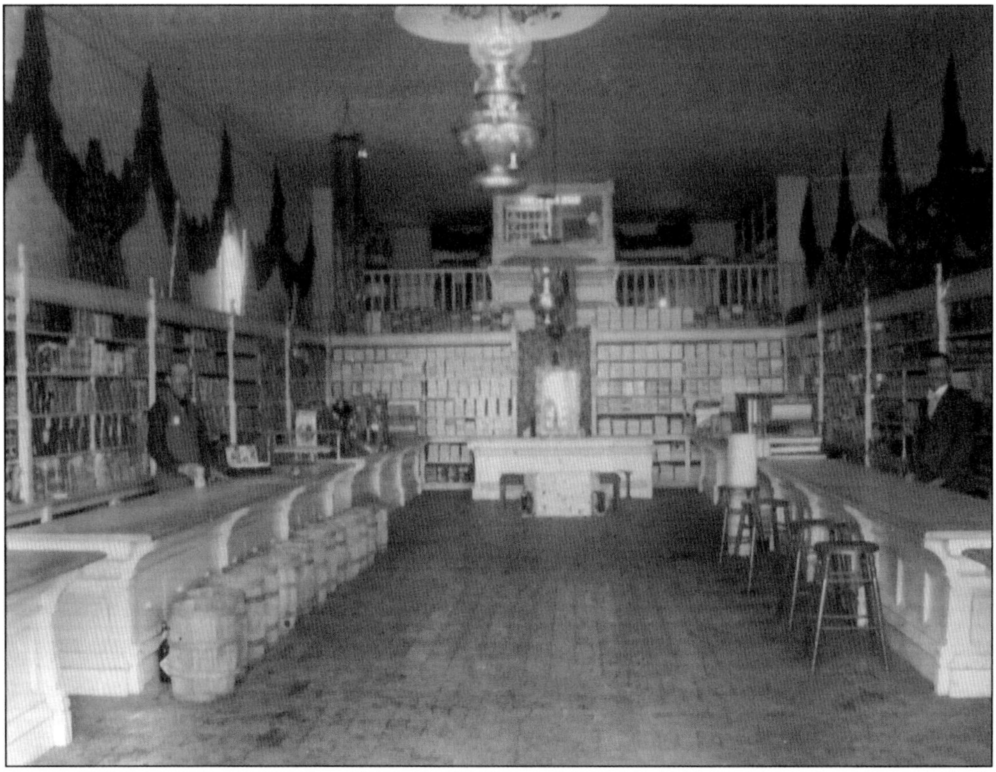

INSIDE MERCANTILE STORE. This photograph was probably taken in the 1890s, because the back is labeled "Pohlman's Store." Pohlman sold hardware, dry goods, canned goods, and produce. Pohlman hired George Burnham to work for him, and in 1902, Burnham bought the business. It was known as the Burnham Store for 60 years. The Burnhams sold the building to Nate DeArmond in 1953, and it became an automobile repair shop. (OB.)

Another View inside the Store. In 1969, Walt Moore and Howard Raish bought the mercantile store and sold antiques. Lorraine Clark bought it in the early 1970s and leased it to Barbara Morgan for an antique mall. When faced with a mandatory retrofitting for earthquake safety, the Clarks sold the building to the City of Temecula. The mercantile fixtures were kept intact until the 2005 renovation. (TVM.)

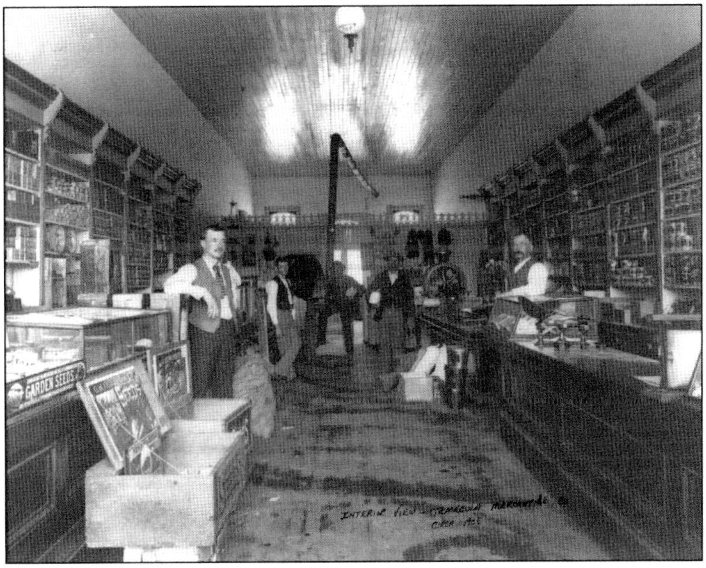

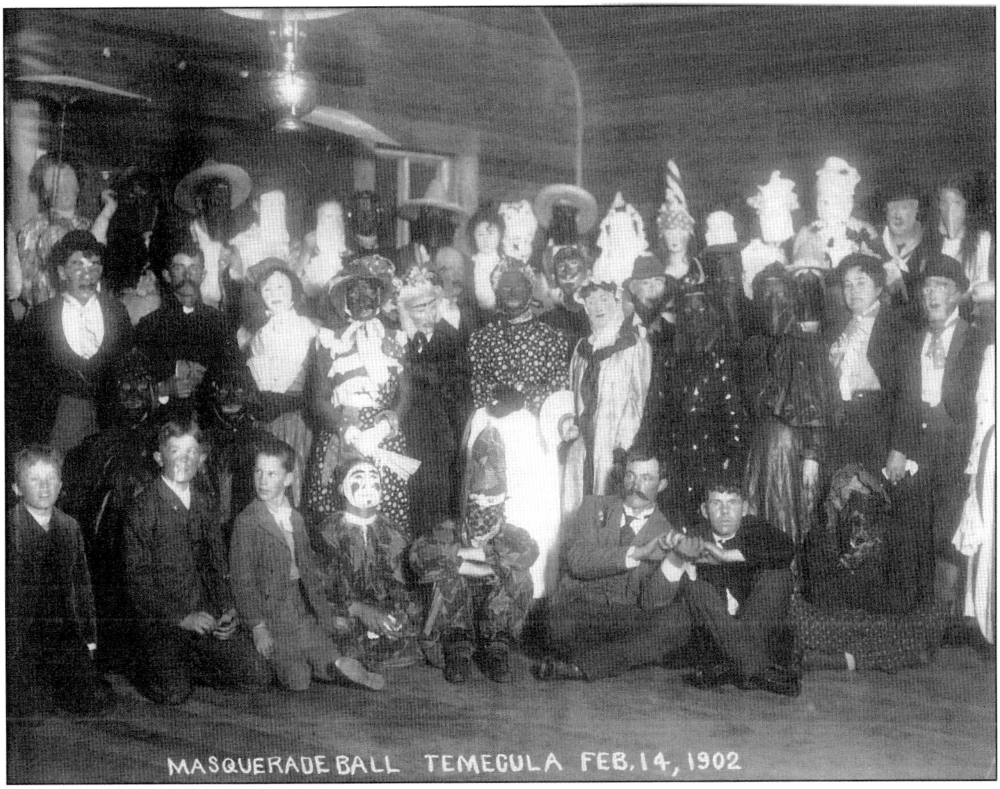

Valentine's Day Masquerade Ball, 1902. The ball was held at the second-floor social room in the livery stable at the northwest corner of Front and Main Streets. The dance floor was polished with wax and then buffed to a shine with bales of hay. The livery provided horse and wagon rentals to people coming to town by train and would also stable horses for visitors in town. (TVM.)

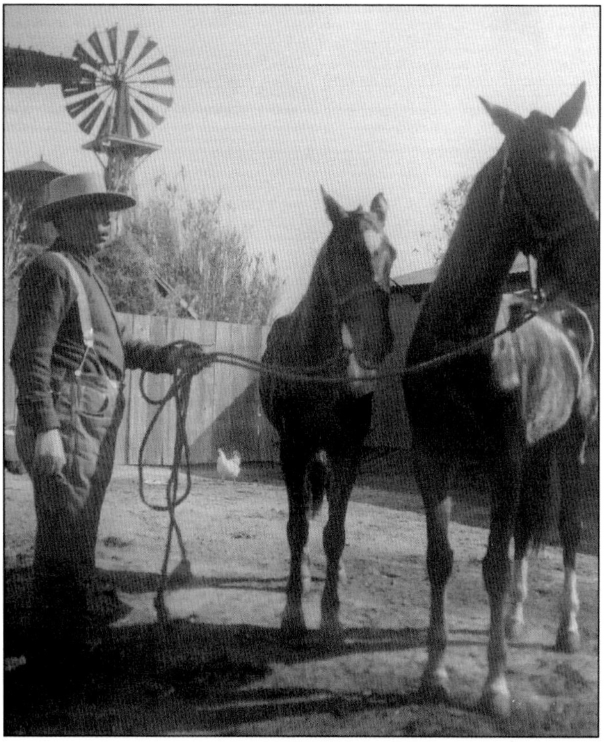

Mac Machado. Entries in Machado Store's ledgers list freight service, tobacco, camphor, axle grease, suspenders, and pickles. He married Alice Vaughn, who came on the train from Iowa in 1884 to join her sisters. Alice was honored as one of the longest residents of Temecula in 1952. (JR.)

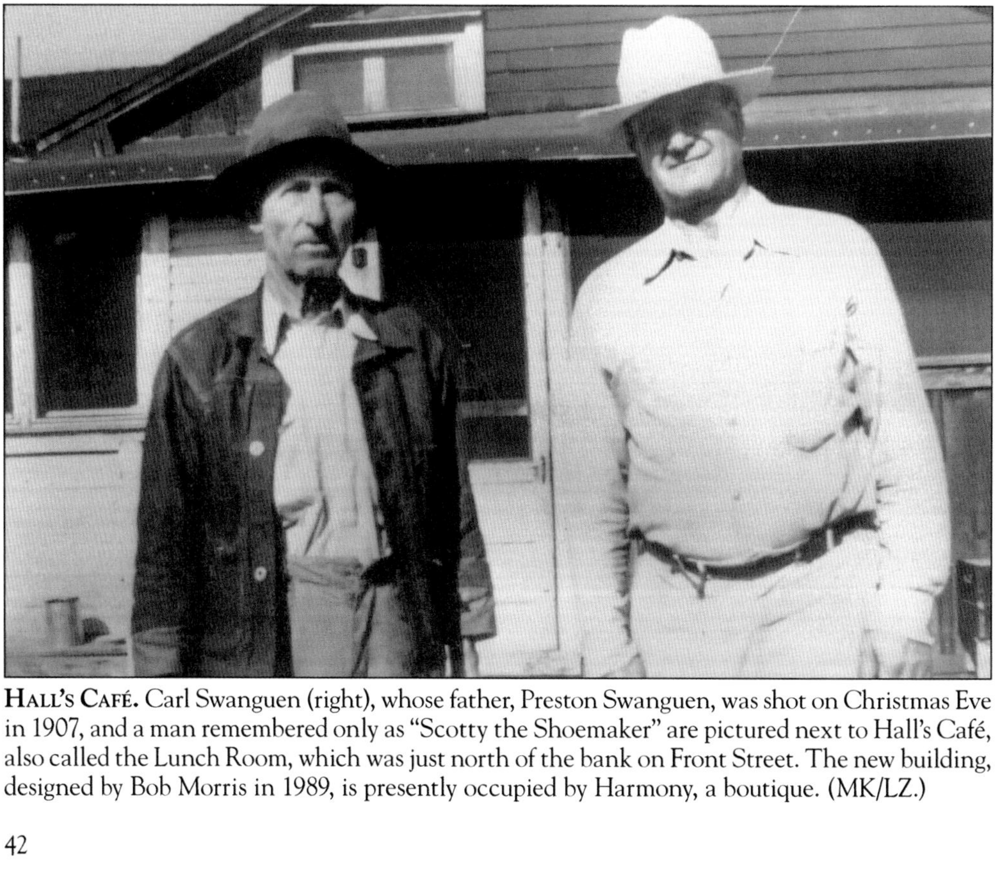

Hall's Café. Carl Swanguen (right), whose father, Preston Swanguen, was shot on Christmas Eve in 1907, and a man remembered only as "Scotty the Shoemaker" are pictured next to Hall's Café, also called the Lunch Room, which was just north of the bank on Front Street. The new building, designed by Bob Morris in 1989, is presently occupied by Harmony, a boutique. (MK/LZ.)

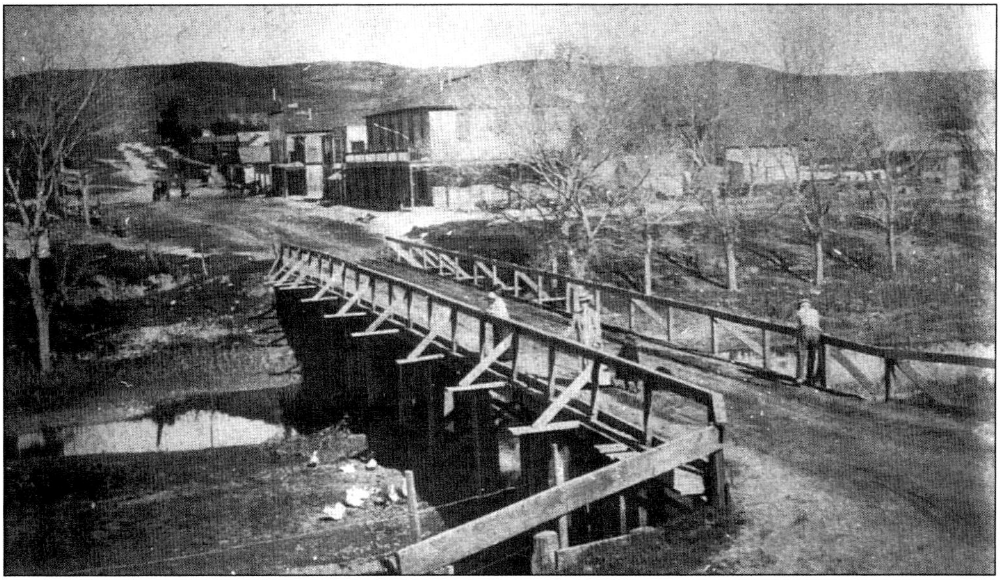

Main Street Bridge. This was the only bridge crossing Murrieta Creek in the early days of Temecula. Before the wooden bridge was replaced in 1945, a temporary culvert was built south of Main Street for automobile traffic. It washed out during a rainstorm, temporarily isolating residents wanting to use their automobiles. Planks were laid across the old pilings so pedestrians could cross the creek. (LB.)

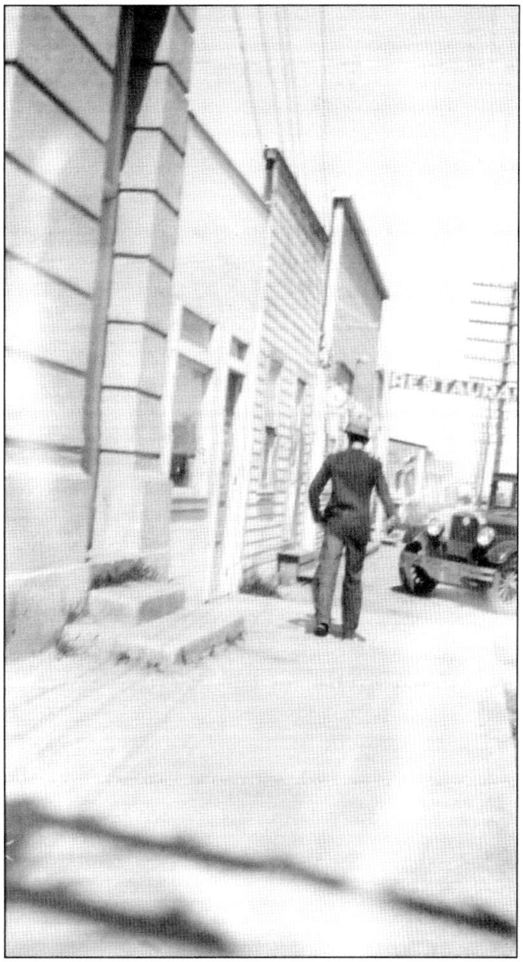

Buildings on Front Street. A businessman is walking from the bank, past the shoe repair shop and toward Hall's Café and an automobile. It is possible the unidentified man was one of the Hollywood moguls who frequented Winkels's blind pig saloon. Illegal slot machines hid behind partitions in cafés in the early 1940s. As motorized vehicles became more commonplace, Front Street became a thoroughfare. (GT.)

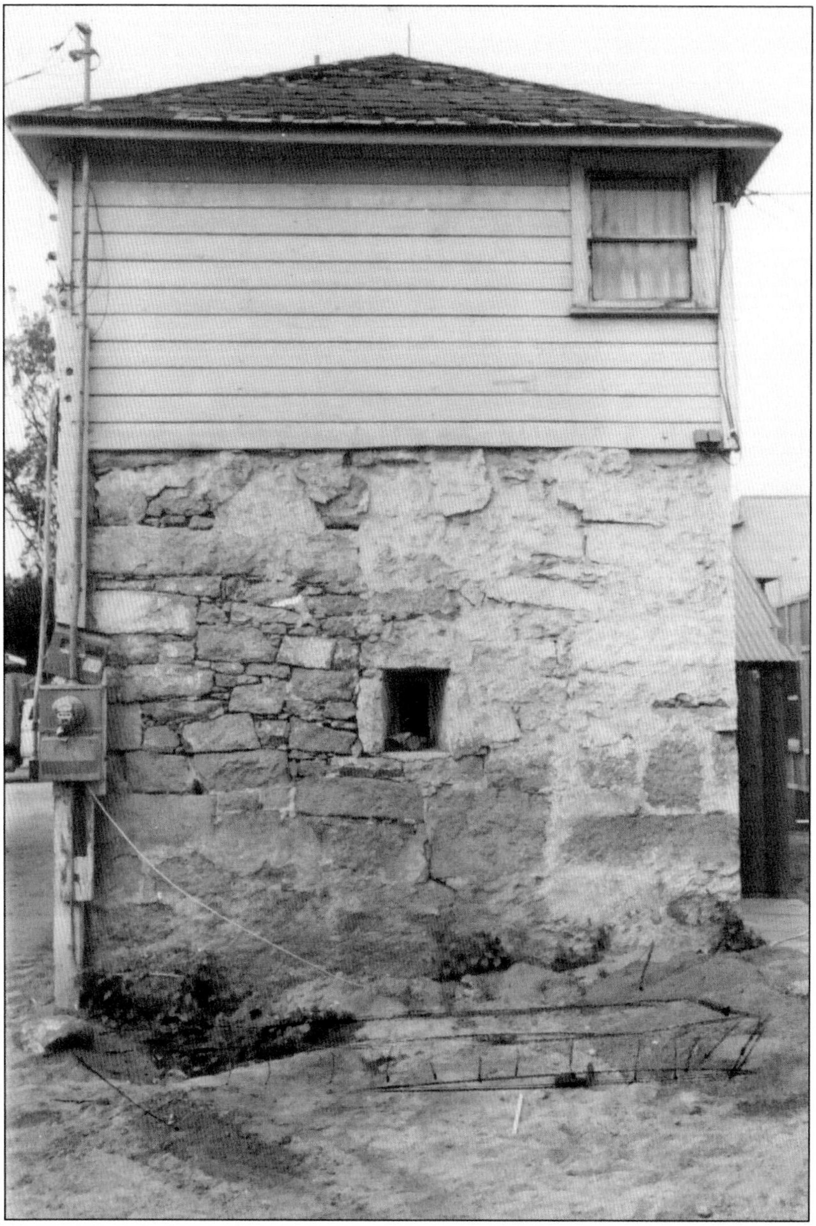

Tank House. Although this outbuilding to the Welty Building now has the sign "Jail" that tourists like to pose by, the structure was probably never used as a jail. When Frank Burnham drew a map from memory, he labeled the building "well." It was most likely a covered well with a mechanism to pump the water up to a storage tank. The base is constructed of Temecula granite, and at one time, there was an apartment upstairs, built after the tank was removed. Regarding a jail in Temecula's historic past, a notation on a 1960s map drawn by an unknown artist says, "[Preston] Swanguen [who was later killed by Horace Magee] had once saved Magee when Magee set jail on fire." Some have speculated that Mary Jane Welty had it constructed for the cold storage of grocery merchandise, and the bars were placed to prevent theft. The Escalliers set a horse trough alongside the building and crushed grapes by walking on them. The wine fermented in tubs outside and wandering livestock would get tipsy after sampling the drink. (TVM.)

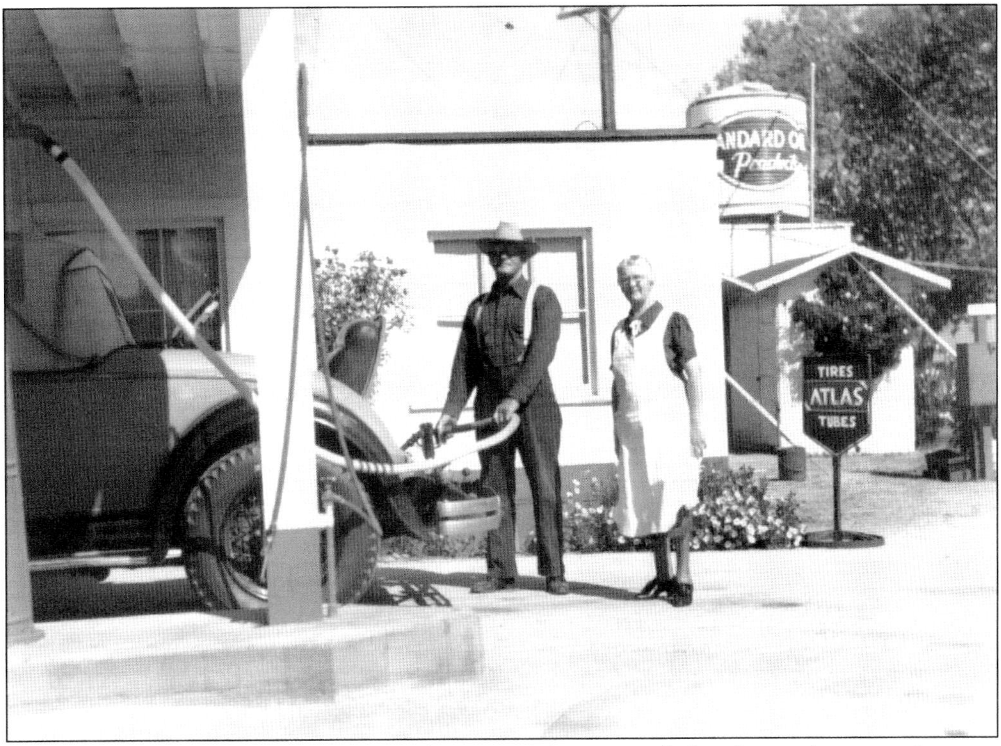

Albert and Mabel Nienke. The Nienkes owned the Temecula Lumberyard next to the train tracks on the west side of Murrieta Creek, a house on the northwest corner of Pujol and Main Streets, and a gas station and store near the Pala Road Bridge. The Nienkes built houses in Old Town and ran a small campground on Highway 395, where it intersected with Pala Road, now named Pechanga Parkway. They had an archery range and a petting zoo. (GO.)

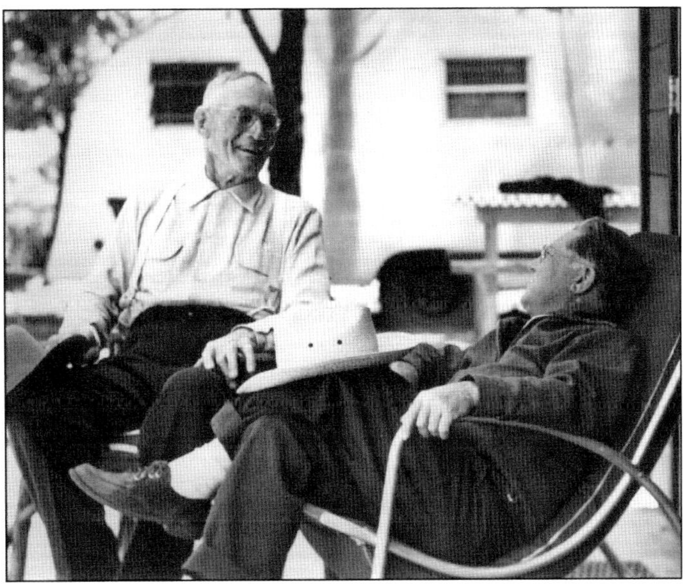

Nienke and Gardner. The famous mystery writer Erle Stanley Gardner (right) said his dog Rip chose Temecula for their home. In 1937, when the author was traveling, Rip had a barking fit. So, Gardner stopped at the Nienkes' (Albert Nienke pictured left) gasoline station and eventually bought a large ranch south of town, the site of the Great Oak tree. When Gardner needed to use a telephone, he came into town and called from the switchboard. (GO.)

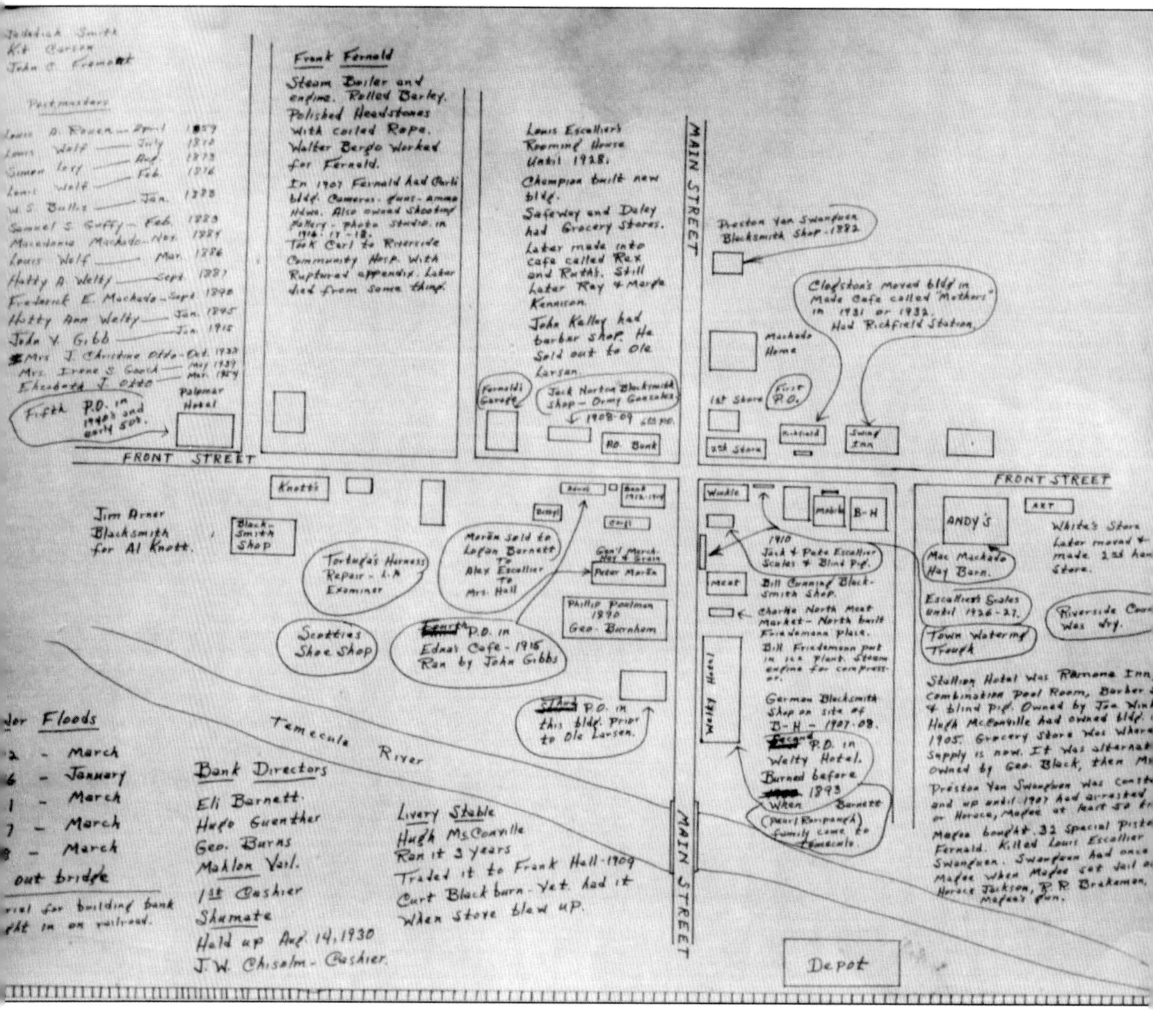

Annotated Map of Old Town. The compiler of this map is unknown. It lists the Art Shack, so it was drawn in the 1960s or later. Helpful lists and other notations give valuable information, like locations of post offices and postmasters and their years of service. It gives information about people with businesses in Old Town, and summaries of events, like the 1907 Christmas Eve shooting, bank robbery, and years of floods. It cites ownership and use of buildings in Old Town. This information, when compared with census records, deeds, newspaper articles, and gossip columns, gives a good picture of the layout of the town and the social lives of the people who lived and worked here. (GT.)

Three

Post Offices

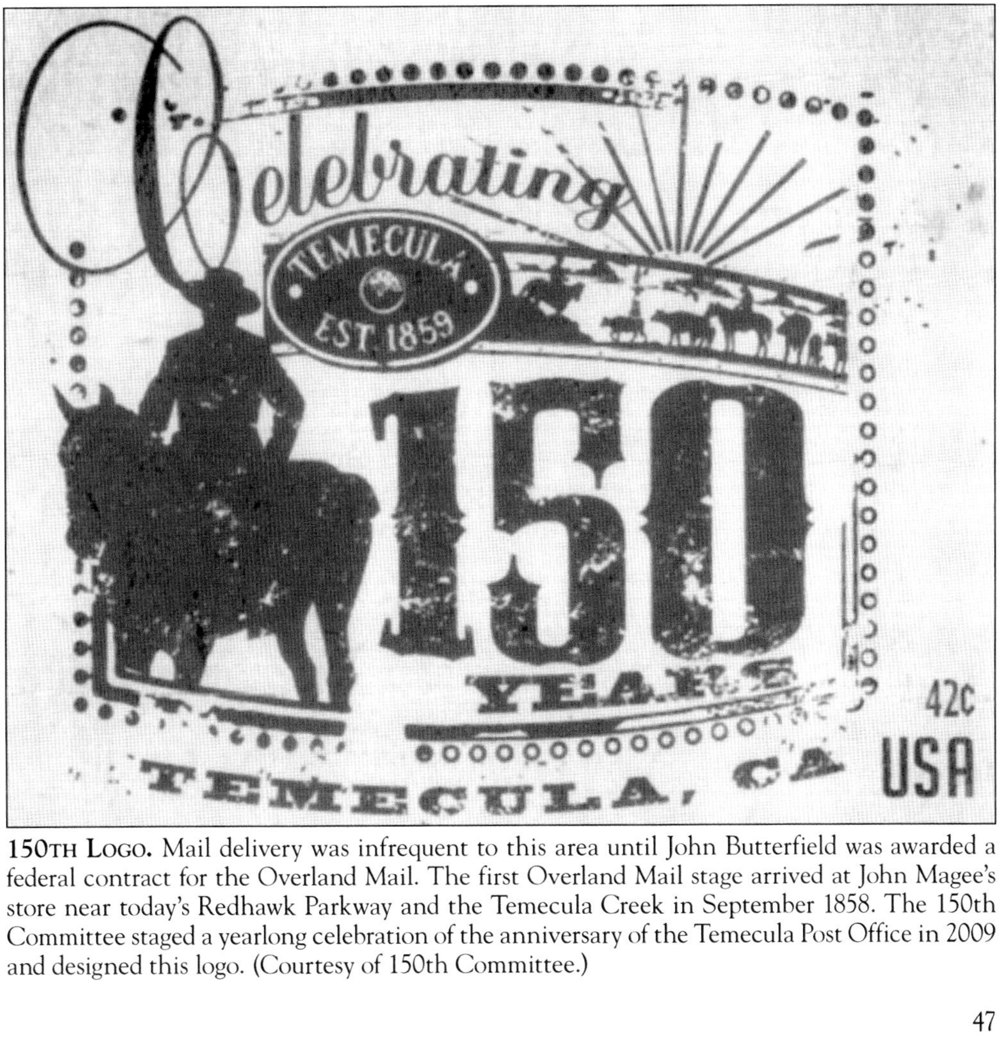

150th Logo. Mail delivery was infrequent to this area until John Butterfield was awarded a federal contract for the Overland Mail. The first Overland Mail stage arrived at John Magee's store near today's Redhawk Parkway and the Temecula Creek in September 1858. The 150th Committee staged a yearlong celebration of the anniversary of the Temecula Post Office in 2009 and designed this logo. (Courtesy of 150th Committee.)

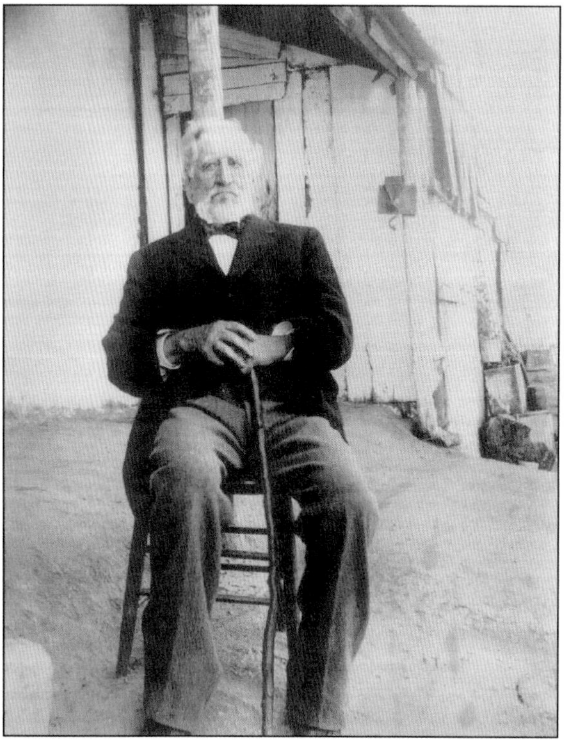

John Magee, Owner of Post Office No. 1. The first US post office in Temecula was established at Magee's Store on April 22, 1859, with Louis Rouen as postmaster. The store was located approximately where the Vail Ranch fire station on Overland Trail is today. Temecula's post office was the first in what would later become Riverside County. Butterfield Mail deliveries were discontinued in November 1862 because of the Civil War and Temecula postal service ended. (JPH.)

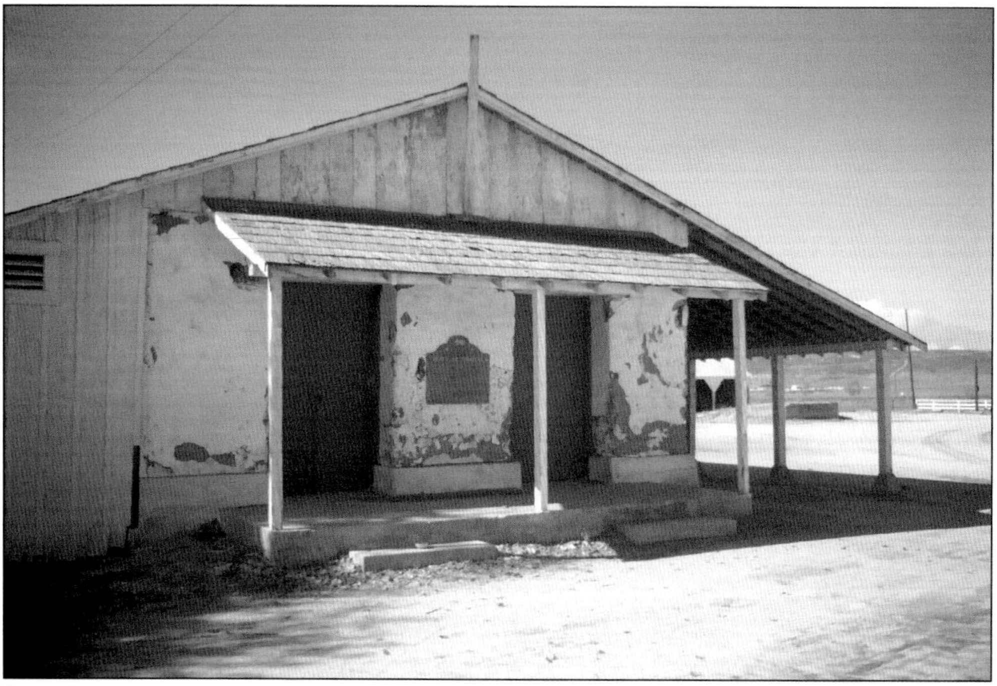

Post Office No. 2. In 1870, prior to the development of the new Town of Temecula, now called "Old Town Temecula," the Wolf Store adobe was the center of town. Louis Wolf served as postmaster at his general store. Mail was brought by stage or horseback three times a week. The store along the Southern Emigrant Trail is still standing near Temecula and Redhawk Parkways. (TVHS.)

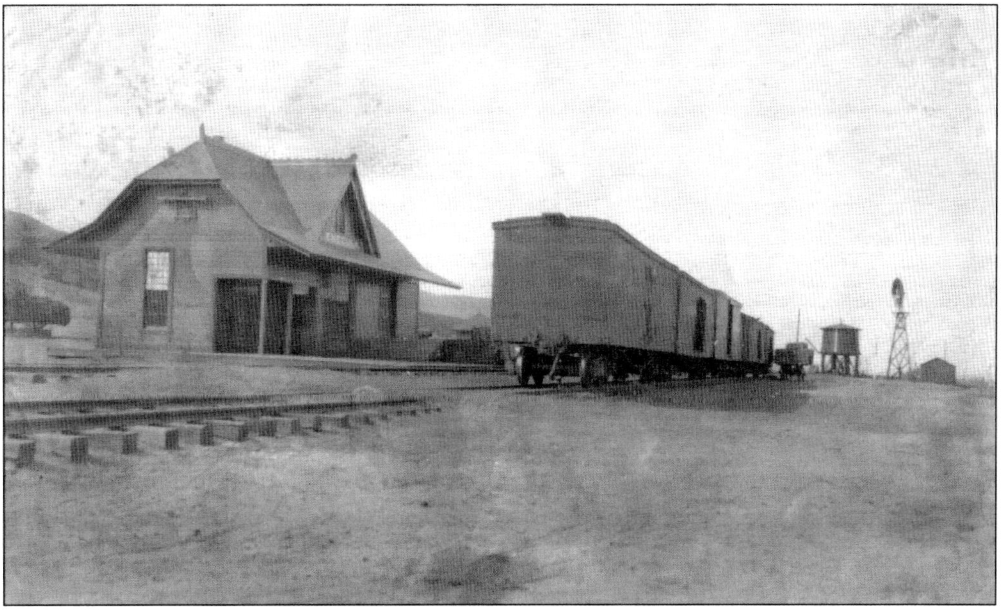

POST OFFICE NO. 3. A post office near the present-day Armstrong Garden Center on Ynez Road, opened and operated between 1880 and 1881, was called the Pujol Post Office; it is not included in the count. In 1883, a temporary train depot served as a post office near the corner of today's Diaz and Winchester Roads. The post office moved to the new depot, pictured, near Pujol and Main Streets in 1883. (GT.)

POST OFFICE DOCUMENT, 1875. This document indicates that the closest post office to the Temecula Post Office was 12 miles away near Fallbrook. It originally listed Temecula in San Diego County, and then it was changed to indicate Riverside County after the new county was formed in 1893. People picked up mail at the post office because there was no home delivery. (NA.)

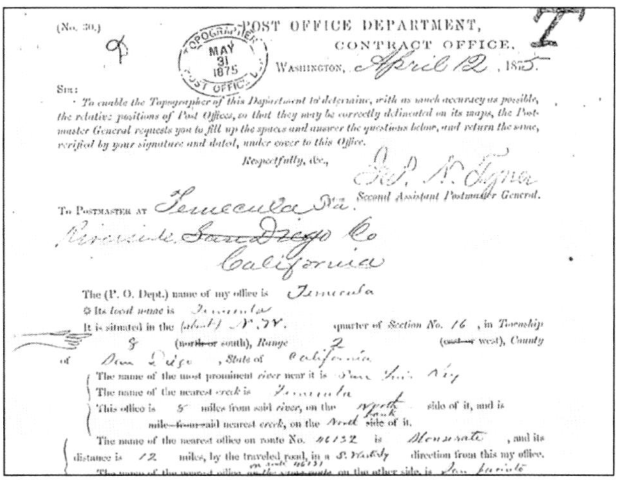

(No. 30.)

POST OFFICE DEPARTMENT,
CONTRACT OFFICE.
WASHINGTON, April 12, 1875.

TOPOGRAPHER MAY 31 1875 POST OFFICE

SIR:

To enable the Topographer of this Department to determine, with as much accuracy as possible, the relative positions of Post Offices, so that they may be correctly delineated on its maps, the Postmaster General requests you to fill up the spaces and answer the questions below, and return the same, verified by your signature and dated, under cover to this Office.

Respectfully, &c.,

[illegible]
Second Assistant Postmaster General.

TO POSTMASTER AT Temecula [illegible]
Riverside ~~San Diego~~ Co
California

The (P. O. Dept.) name of my office is Temecula
Its *local name* is Temecula
It is situated in the [illegible] N. W. quarter of *Section No.* 16, in *Township* 8 (~~north or~~ south), *Range* 2 (~~east or~~ west), *County* of San Diego, *State* of California
The name of the most prominent *river* near it is [illegible]
The name of the nearest *creek* is Temecula
This office is 5 miles from said *river*, on the North bank side of it, and is mile ~~from~~ said nearest *creek*, on the North side of it.
The name of the nearest office on route No. 46132 is [illegible], and its distance is 12 miles, by the traveled road, in a S. Westerly direction from this my office.
The name of the nearest office [illegible] on the other side, is [illegible]

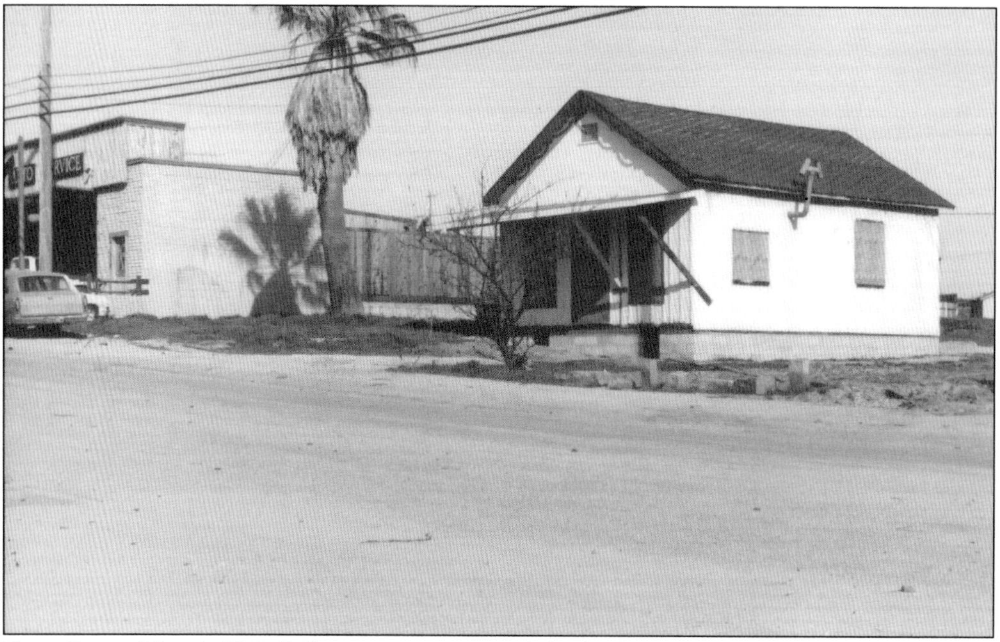

POST OFFICE NO. 4. W.S. Bullis was postmaster while this building behind the Machado Store was the Temecula Post Office, beginning in 1884. The structure, possibly built as a post office, is still standing. It has been an upholstery shop, a beauty salon, and a deli. At present, it is the Public House restaurant, specializing in locally grown foods and brew on tap. (TVHS.)

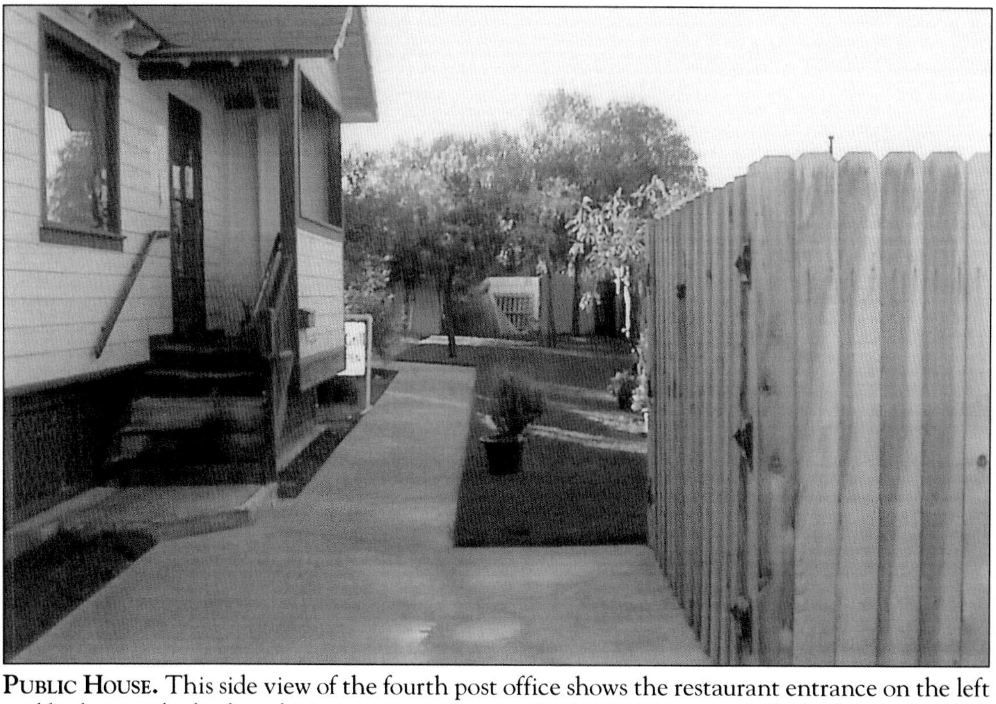

PUBLIC HOUSE. This side view of the fourth post office shows the restaurant entrance on the left and looks into the backyard prior to renovations in the 2000s. Now gated, the back area provides an alfresco dining area where musicians perform on a small stage. It is located at 41971 Main Street and is in view of the Temecula Civic Center. (DF.)

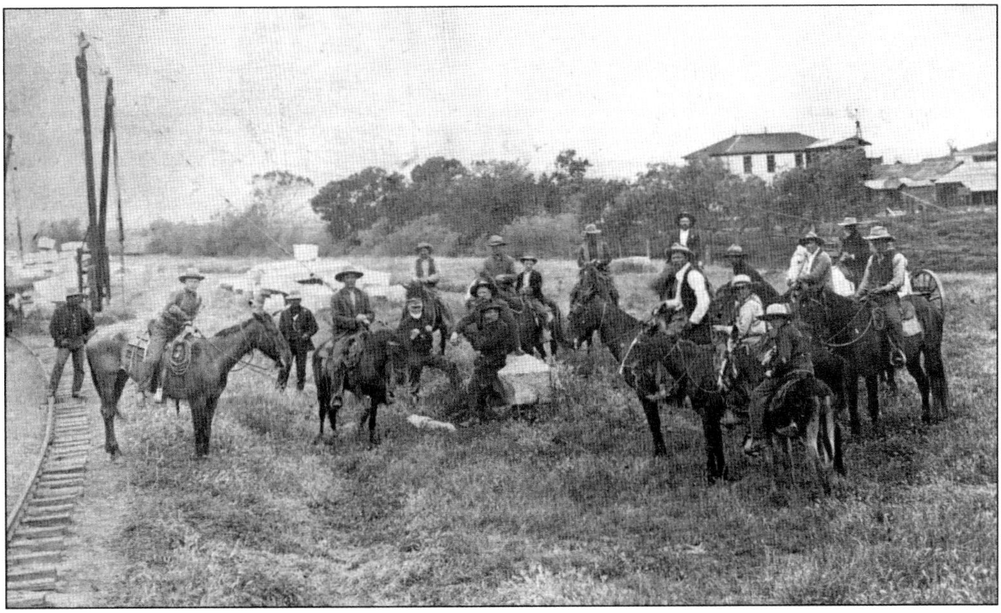

Postal Patrons, 1894. The Temecula Post Office served the residents of the small village, including the stationmaster, shopkeepers, hoteliers, stonemasons, quarrymen, blacksmiths, liverymen, and those who provided entertainment with billiards, cards, and strong drinks. Mail was kept at the post office until the recipient came for it. Travelers received mail addressed to General Delivery, Temecula, California. (TVHS.)

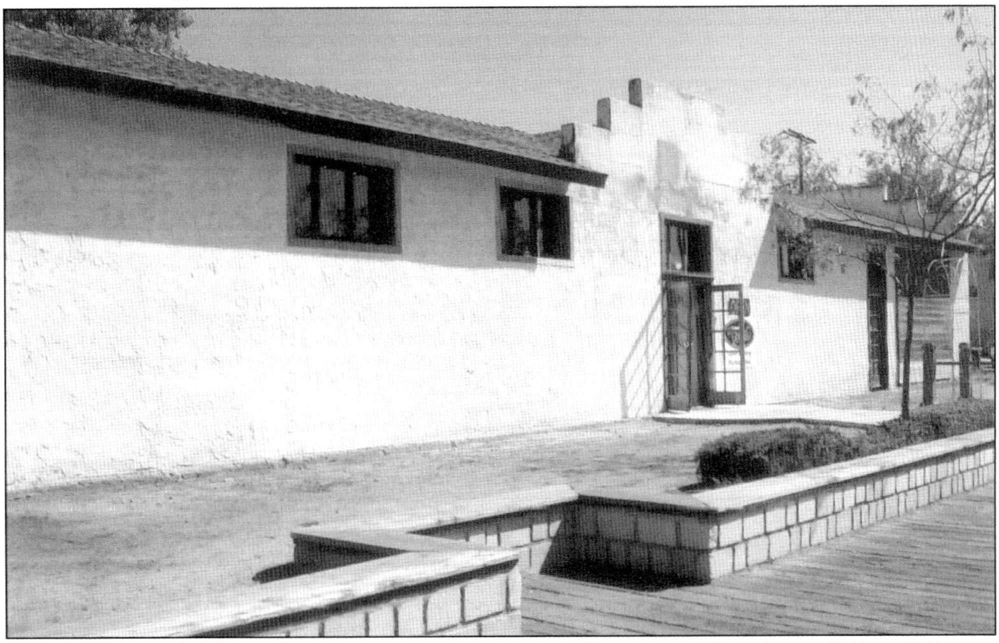

Post Office No. 5. The first Machado Store was thought to house the Temecula Post Office in 1886. Other early postmasters were Simon Levi in 1873 and Samuel Guffy in 1883. Machado built the store, shown in the photograph, in 1909 of terra-cotta bricks after the original one burned. Machado Store's receipts from the 1910s identify his store as the Mission Store, selling granite curbing and Mission Indian baskets. (DF.)

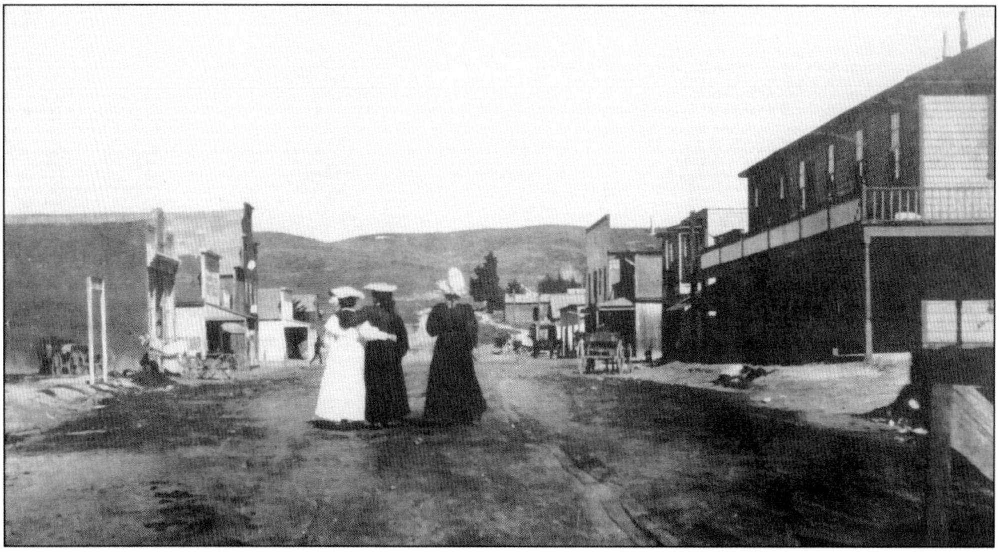

POST OFFICE NO. 6. The post office was housed in the Welty Hotel beginning in 1887. The structure was originally built for train passengers. Some of the lumber used to rebuild the hotel after a fire in 1891 was salvaged from the Santa Gertrudis School. This photograph shows young ladies in front of the Welty Hotel and also shows the fourth and fifth post offices in the background. (TVM.)

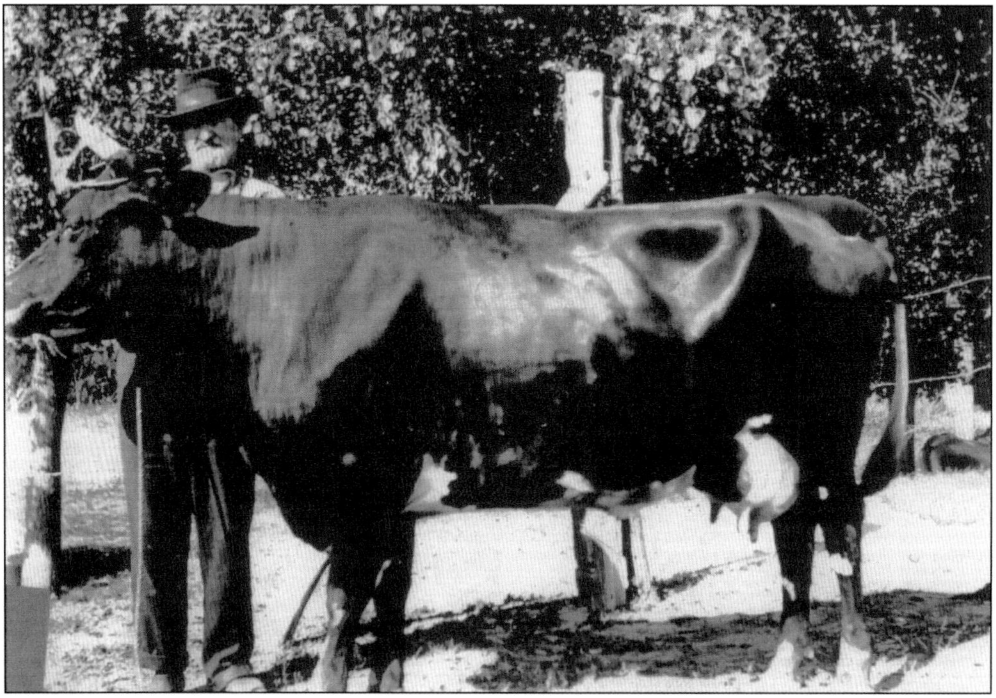

JOHN WELTY OUTSIDE OF POST OFFICE NO. 7. After being in the Welty Hotel for eight years, the post office moved to the Welty home in 1895 and was there for 20 years. The home (not shown) was across the street from the hotel and was later owned by Ole Larson. Welty and his wife, Mary Jane, came to California in 1866. Pennypickle's Workshop, the Temecula's Children's Museum, is at that location now. (JR.)

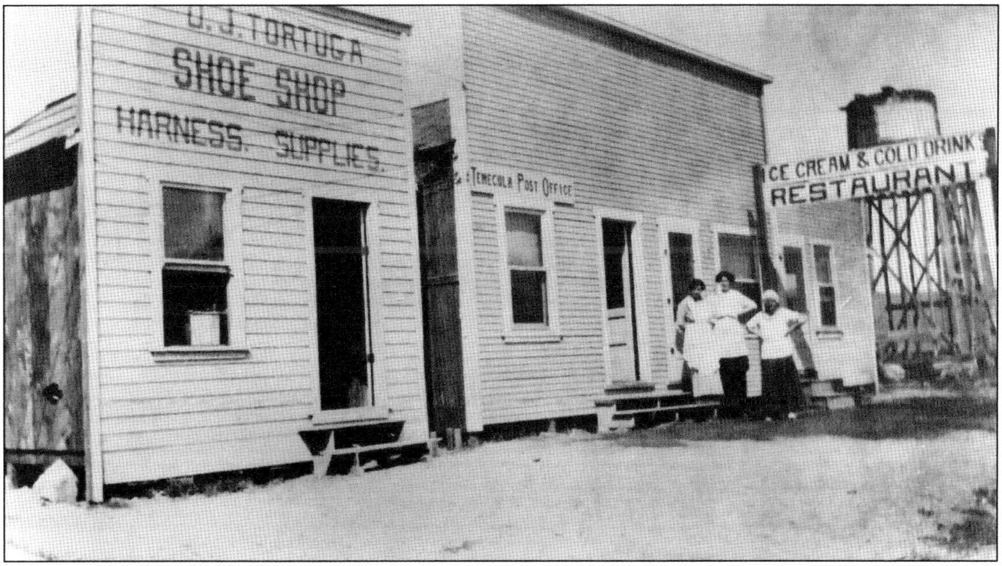

POST OFFICE NO. 8. John Welty's daughter Hattie was the postmaster in this building, the first constructed specifically for use as a post office, in 1915. Over the years, it was also the telephone office and bus station. The building later was Hall's Café. It was next to the present-day Bank of Mexican Food Restaurant. (MK/LZ.)

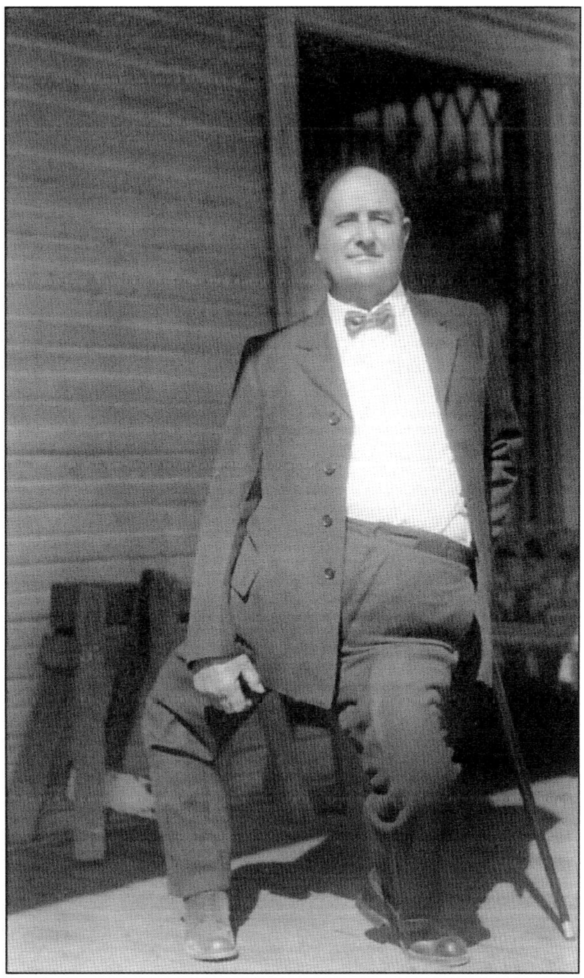

POSTMASTER JOHN V. GIBB. After Hattie Welty resigned, Gibb, a double-amputee with no family, served as postmaster from 1915 until the time of his death in 1938. A small bedroom in the rear of the building, shown above, accommodated the telephone operator, who slept next to the switchboard. Tortuga's shoe shop was next door on Front Street. (MK/LZ.)

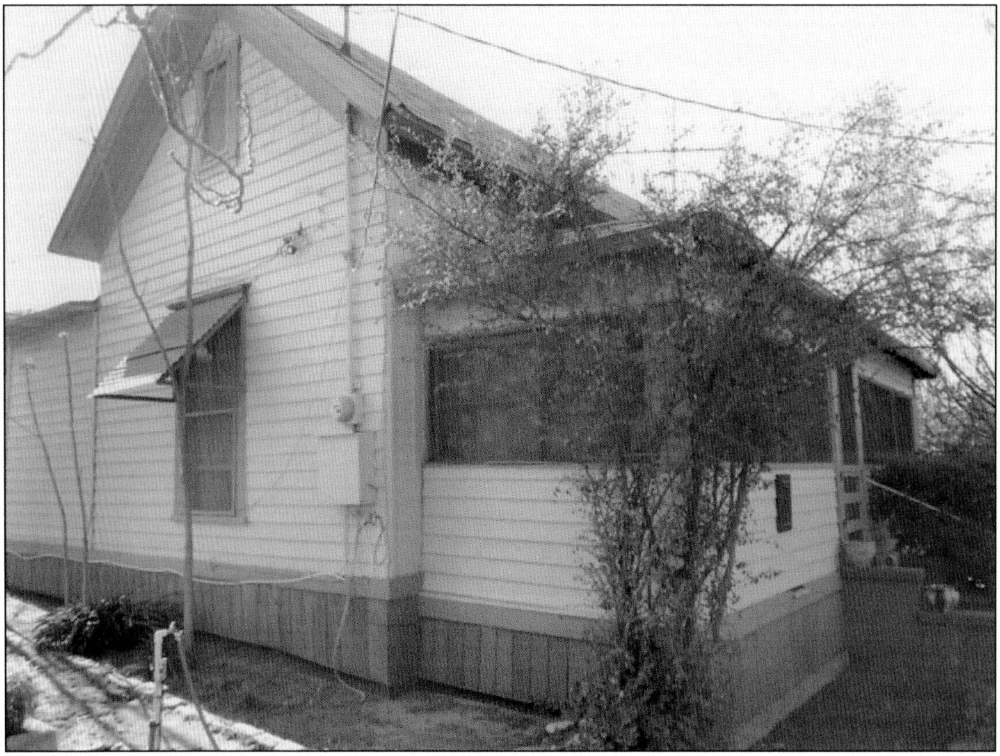

Post Office No. 9. The Temecula Post Office moved to Postmaster Christine Otto's home in 1938. This private home on Pujol Street has a historical society commemorative plaque on it. The original historical society placed six plaques throughout Old Town. The present Temecula Valley Historical Society has continued placing plaques at noteworthy locations in Old Town. (LB.)

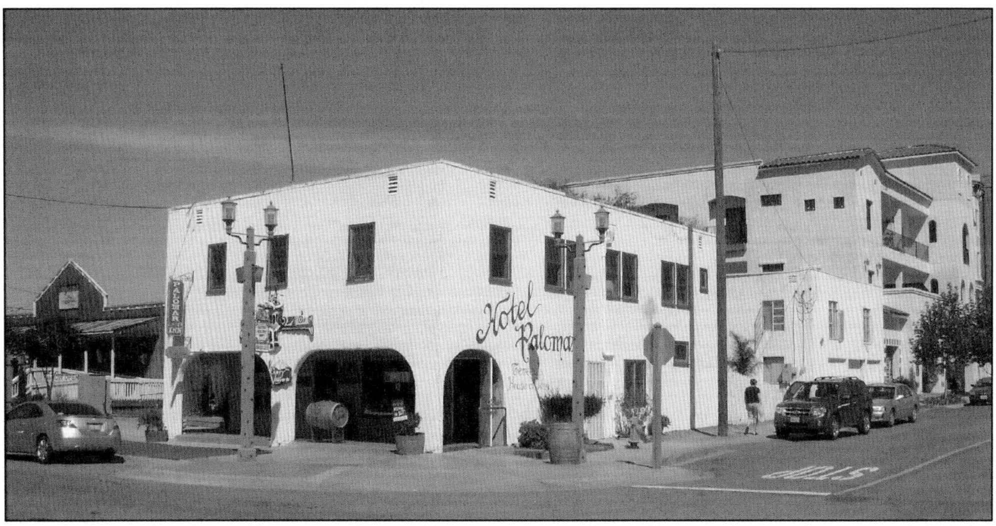

Post Office No. 10. The Palomar Hotel, in continuous use since 1928, housed the post office longer time than any other facility, from 1939 to 1974. In the background is the architecturally compatible Palomar Heritage Building, built with white stucco arches in 2008 with apartments above retail space. In 1967, a postal annex opened in the Rancho California Plaza on the east side of the rerouted Highway 395. (JH.)

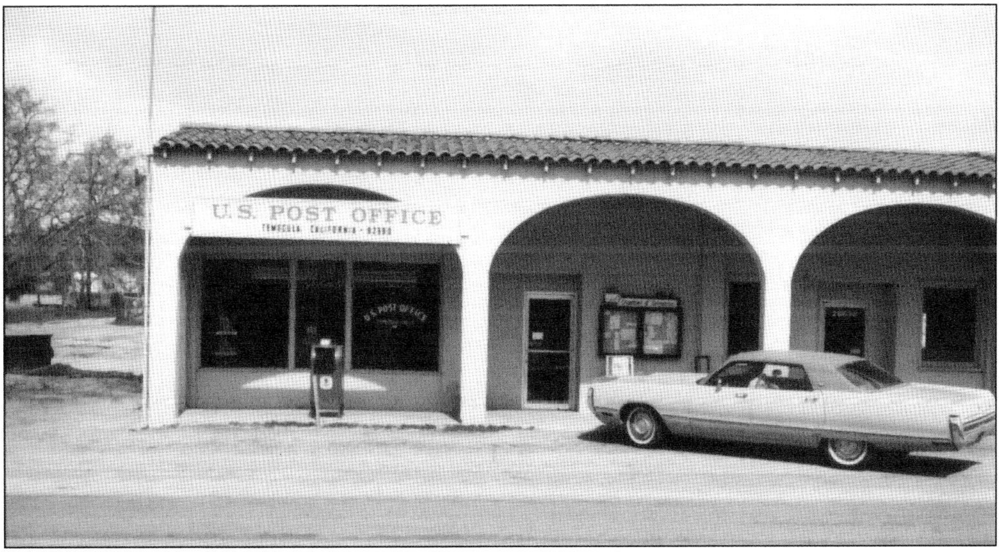

Post Office No. 11. A Riverside County marker at this location said, "The Temecula Post Office, first in Riverside County, was established in 1859 three miles southeast of here on the Butterfield Stage Route. When California Southern Railroad was built through here in 1882, the post office moved and the town followed. Both locations are successors to Temeku, a Luiseno Indian Village one mile south of here." (JJ.)

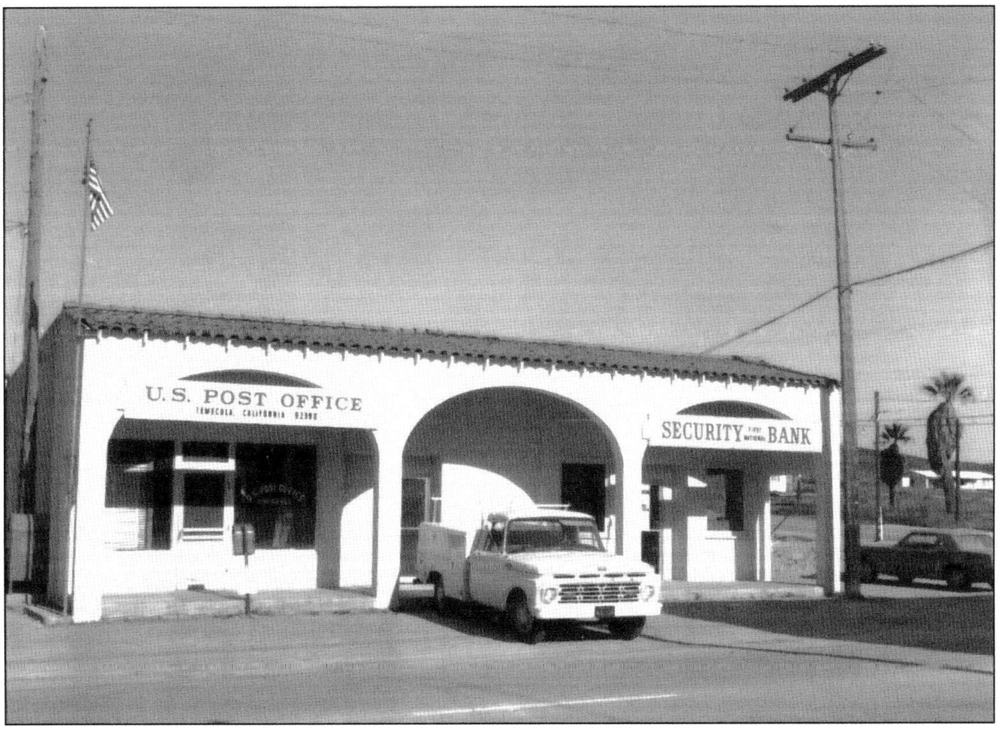

Post Office and Security Bank. The post office was located in the north end of the Champion Building for six years, beginning in 1974. As the town grew, the facility was unable to accommodate the volume of mail, which had to be sorted on the floor until a new post office was built. The sign mentioned above was located in front of this post office. (JJ.)

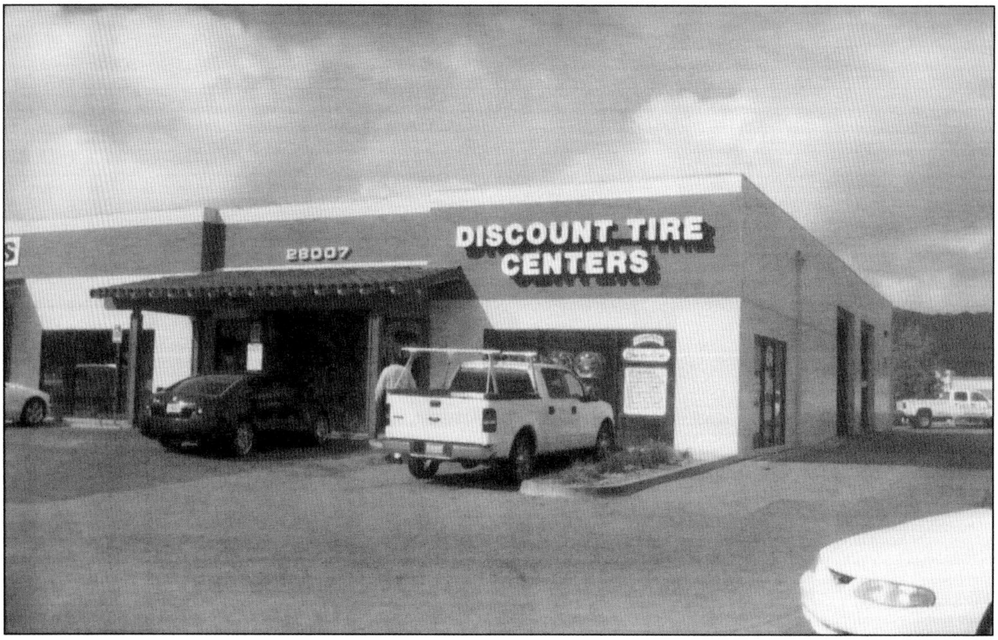

POST OFFICE NO. 12. When the Champion Building closed for remodeling in 1980, the Temecula Post Office moved to this building in an industrial park on Front Street until the Old Town Post Office was completed in 1981 to meet the needs of the growing community. This is now a Discount Tire Center. (DF.)

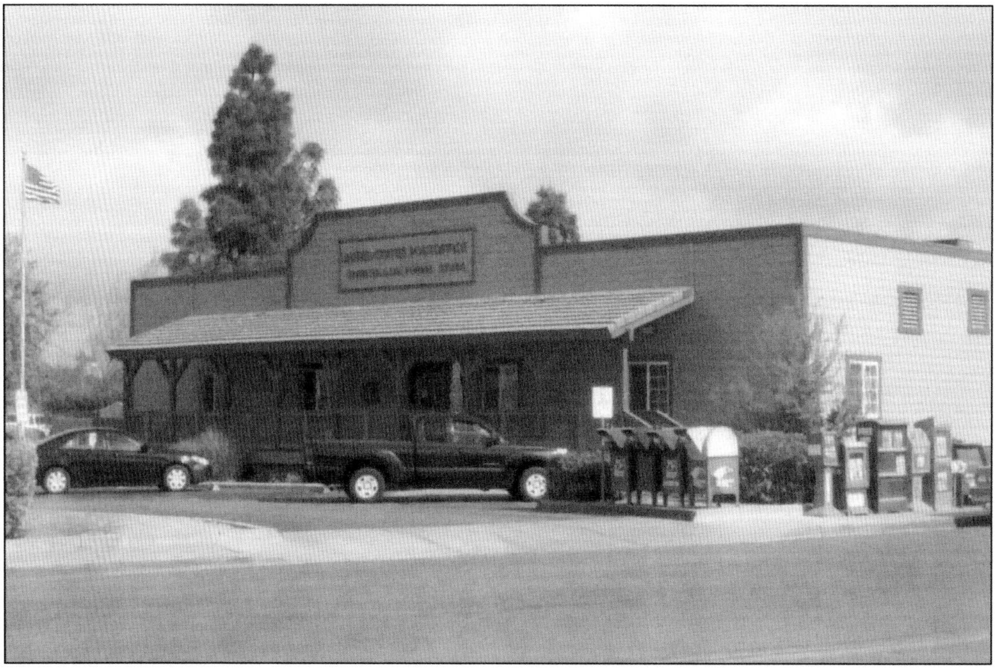

POST OFFICE NO. 13. The 4,800-square-foot Old Town Post Office on Moreno Road and Front Street opened in 1981 with a Western facade; it is still open for business as a branch post office. Bob Gurney was the first postmaster to serve from this facility, which cost about $280,000 to build. Some of the earliest residents of Temecula still have single digit post office boxes here. (DF.)

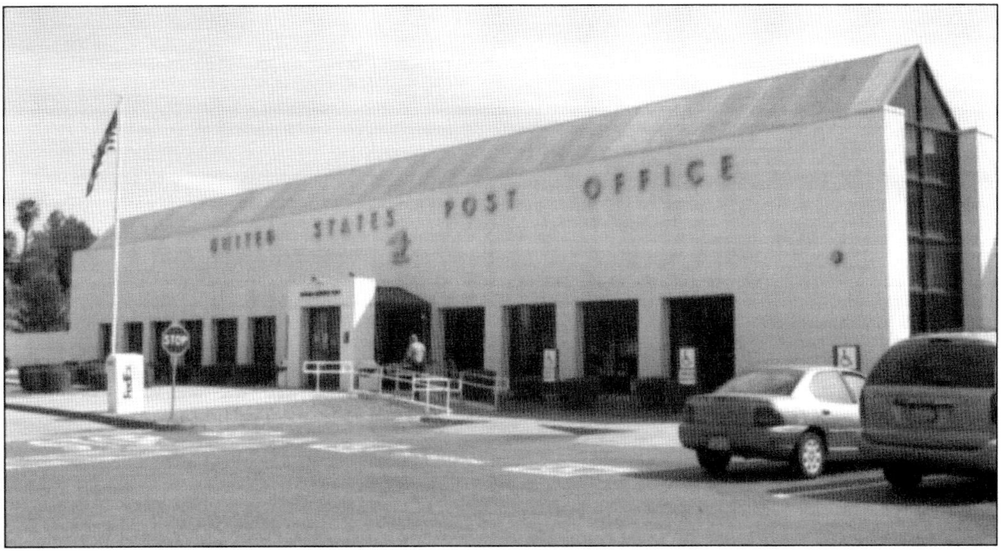

POST OFFICE NO. 14. This, the current main post office, opened in 1991 and is the hub for postal business. Located at the corner of Rancho California and Margarita Roads, it serves a population of over 100,000 residents. The 13th post office and four annexes share the workload. The post office opened on September 25, 1991, and the main postal zip code is 92591. (BM.)

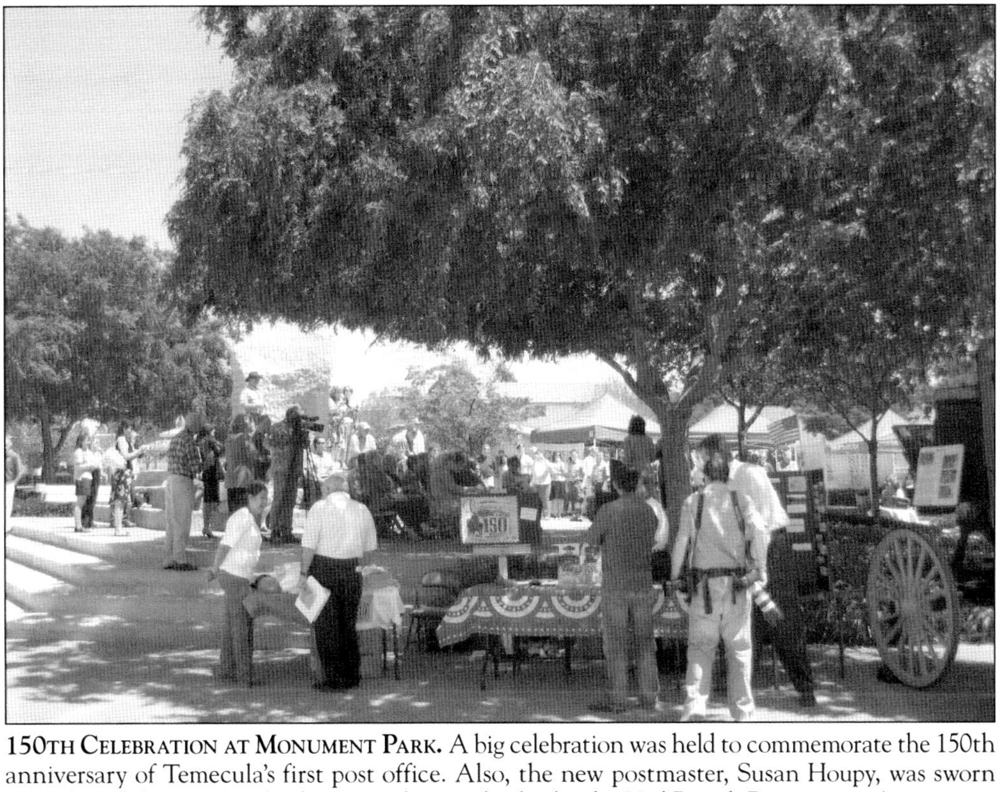

150TH CELEBRATION AT MONUMENT PARK. A big celebration was held to commemorate the 150th anniversary of Temecula's first post office. Also, the new postmaster, Susan Houpy, was sworn in at the celebration. In the foreground was a display by the Vail Ranch Restoration Association and the Temecula Valley Historical Society. A special commemorative stamp was made for use as a cancellation stamp upon request for that day only. (RF.)

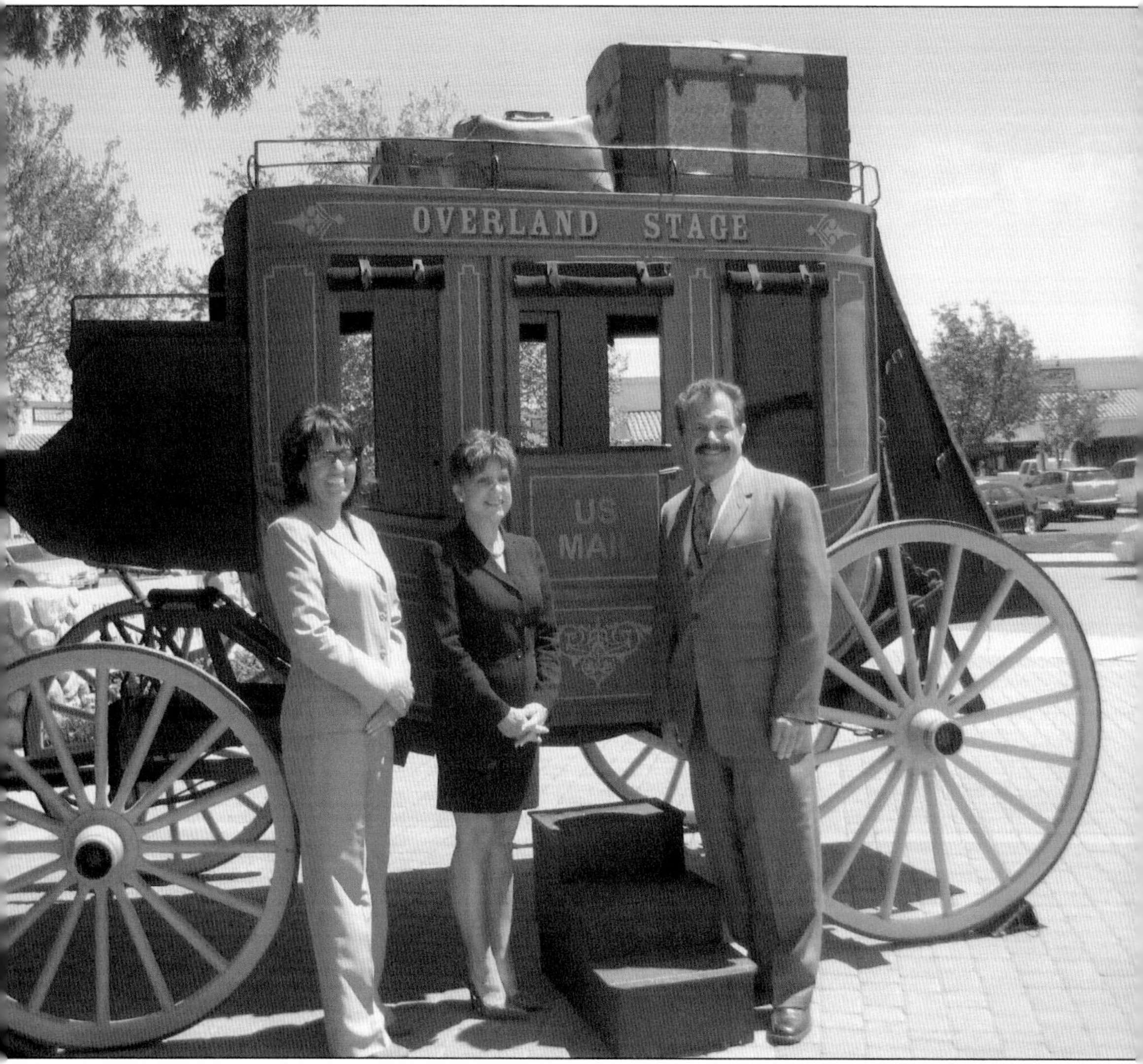

New Postmaster, 2009. After her swearing in on April 22, 2009, Postmaster Susan Houpy (left), Temecula mayor Maryann Edwards (center), and San Diego District postal manager Dallas Keck posed by the replica stagecoach owned by the Vail Ranch Restoration Association to honor the Butterfield Overland Mail that first carried regular deliveries to Temecula. Temecula's post office has the distinction of being one of the oldest inland post offices in Southern California. (RF.)

Four

Development of the Town

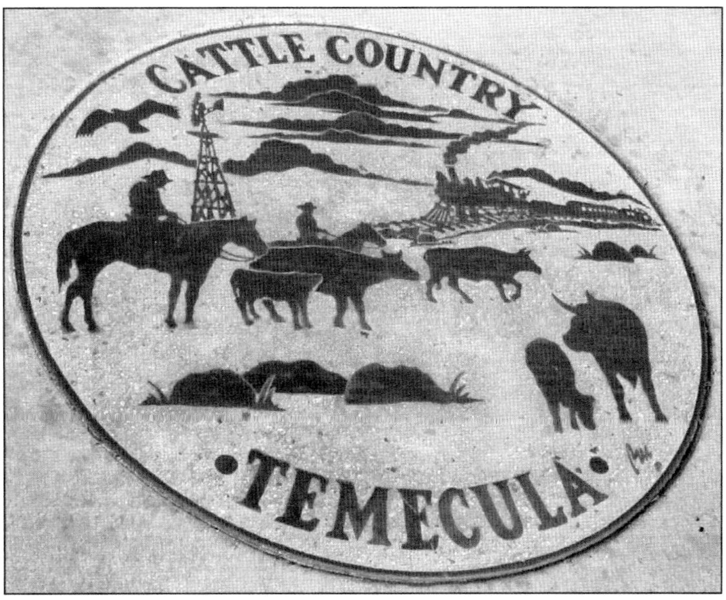

Cattle Country Medallion. Old Town Temecula grew as a stop on the railroad to service the cattle town. Saloons, banks, and general stores catered to ranchers, cowboys, and farmers. Little by little, the character of the town was changing and needed schools and churches to take care of the growing population. As traffic increased on Front Street, businesses started to support the travelers. (BM.)

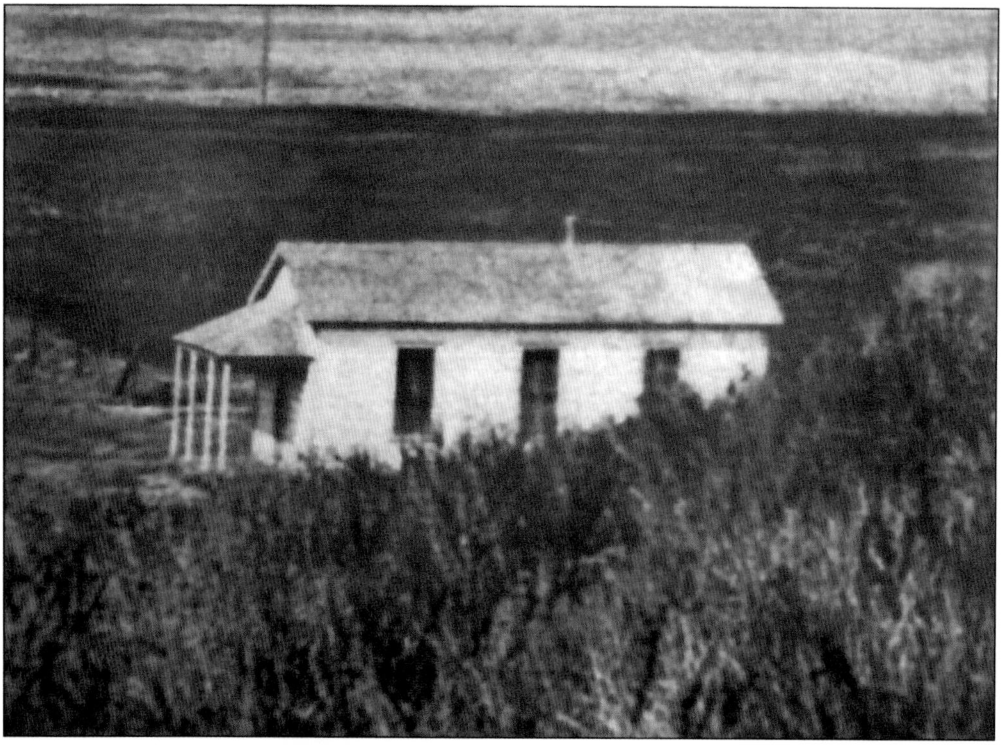

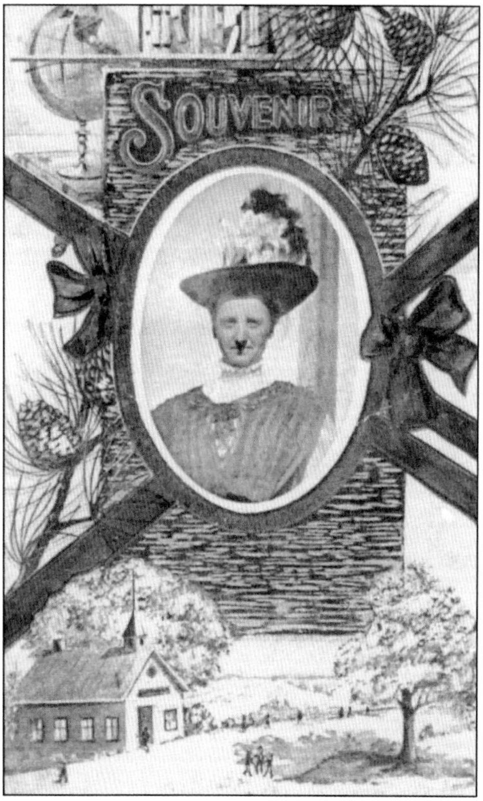

LITTLE TEMECULA SCHOOL. This school was on Loma Linda Road, formerly called Magee Road, in the Little Temecula Rancho. In 1874, Jacob Bergman and Louis Wolf were trustees of the school; the teacher was D.B. Armick. Wolf may have had a previous school at the Wolf Ranch. Thomas Brady, James Banks, and John Magee were trustees in 1885. School was held at this location from 1873 through 1917. (TVM.)

GRADUATION LEAFLET, 1909. Teacher Annie Grace Barwise presided over students at the little school. Walter Daly Knight was the only student graduating from eighth grade in 1909. There were four books in the school library in 1874 and 176 books in 1887. The building was 16 by 32 feet in size with a 15-foot ceiling, and later a second outhouse was constructed. Teachers reported poor outhouse ventilation, which was improved over time. (TVHS.)

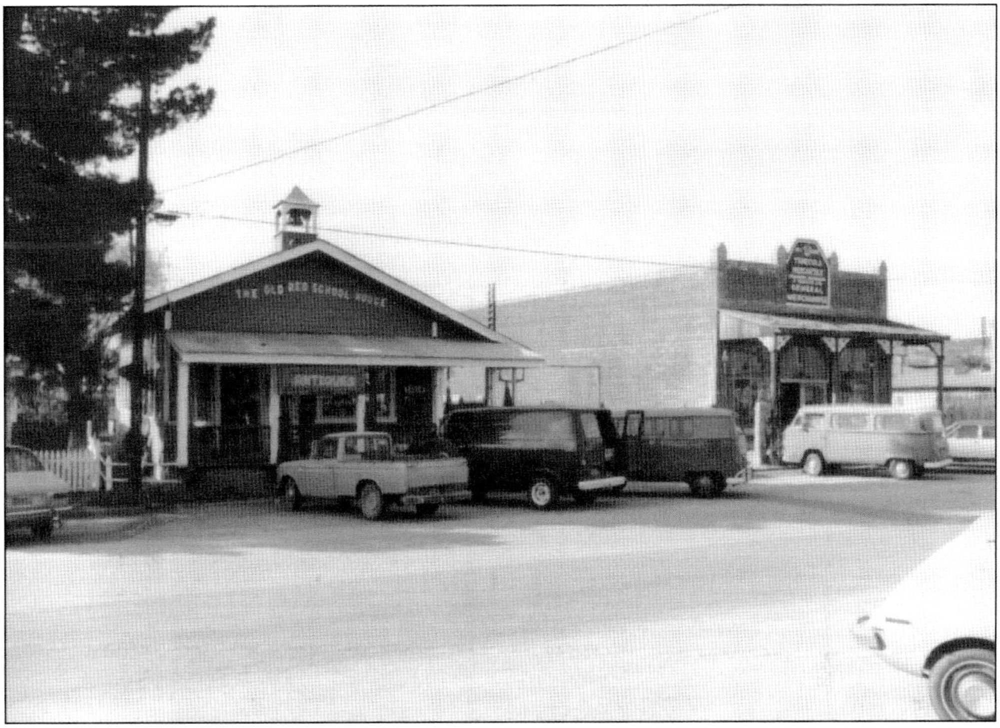

Old School on Main Street. In 1938, this old school was moved from Pala and Loma Linda Roads and was added to the Mission-style school, which was built in 1915. When the Mission-style school burned to the ground, this school was saved and moved to Main Street. It was used by several businesses before it, too, went up in flames in 1979. Pennypickle's Workshop is now on the site. (TVM.)

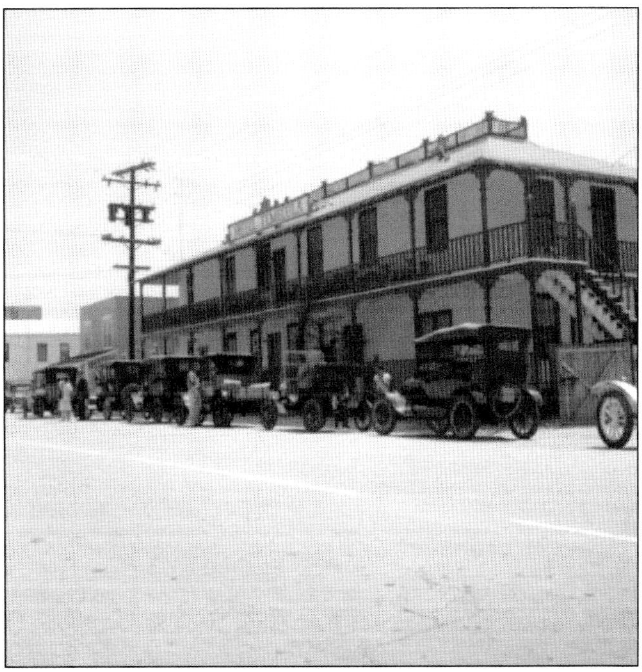

Welty Hotel. To avoid a conflicting school name, the first school district in Old Town was named the Pujol School District. Until funds were raised and the building was erected, classes were held in the Welty Hotel, approximately from 1888 until 1889. The students probably met in the dining room of the hotel, which also served as the post office at the time. (TVM.)

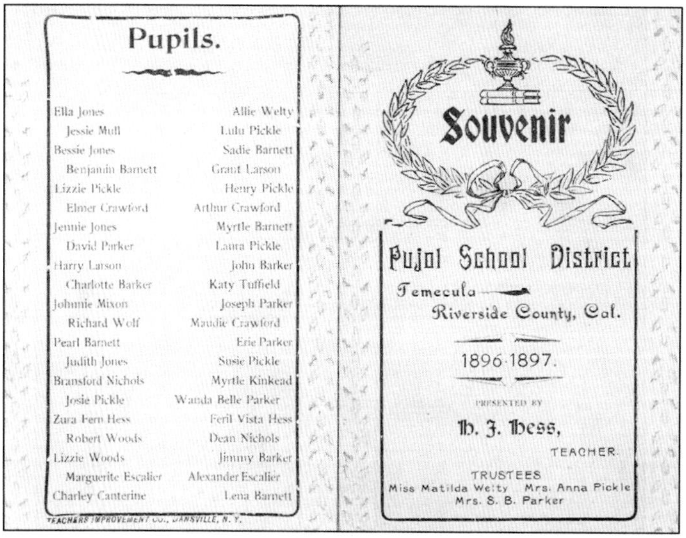

Pupils.

Ella Jones	Allie Welty
Jessie Mull	Lulu Pickle
Bessie Jones	Sadie Barnett
Benjamin Barnett	Grant Larson
Lizzie Pickle	Henry Pickle
Elmer Crawford	Arthur Crawford
Jennie Jones	Myrtle Barnett
David Parker	Laura Pickle
Harry Larson	John Barker
Charlotte Barker	Katy Tuffield
Johnnie Mixon	Joseph Parker
Richard Wolf	Maudie Crawford
Pearl Barnett	Erie Parker
Judith Jones	Susie Pickle
Bransford Nichols	Myrtle Kinkead
Josie Pickle	Wanda Belle Parker
Zura Fern Hess	Feril Vista Hess
Robert Woods	Dean Nichols
Lizzie Woods	Jimmy Barker
Marguerite Escalier	Alexander Escalier
Charley Canterine	Lena Barnett

TEACHERS IMPROVEMENT CO., DANSVILLE, N. Y.

Souvenir

Pujol School District

Temecula

Riverside County, Cal.

1896-1897.

PRESENTED BY

H. J. Hess,

TEACHER.

TRUSTEES

Miss Matilda Welty Mrs. Anna Pickle

Mrs. S. B. Parker

Souvenir of Pujol School District, 1897. The district served 42 students living in the Old Town area that year, some with familiar surnames of Wolf, Barnett, and Escallier. The building, constructed in 1889 for $500, sat near the location of today's Temecula Valley Museum. To make room for a new school, this building was moved to two lots, purchased for $95, on Fourth Street in 1915. (ROM.)

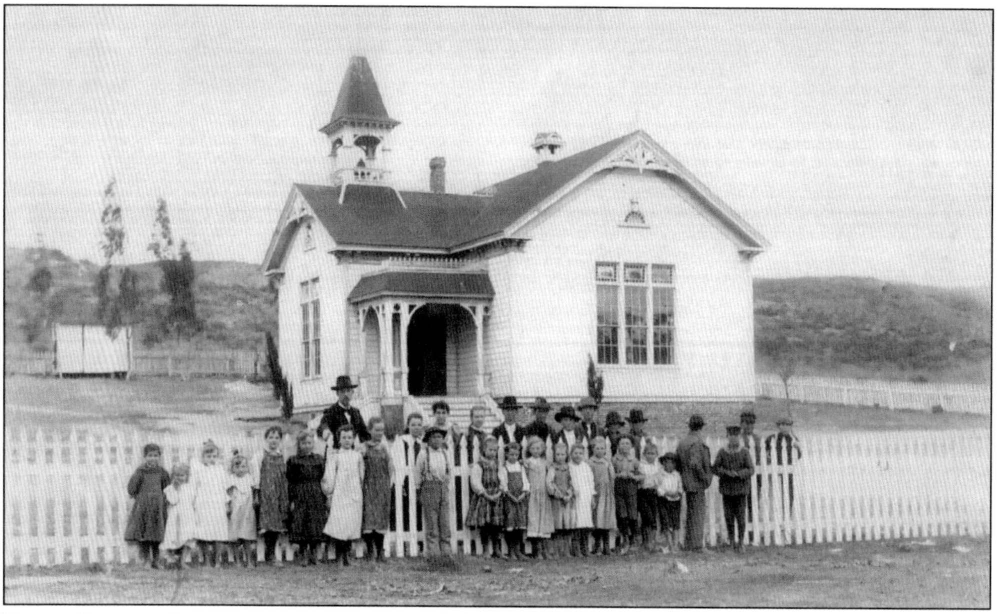

Pujol School Students, 1896. None of these students are identified. The school originally sat near today's Temecula Valley Museum and was moved to Fourth Street to make room for the Temecula Union School. It was moved again in 1986 to the Santiago Road campus of the Temecula Community Church. Restored with 1889 school decor, it is one of the few historical buildings that has not been architecturally changed. (ROM.)

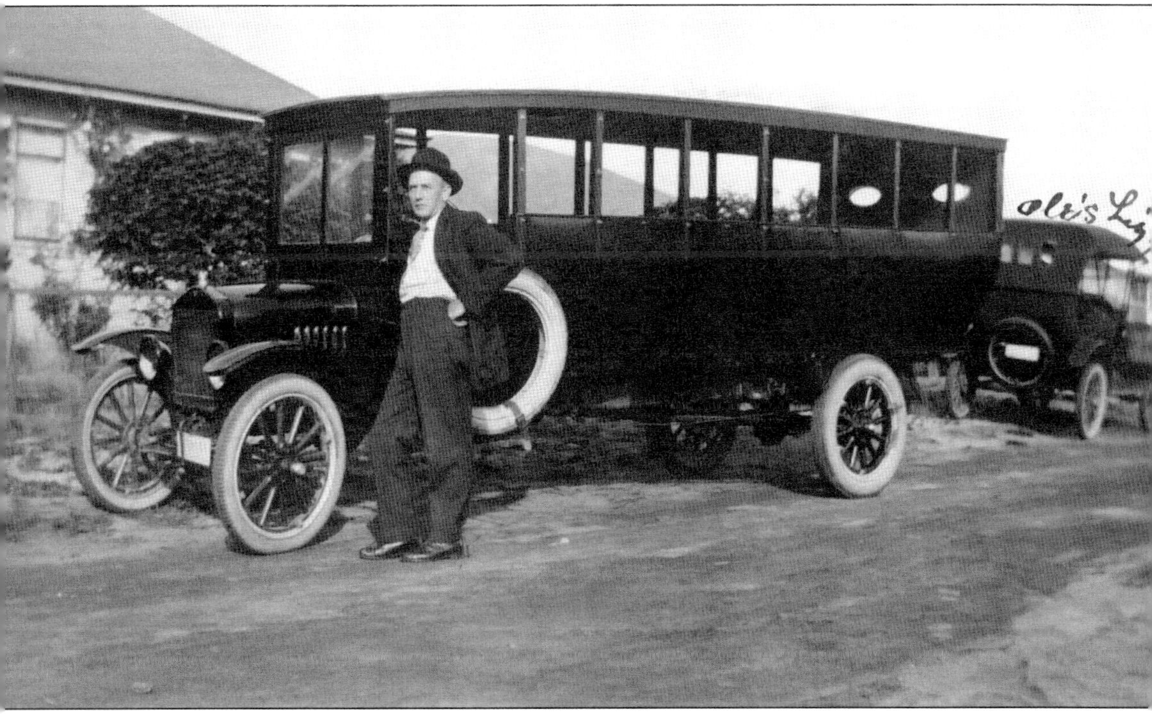

School Bus and Tin Lizzy. Someone wrote on the photograph, "Al Otto and the Temecula School bus with Ole Larson's tin lizzy behind." Al Otto was a school bus driver and custodian for 27 years, beginning in the spring of 1922. He drove the newest Model T Ford bus, which was open but equipped with isinglass curtains that rolled down in case of rain. On his bus, he carried children who later became community leaders and school board members of Temecula and Elsinore School Districts. Richard Barnett, Margaret Roripaugh Ramsay, Albert Ceas, Margie Kitch, and Sarah Clogston, to name just a few, were passengers on his bus. (TVM.)

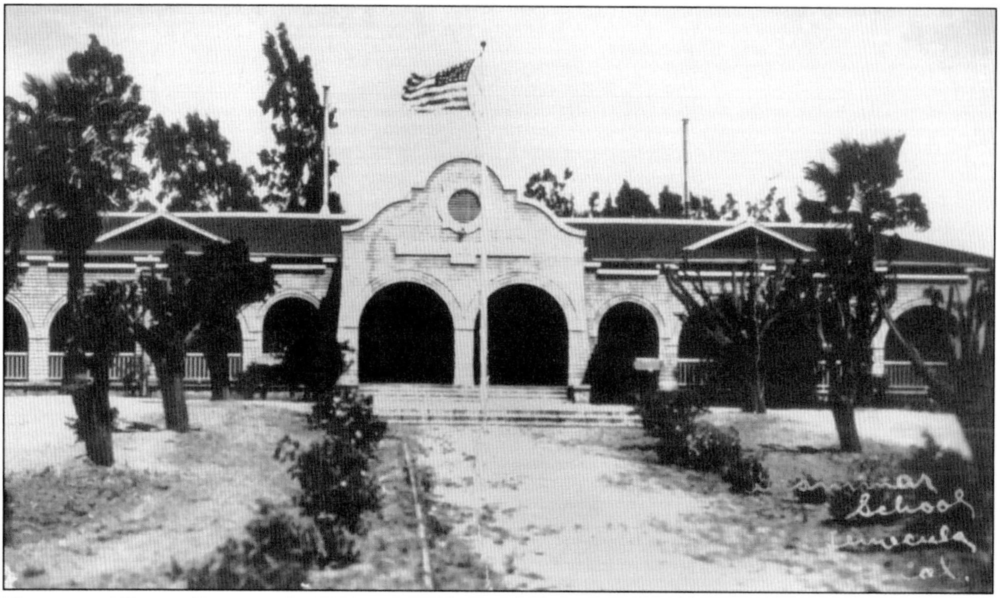

TEMECULA UNION SCHOOL. In 1914, a new Temecula Union School District merged the Temecula, Pujol, and Santa Gertrudis School Districts. The Temecula School was built in 1914 for $10,000. The building was designed in the Mission style by architect Stanley Wilson. Wilson also designed the Mission Inn in Riverside. Both the Temecula School and the Mission Inn were connected by the Inland Highway, also known as Mission Road. (JJ.)

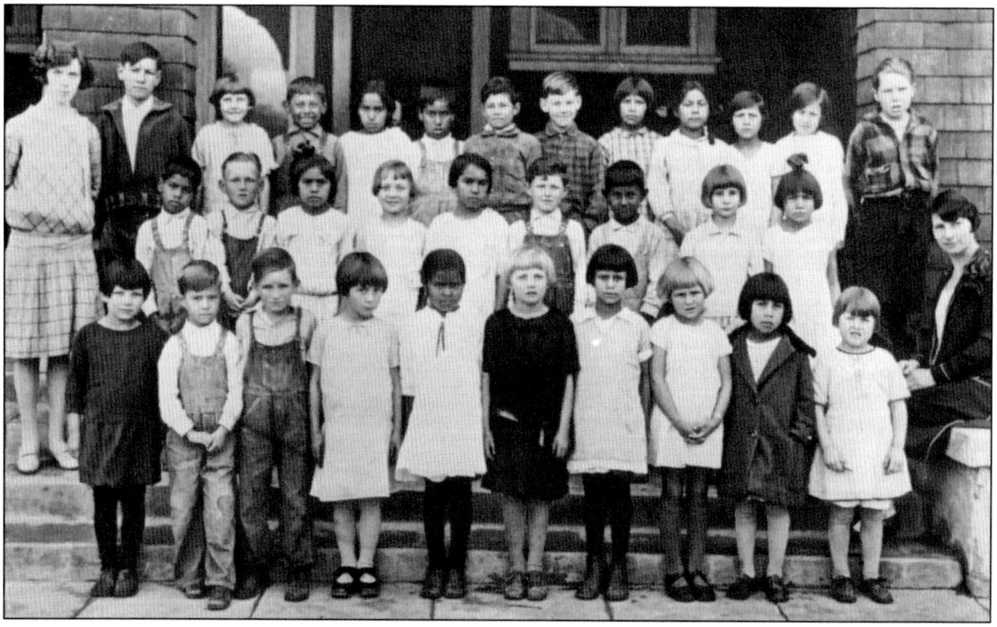

TEMECULA STUDENTS, 1925. Students attended this school for grades one through eight and then attended Elsinore High School. Some of the 45 students in this photograph are Tony Tortuga, Billy Friedemann, Jimmy Arviso, Harry Helms, Horace Parker, Vern Otto, Mildred Sweet, Vera Knott, Margaret Roripaugh, Marjorie Swanguen, Annie Speziali, Peggy Walters, Don Clogston, Bennie Hitt, Francis Barnett, Lloyd Arviso, and Leon Servell. The teachers were Mrs. Cantarini and Mrs. Murray. (GT.)

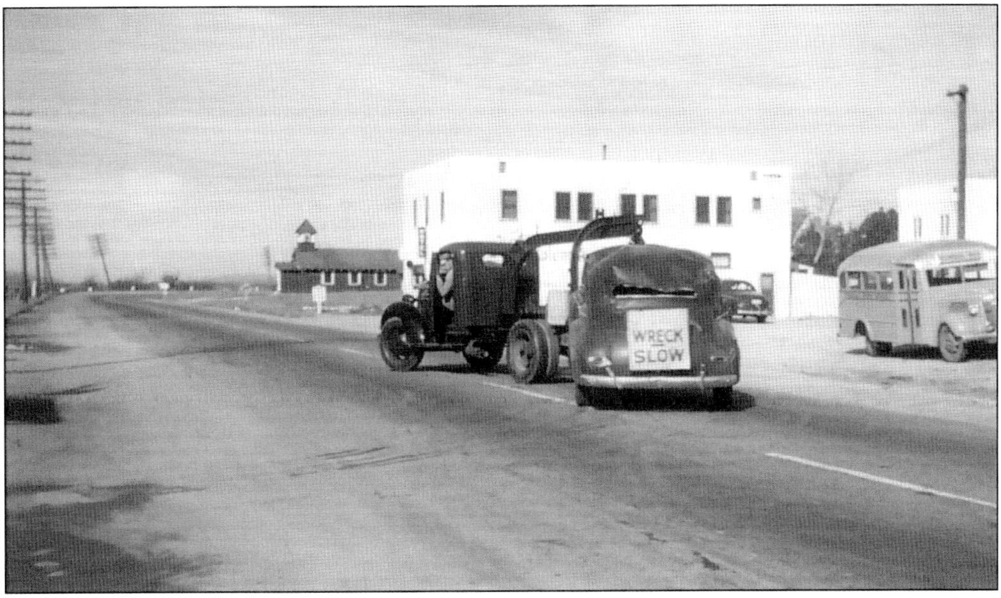

Tow Truck and School Bus. Johnny Munoa is seen driving Knotts Garage Tow Truck, a 1937 Chevrolet truck, north on Front Street pulling a disabled car. The unpainted Catholic church in the background was on Sixth and Front Streets. A school bus was parked across from the Palomar Hotel. Until the 1970s, a bus carried students from Pechanga, Temecula, Murrieta, Wildomar, and Alberhill to high school in Elsinore. (JK.)

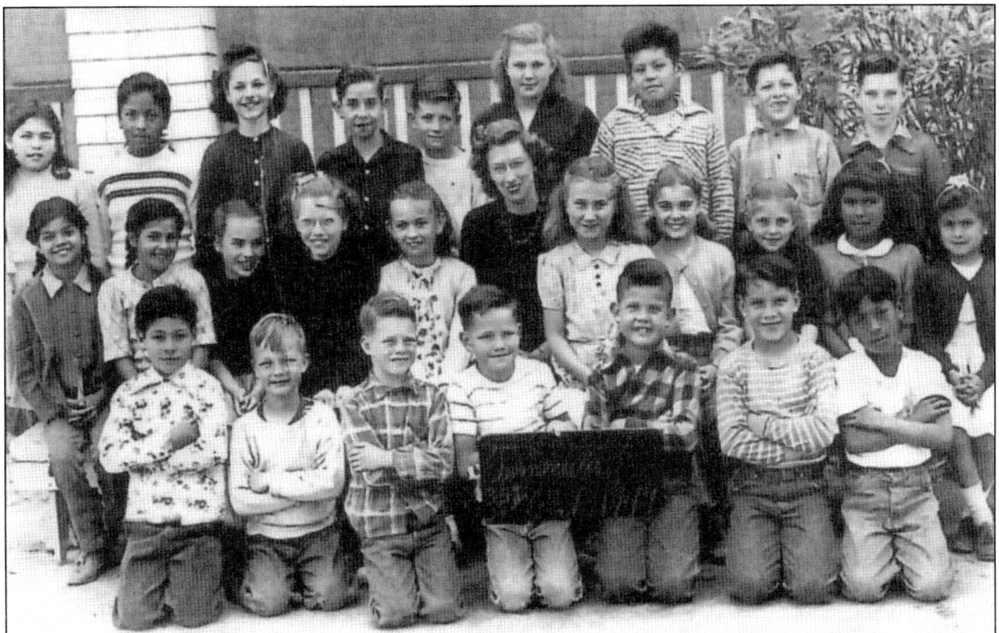

Temecula Students, 1949. At the time, this was the only school in Temecula. By 2012, there were 34 public schools in Temecula and several private schools. Students from the following families are shown: Mora, Friedemann, Knott, Ramirez, Navarro, Roripaugh, Emerson, Archambeau, Robinson, Rodriguez, Ceas, Barnett, Young, Martin, Calac, and Hoth. The teacher was Ann Louise Knott, a relative of the local Knotts, who came from South Dakota. (DB.)

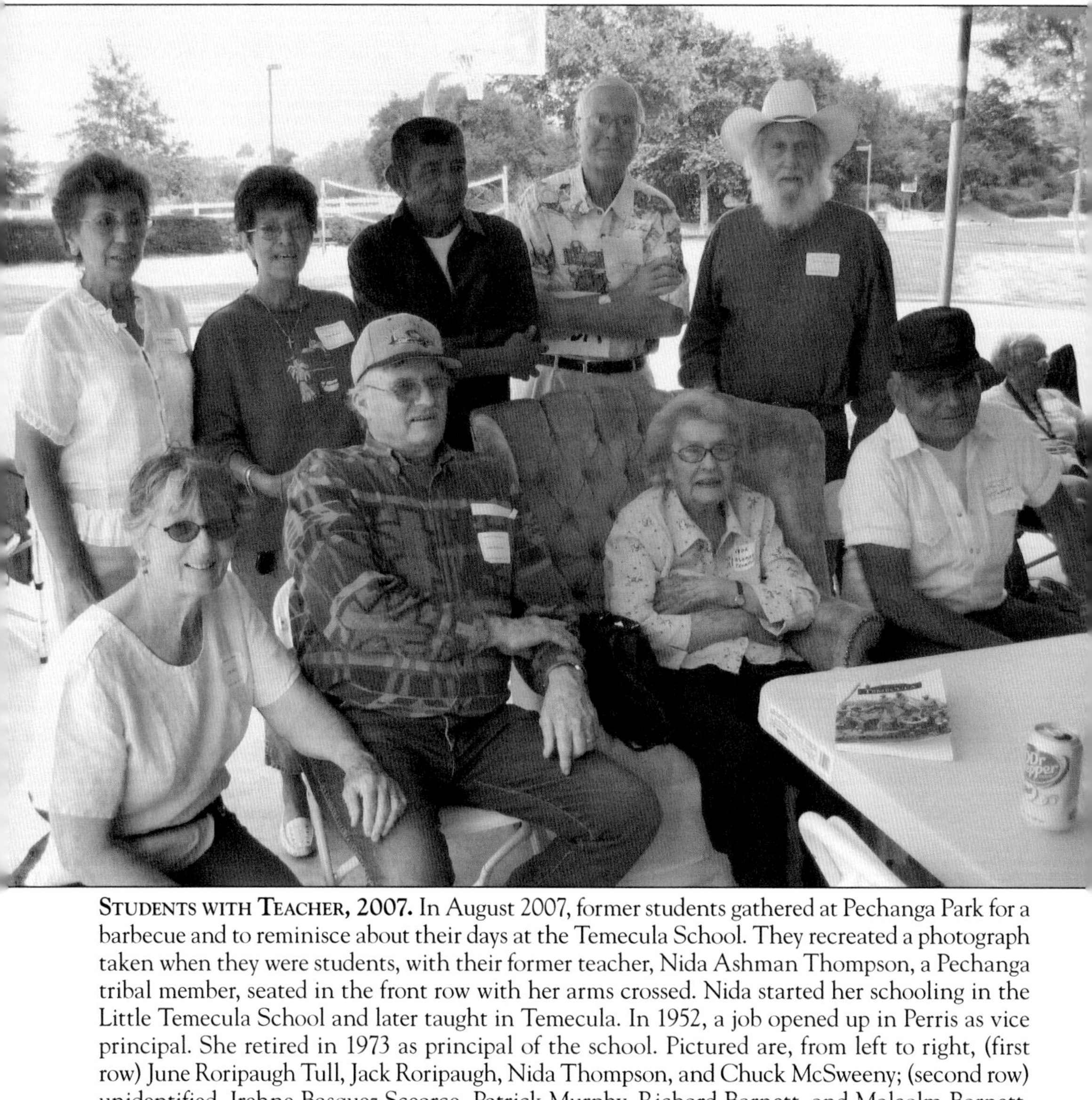

Students with Teacher, 2007. In August 2007, former students gathered at Pechanga Park for a barbecue and to reminisce about their days at the Temecula School. They recreated a photograph taken when they were students, with their former teacher, Nida Ashman Thompson, a Pechanga tribal member, seated in the front row with her arms crossed. Nida started her schooling in the Little Temecula School and later taught in Temecula. In 1952, a job opened up in Perris as vice principal. She retired in 1973 as principal of the school. Pictured are, from left to right, (first row) June Roripaugh Tull, Jack Roripaugh, Nida Thompson, and Chuck McSweeny; (second row) unidentified, Irehne Basquez Scearce, Patrick Murphy, Richard Barnett, and Malcolm Barnett. Nida was 96 years old when this photograph was taken and lived to be 100. (RF.)

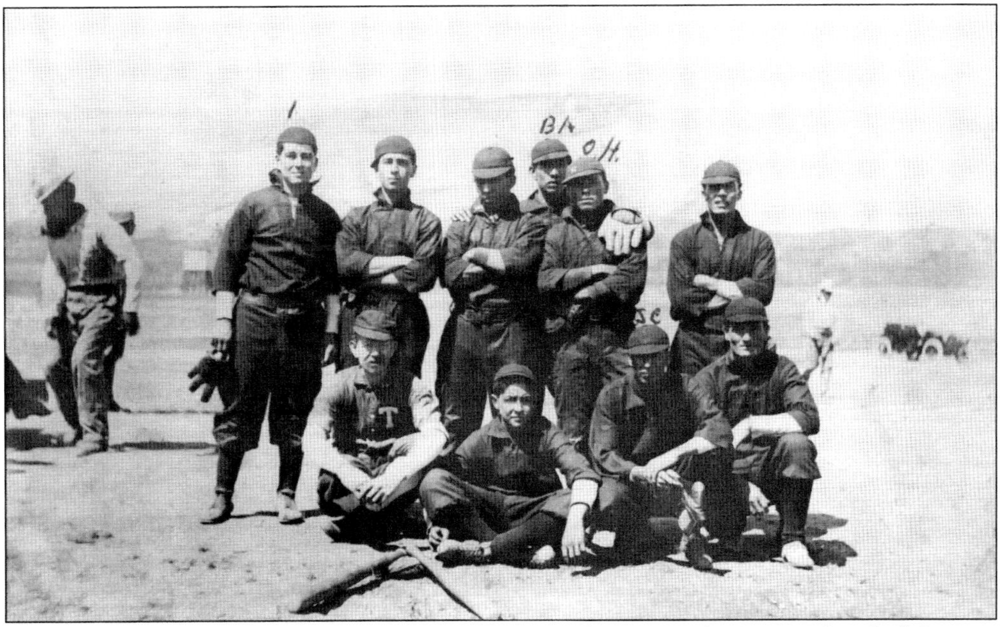

1926 Baseball Team. The Temecula Indians won the Riverside County Baseball League championship in 1921, the year the league organized. Players are, from left to right, (first row) Charles McVicker, Charles Escallier, Steven Connley, and Elzie Freeman; (second row) Alex Escallier, Willie Arrow, Saturnino Calac, Ben Amago, Otto Hungary, and Albert Golsh. (JM.)

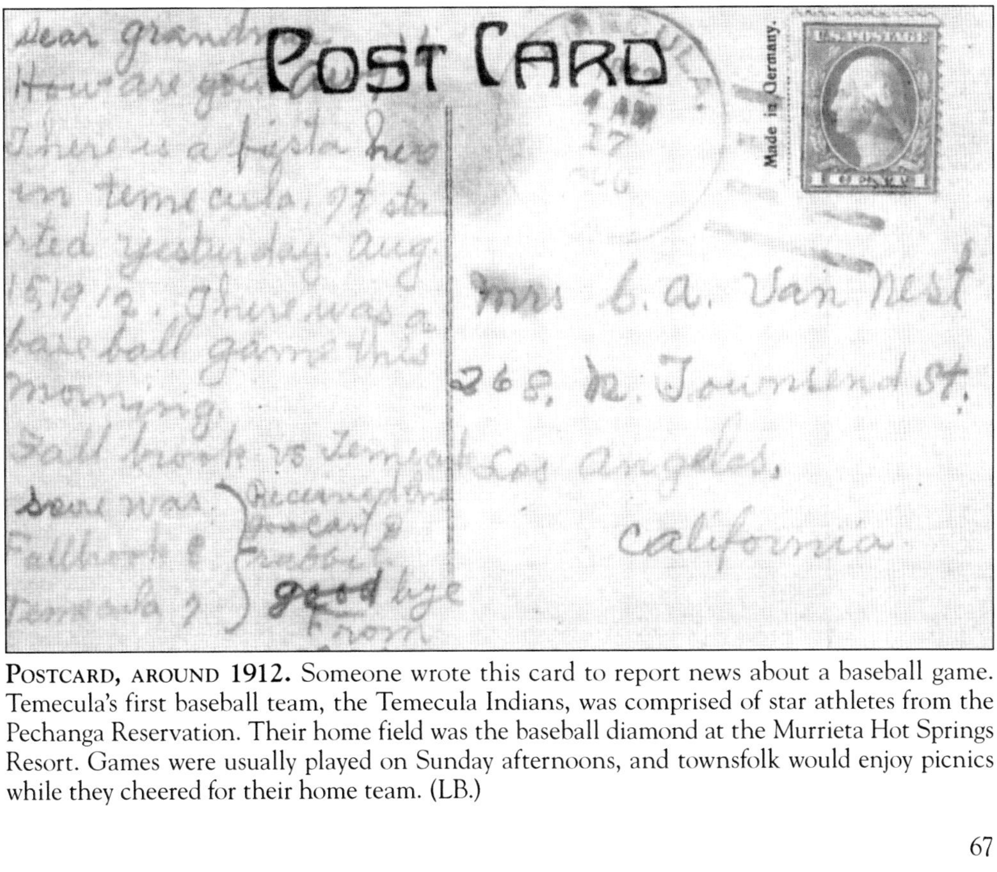

Postcard, around 1912. Someone wrote this card to report news about a baseball game. Temecula's first baseball team, the Temecula Indians, was comprised of star athletes from the Pechanga Reservation. Their home field was the baseball diamond at the Murrieta Hot Springs Resort. Games were usually played on Sunday afternoons, and townsfolk would enjoy picnics while they cheered for their home team. (LB.)

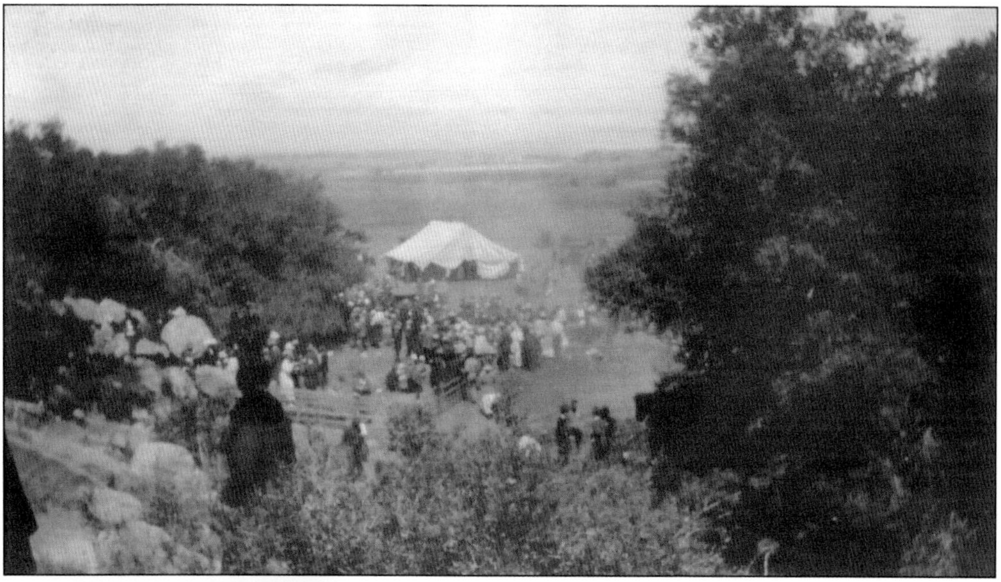

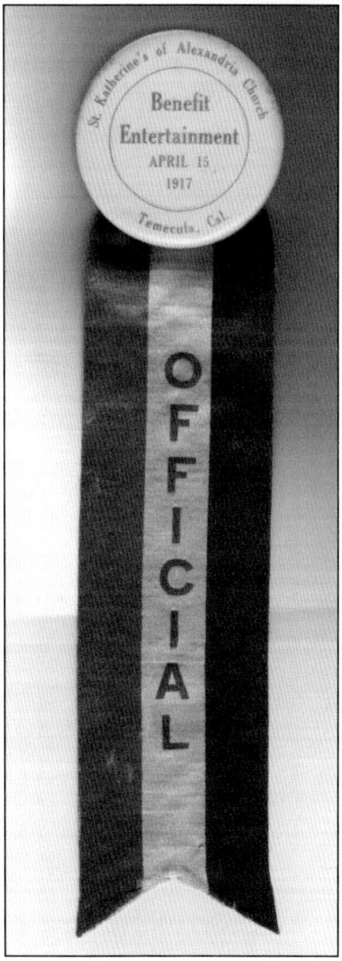

Barbecue for St. Catherine's Church, 1917. Mac Machado donated two lots and the Santa Fe Railroad donated four lots for a church at the corner of Front and Sixth Streets. On April 15, 1917, a barbecue benefit was put on with Mahlon Vail donating a steer and a location for the barbecue at the Pauba Ranch. Notable athletes and gamblers came from Los Angeles for the event. (MC.)

Ribbon from 1917 Church Barbecue. Around 800 people in 200 automobiles converged on the Pauba Ranch to enjoy the food, music, and sporting events, which included wrestling, boxing, and bronco busting by Vail Ranch cowboys. Joe Winkels supplied libations. A gambling concession brought in more than enough money to cover the cost of the new church building. Rev. J.J. Burri bought a car for himself with the excess funds. (LB.)

St. Catherine's Catholic Church. This, the first church in Temecula, a 36-by-26-foot wood-frame structure, cost about $12,000 to build and furnish. It was moved to Sam Hicks Monument Park and is now known as the Chapel of Memories. Today, it is primarily used as a wedding chapel, with a record of 55 weddings in 2011, benefitting the Temecula Valley Museum. There are over 40 houses of worship in Temecula today. (JK.)

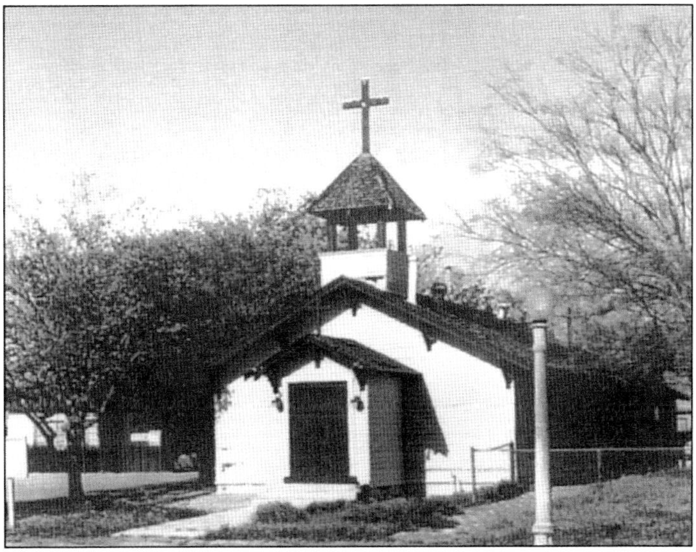

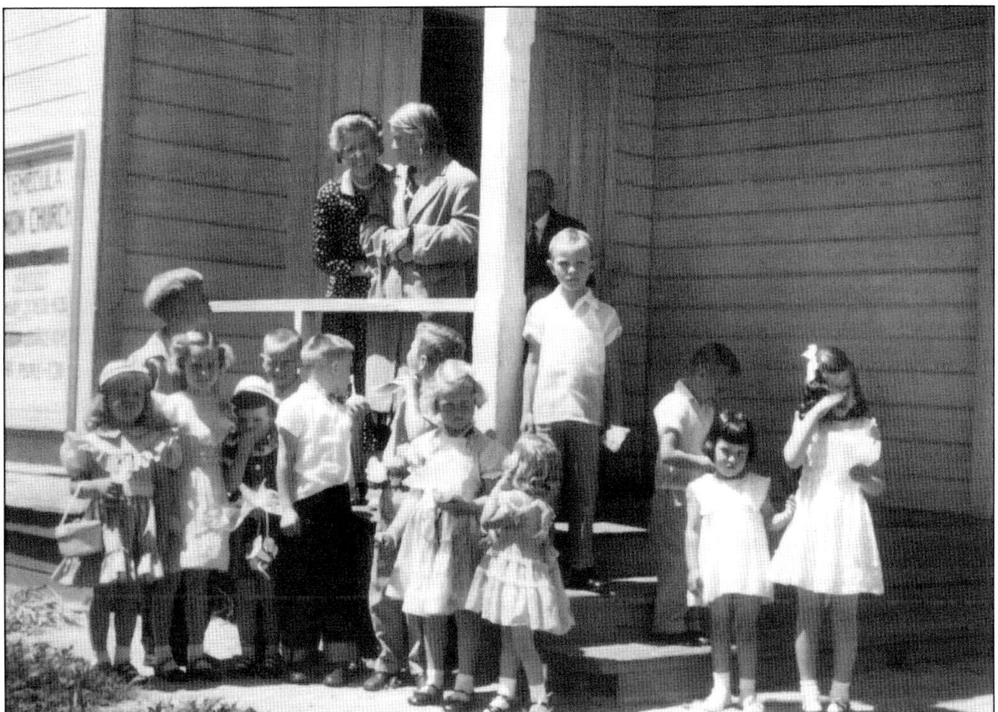

Temecula Union Church. The former Pujol Schoolhouse was used by the Protestant church in the 1950s. These unnamed adults and children posed by the front door after a service. Several groups used the building, which is now located on Santiago Road as part of the Temecula Community Church. Other church buildings built in Temecula by 1990 were Rancho Community on Vallejo Road and Hope Lutheran on Rancho California Road. (JJ.)

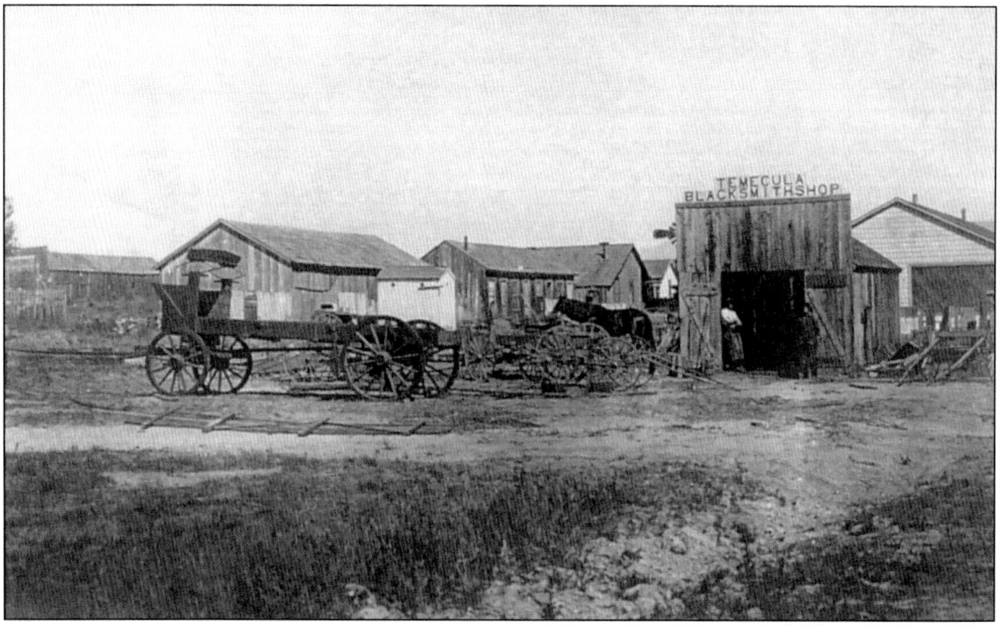

Temecula Blacksmith Shop. Old maps show a least four blacksmith shops in Old Town. This one was possibly located across from today's Serendipity Antiques Etc. store. A smith would work over hot coals shaping metal pieces that would become hardware for wagons or for implements. Blacksmithing was an important part of daily life in the days when everything was made from wood or metal and before motorized vehicles became popular. (TVM.)

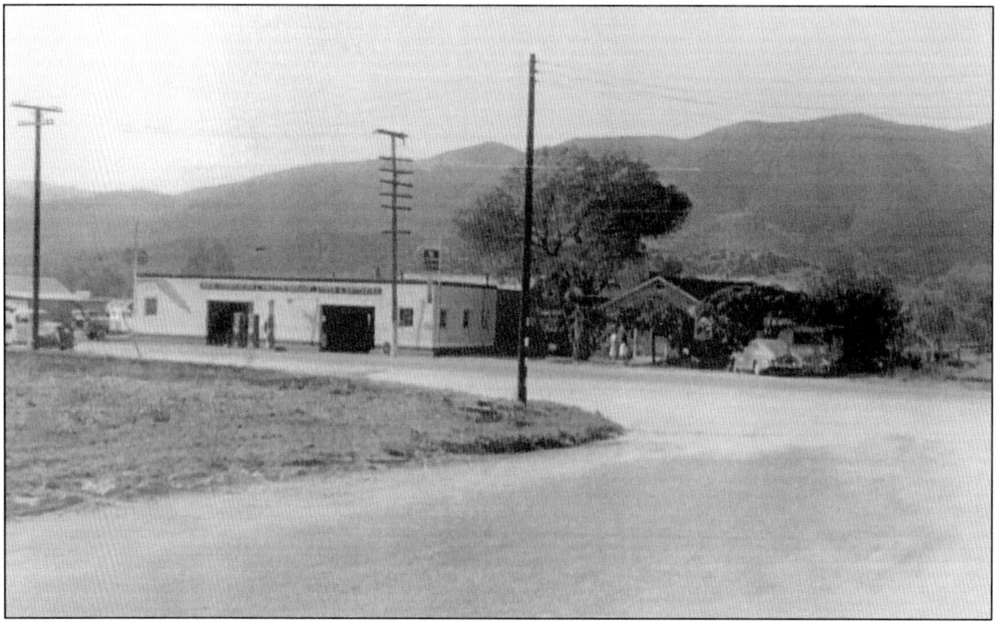

Al and Freda Knott. The Knott Garage and home at the corner of Fifth and Main Streets was at the edge of town. With the growing use of motorized vehicles, blacksmiths like Al Knott shifted to selling gasoline and doing automotive mechanical repair work. The building was used until the flood of 1992. Their house next door was later converted to a tearoom and is presently an antique store. (JK.)

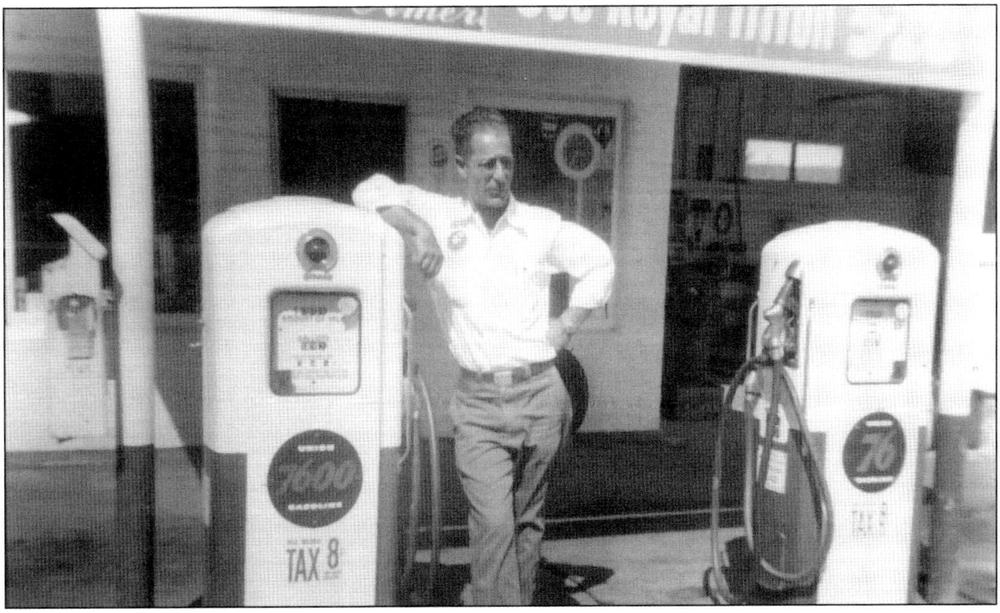

OTTO'S 76 STATION. This station was at the southeast corner of Third and Front Streets, in front of what is now Butterfield Square. Al Otto moved to Temecula in 1936 and first worked for the First National Bank of Temecula and then for author Erle Stanley Gardner. Otto rented the Nienkes' house, which was moved from Murrieta in 1920 to 28717 Pujol Street. (JJ.)

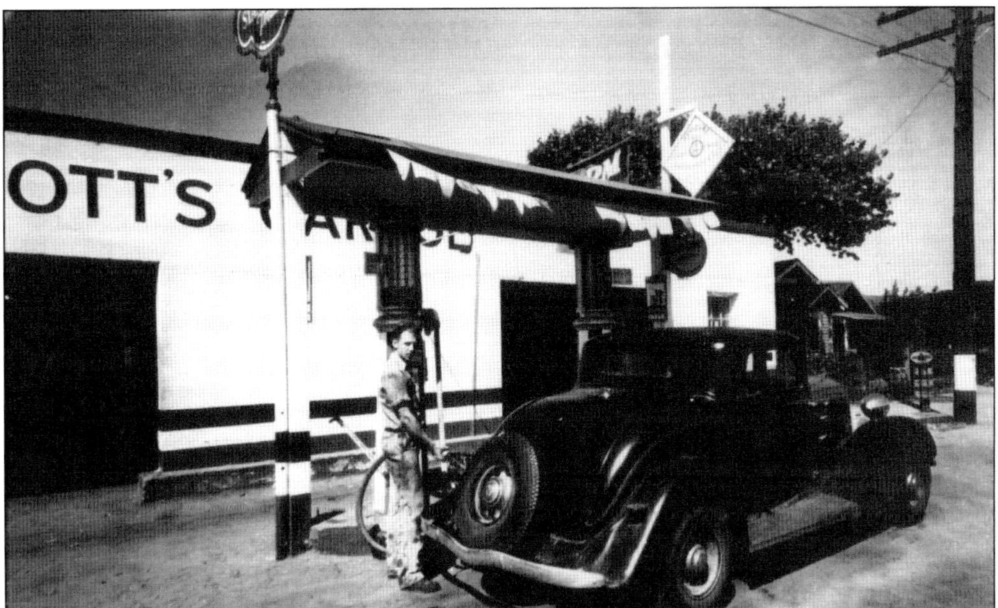

KNOTT'S STATION. US Highway 395 went down Front Street from 1934 through 1948, going through other little towns between Mexico to Canada. Knott's Garage, the Palomar Hotel, and the Swing Inn Café depended on business from motorists who drove through town on the two-lane highway. Temecula, a sleepy, little town with dirt side streets, had a population of about 200 during that time. (JK.)

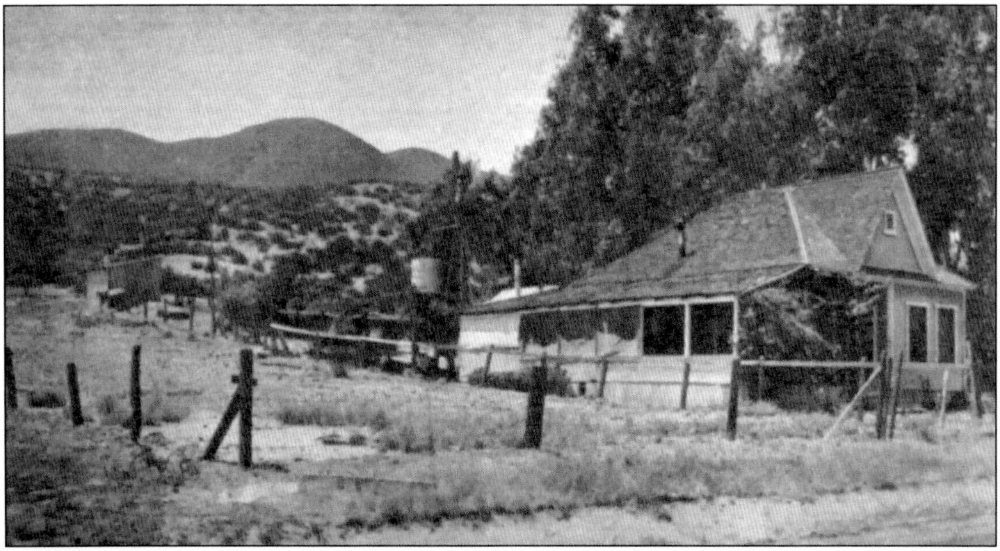

McNeill House. In 1936, Al Knott leased his blacksmith shop to John D. McNeill for $36 a month. McNeill, a Massachusetts native, lived with his wife and five children in this house on Pujol Street. He was muscular and strong and wore thick glasses. He dressed in overalls and a denim shirt for work. No one knew about his past. (DR.)

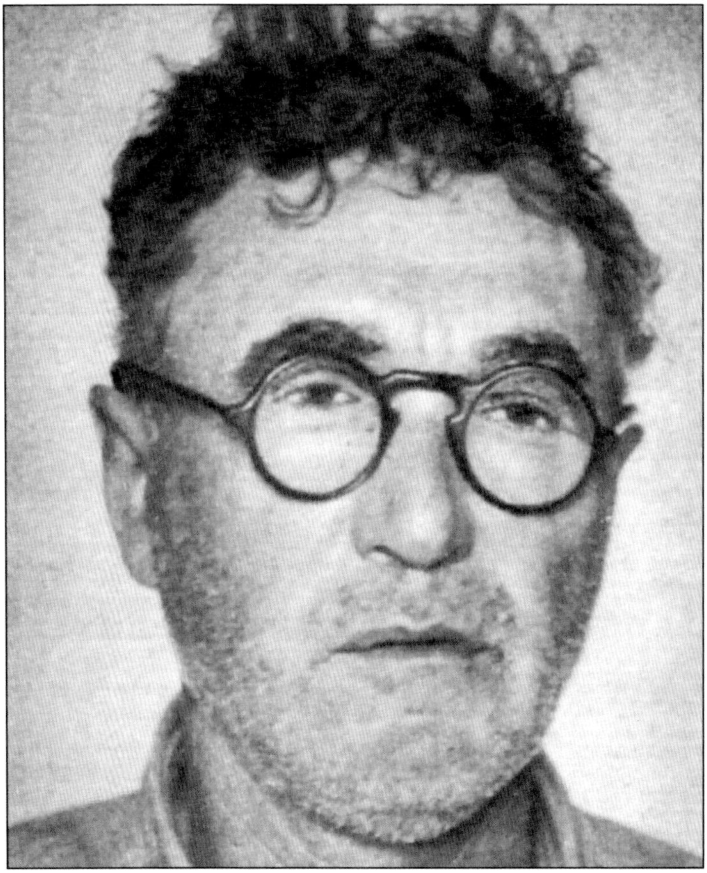

John McNeill. On August 13, 1936, the Riverside County Sheriff's Office received a call from McNeill—"My wife's been murdered! Please hurry!" He said that when he arrived home for lunch he found his wife lying on the floor. When the officers arrived, they learned emergency personnel had moved Melva McNeill, who was still clinging to life, to a hospital in Riverside. She died that evening without regaining consciousness. (DR.)

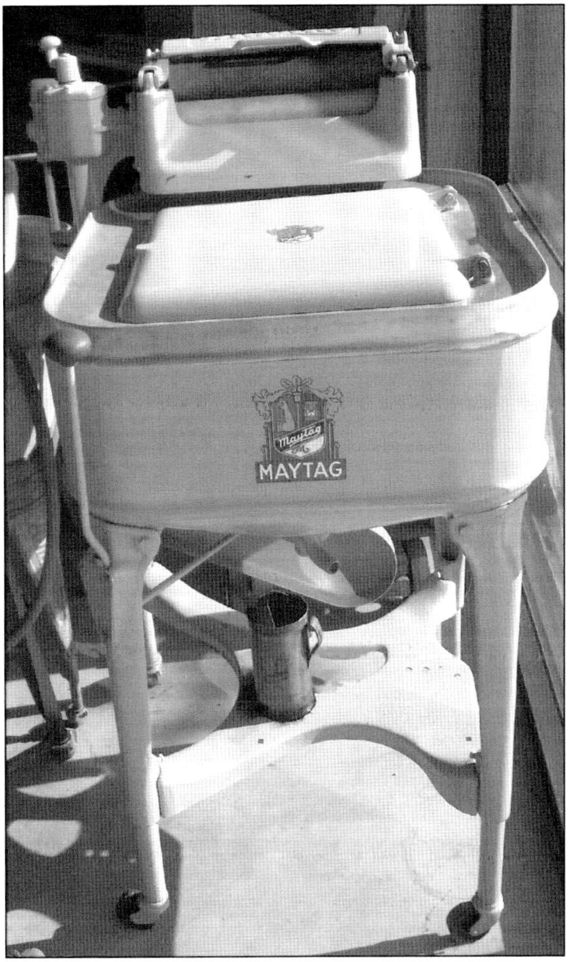

Wringer Washing Machine. During the investigation, Deputy Paul E. Pierre found a newspaper-wrapped bundle buried beneath the firewood in a box behind the kitchen stove. In the bundle, he found two rubber-covered rollers from the wringer of a washing machine. One roller was covered in blood. The murder weapon had been found. A little mongrel dog led Deputy Pierre to McNeill's rabbit hutches and began digging a hole. (RF.)

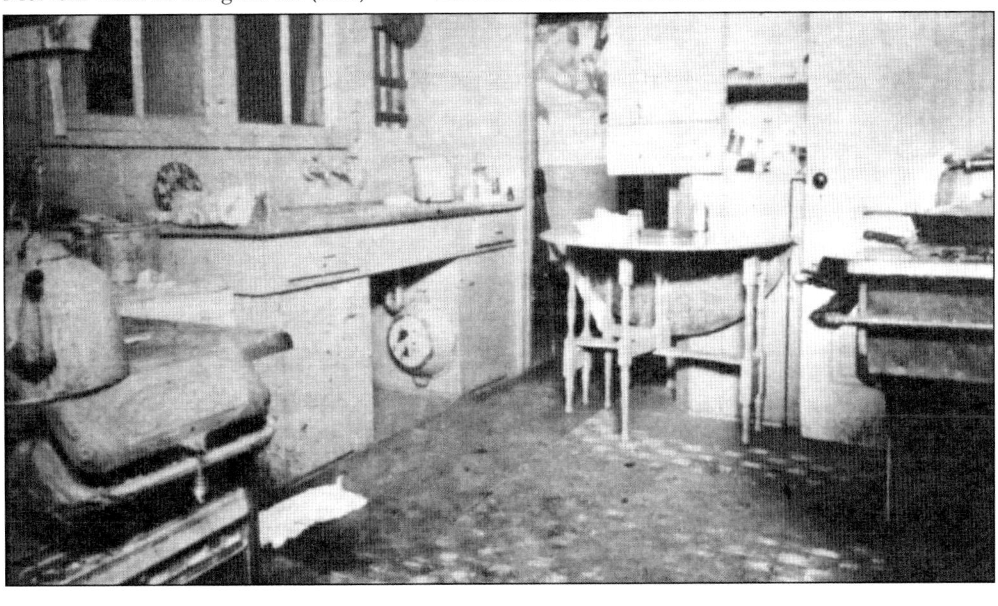

Inside McNeill House. McNeill tried to blame the crime on migrant farm workers, but the dog dug up a bundle of bloodstained clothing that was McNeill's according to several witnesses. He was arrested, tried, and convicted of his wife's murder. McNeill was sent to San Quentin prison, a place he had been before as Daniel McMaster on forgery charges. On July 9, 1937, McNeill went to the gallows. (DR.)

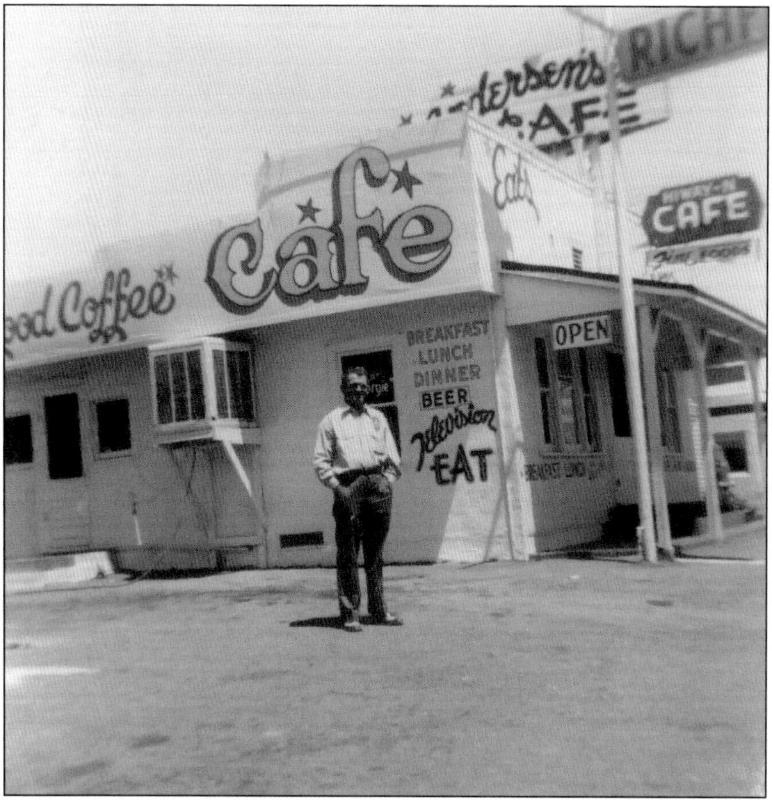

ANDERSONS CAFÉ. Harold "Andy" Anderson, a realtor, is standing in front of his café, which he later sold to Tommy Hotchkiss, who renamed it the Swing Inn Café. Anderson owned seven motel units, the café, the adjacent gas station, and a house behind the café. Tall billboards advertising his café and gas station were visible from the realigned highway outside Old Town and attracted motorists onto Front Street for services. (IH.)

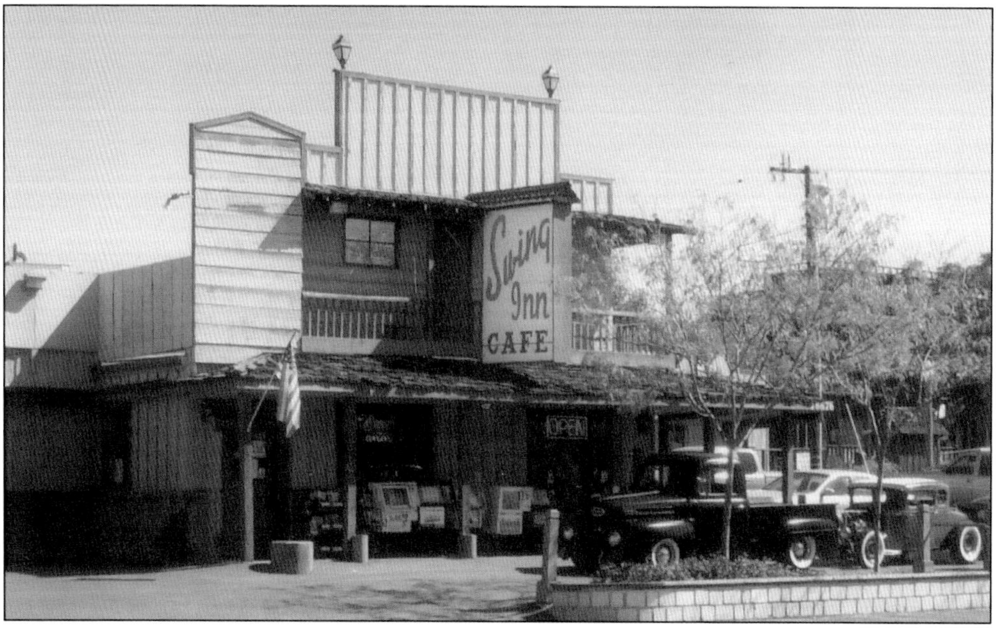

SWING INN CAFÉ. The café served motorists and people who stayed in the row of motel cottages called the Swing Inn, located where Butterfield Square is today. In the 1970s, owner Tommy Hotchkiss changed the facade, making the first move to start a Western 1890s motif theme in Old Town. Bob Morris also promoted the historical theme. (JH.)

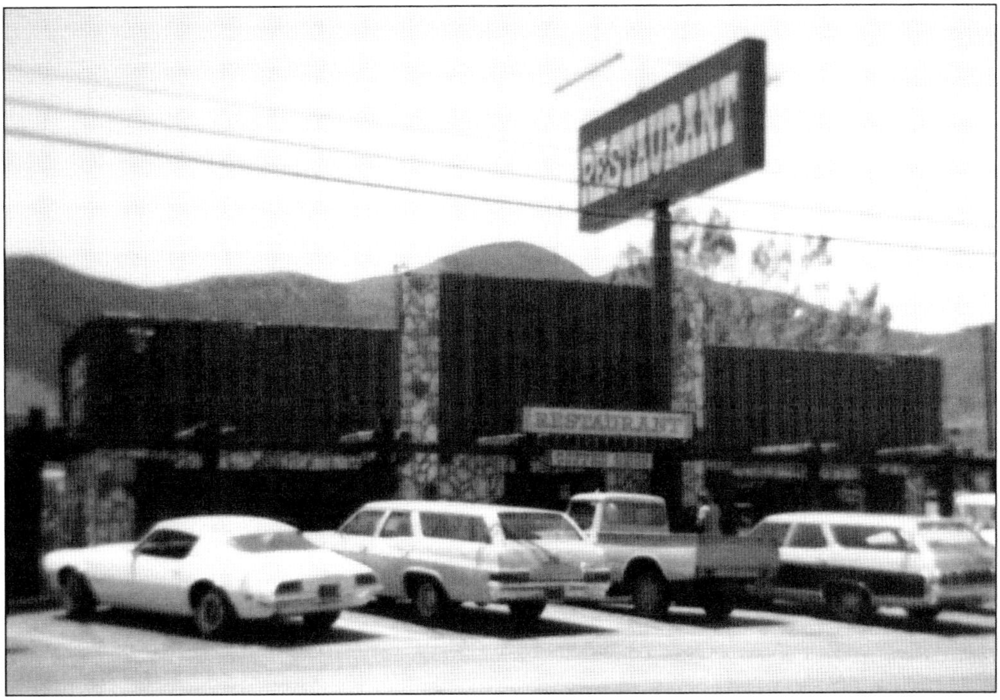

B-H RESTAURANT. "B-Bar-H" was one of the most popular 24-hour cafés along Highway 395. Fishermen stopped for a meal on their way to Lake Henshaw, and locals met to eat and play slot machines. It was named for Bill and Herta Ferrel, the original owners. A truck weigh station was adjacent to it. It was located on the present-day site of the Quilt Shop. (TVM.)

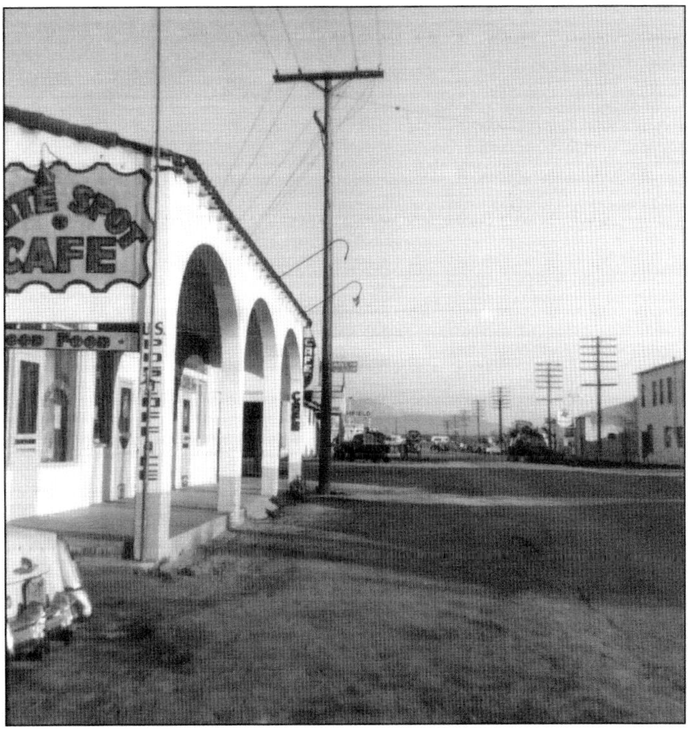

RITE SPOT CAFÉ. The café at the south end of the Champion Building was built in Mission Revival style, using Alberhill bricks, by Allen Champion in 1928. The café served breakfast and lunch. Connie and Bob Dawes first owned the B-H, then the Rite Spot Café. It was later a plumbing supply store and then Security Bank. The building is still standing next to today's Rosa's Cantina. (JJ.)

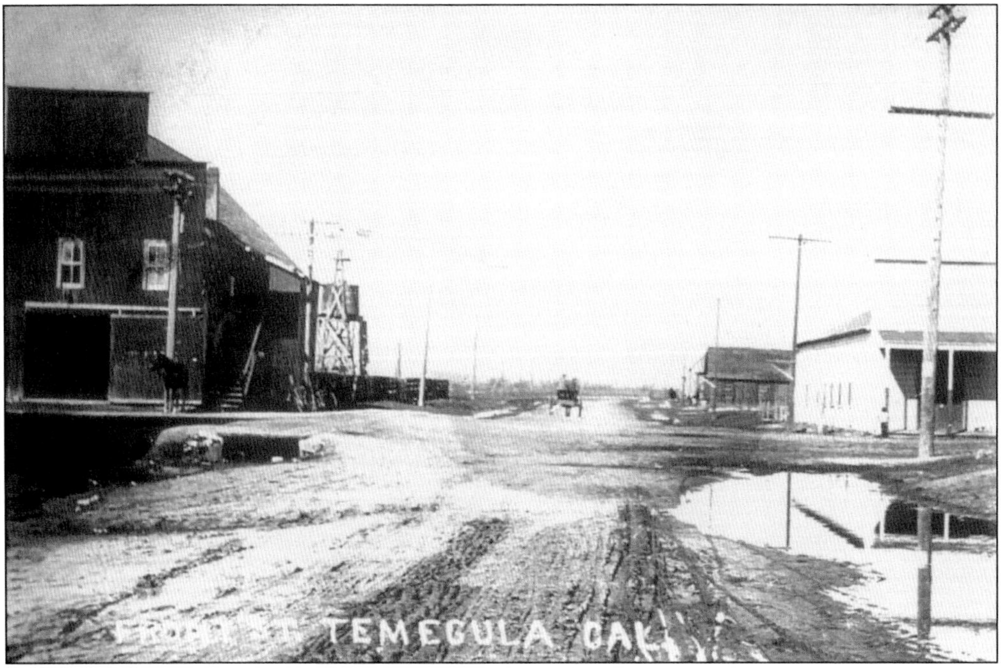

Past the Livery Stable. Ole Larson worked for the McConville livery from 1906 through 1909. The livery kept horses and harness supplies and also had the first telephone in town. Larson slept in a room by the telephone switchboard, which he turned off when he needed to curry horses. As switchboard operator, Larson connected incoming calls to the Vail Ranch, rock quarries, and to Murrieta. (LB.)

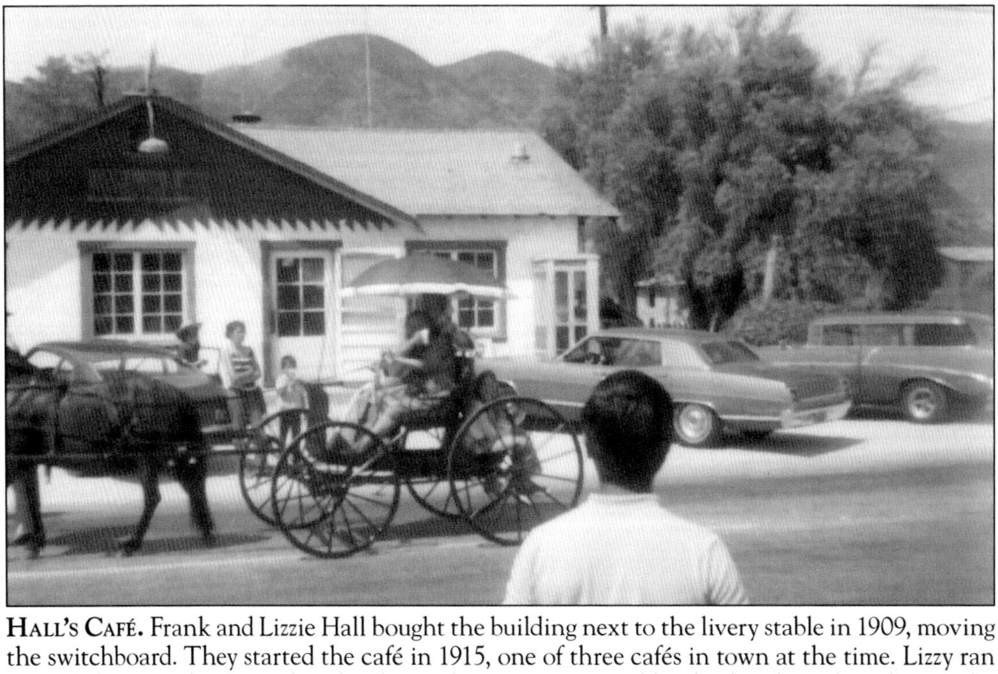

Hall's Café. Frank and Lizzie Hall bought the building next to the livery stable in 1909, moving the switchboard. They started the café in 1915, one of three cafés in town at the time. Lizzy ran it until she retired in 1939; her daughter Edna Swanguen and her husband, Carl, took over the business. They closed the café in 1954. It stayed open as a bus station. (TVM.)

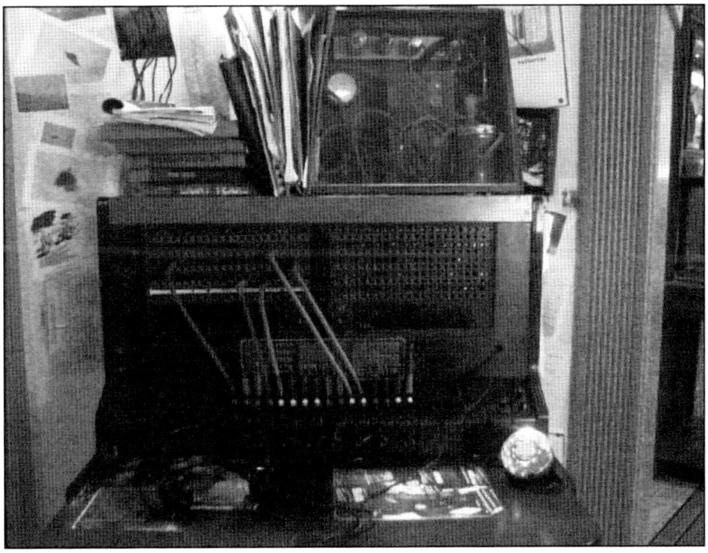

Old-Fashioned Switchboard. A person would lift the handle of a telephone and an operator would ask the number or person they wanted to call. The operator would connect cables on her board so they could speak. As many as four families shared a party line. Edna Swanguen manned the board 24 hours a day, sleeping next to the board until it was replaced by dial telephones in 1961. (LB.)

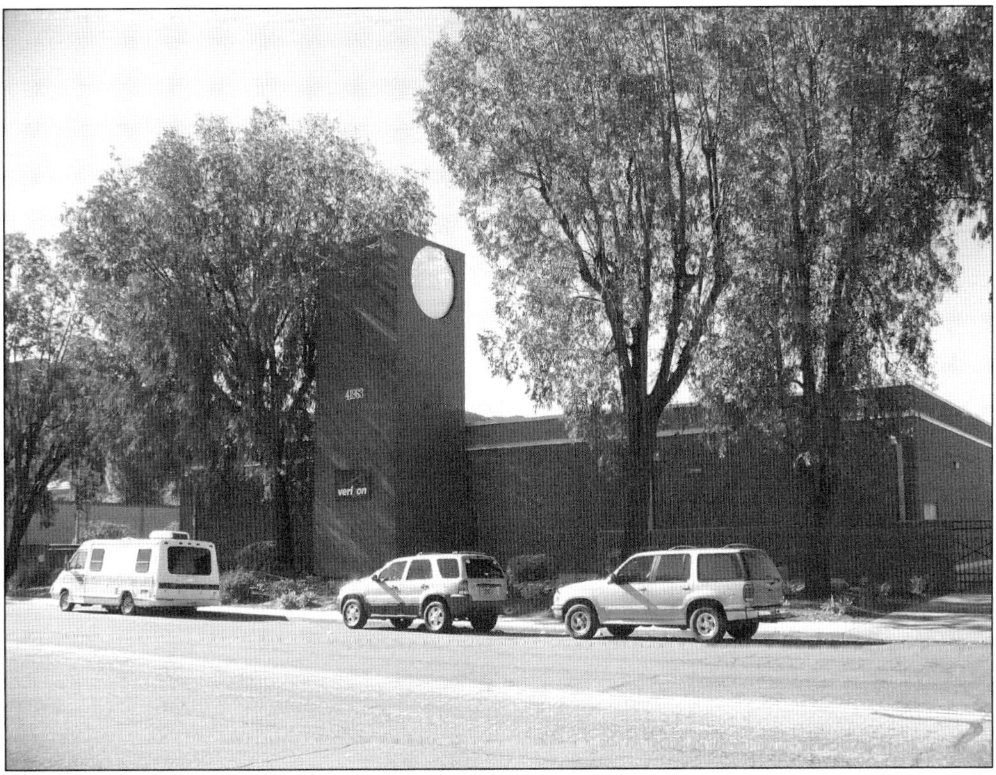

Verizon Telephone Office. When the telephone system could not keep up with incoming calls generated by the rapid population growth of Rancho California, this building was constructed for 1.5 million dollars. New computerized mechanisms were installed to meet the escalating demands. The 40-foot microwave tower was built in 1980 from wood with a Western style complementary to Old Town. This building is behind the Old Town Post Office. (JH.)

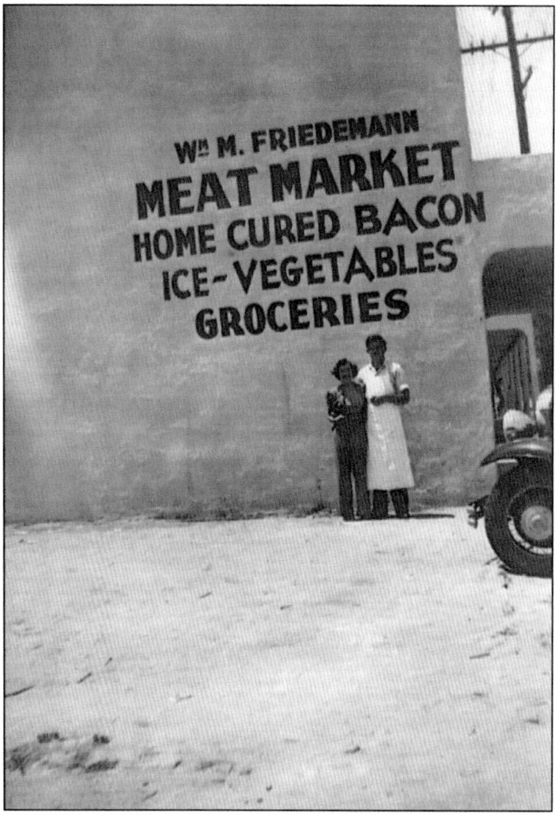

FRIEDEMANN'S MEAT MARKET, MAY 1939. Bill and Pat Coogan Friedemann posed on the side of the old meat market. It was located in the Main Street Emporium antique center next to the Temecula Hotel on Main Street. The *Elsinore* newspaper published a local news note when they installed a cold storage plant for meats, a modern refrigeration unit, in 1923. (TVM.)

MAIN STREET EMPORIUM. In 1974, Tom and Katie Longfellow bought the Friedemann Building, the previous location of the Temecula Meat Market. Their renovations, completed in 1976, incorporated the Friedemann Meat Market into its overall 1890s Western theme. Artifacts from an old blacksmith shop at that location were discovered during renovation and now hang on walls for display. (TVM.)

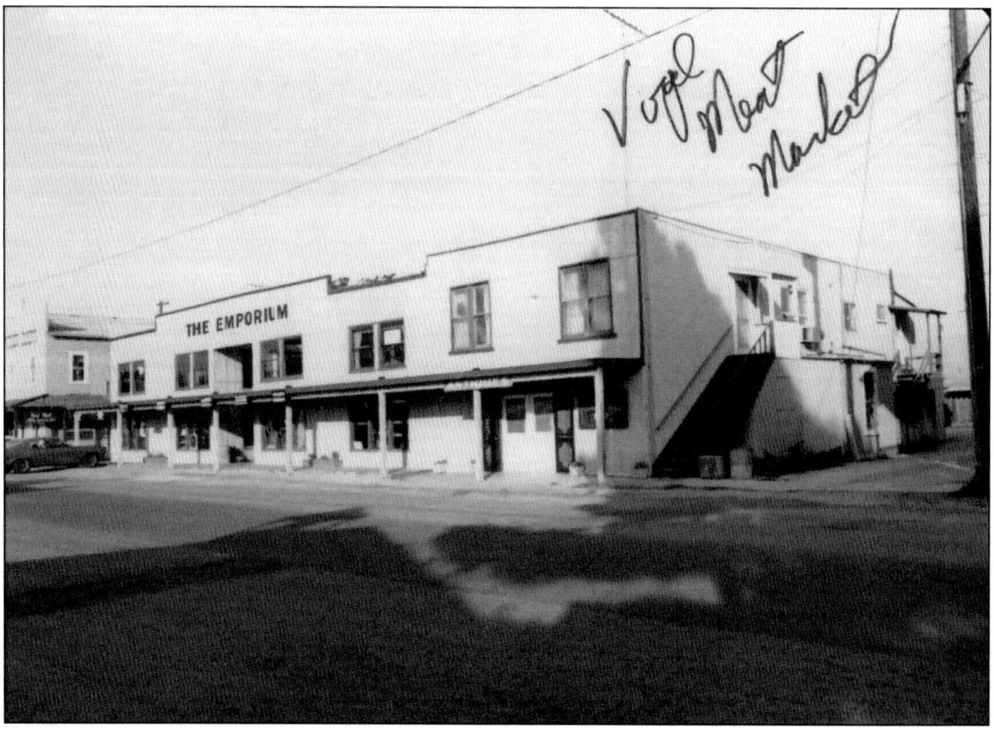

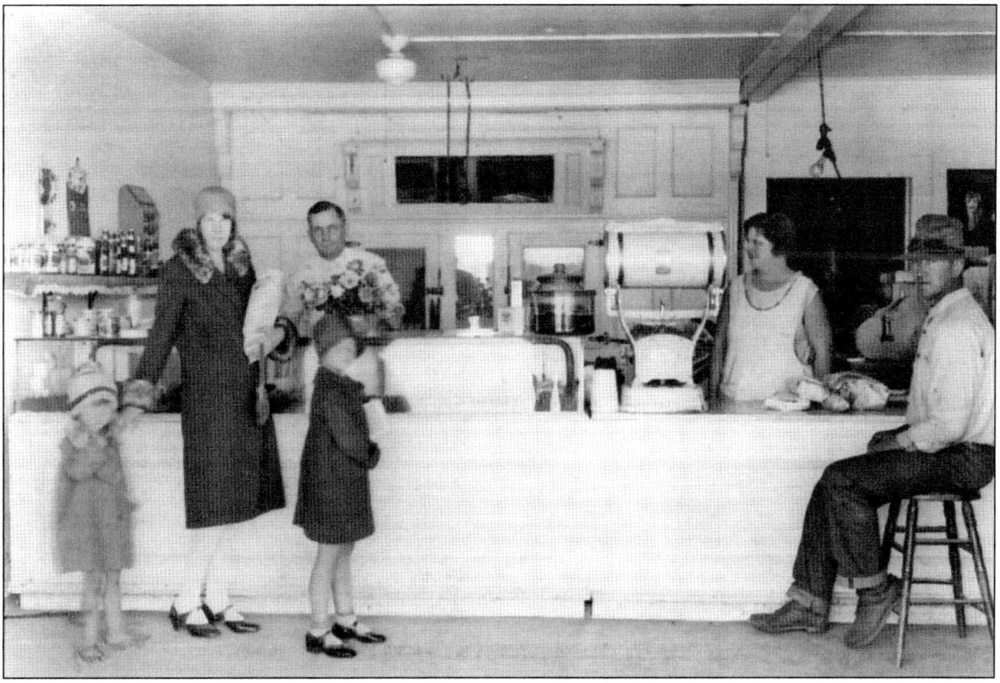

INSIDE FRIEDEMANN'S MARKET. This photograph with a Norman Rockwell feel captured the scene where Will and Jessie Friedemann waited on customers inside of the Temecula Meat Market. Locals lovingly joked that Jessie had the most expensive thumb in the valley when she wrapped and weighed meat orders. (TVM.)

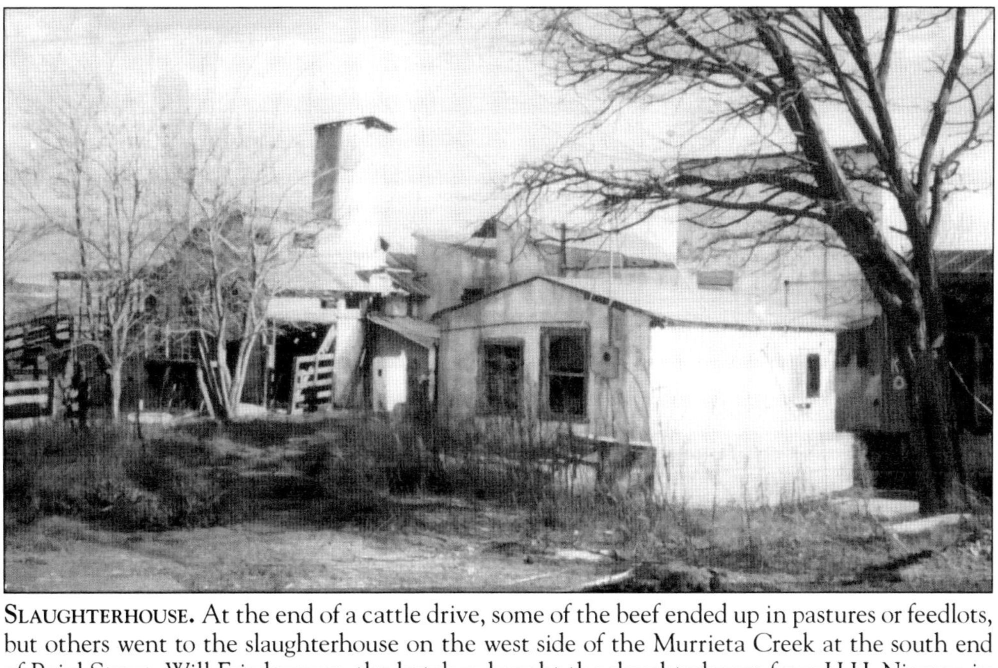

SLAUGHTERHOUSE. At the end of a cattle drive, some of the beef ended up in pastures or feedlots, but others went to the slaughterhouse on the west side of the Murrieta Creek at the south end of Pujol Street. Will Friedemann, the butcher, bought the slaughterhouse from H.H. Nieman in 1910. Friedemann also delivered ice around town for home iceboxes before people owned electric refrigerators. (TVM.)

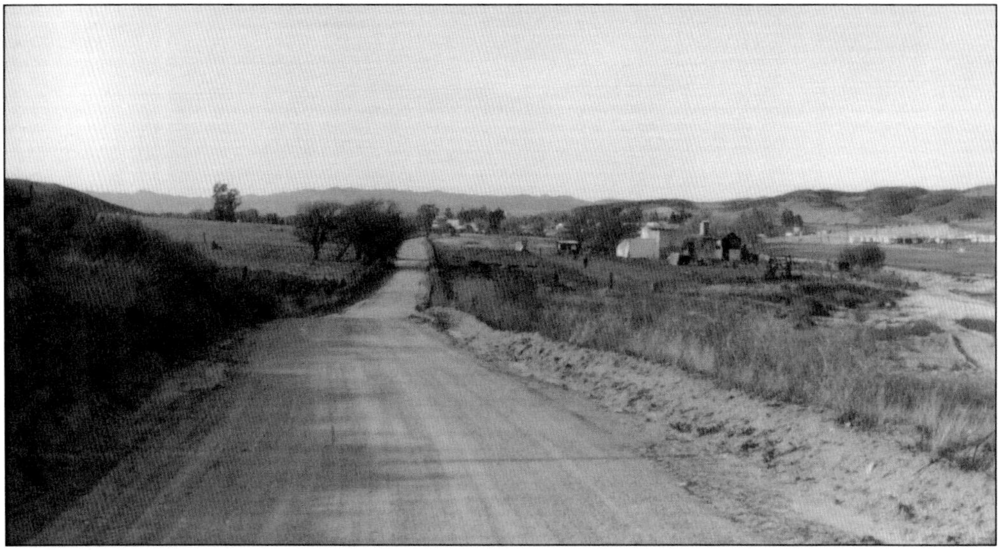

Looking North on Pujol Street, 1974. Pujol Street was once considered a prestigious place to live; all the local businessmen lived there. Before electricity came in, Friedemann had a generator at his house. A resurgence of building started in the 2010s with new townhouses and apartments across from the Boys & Girls Club. (TVHS.)

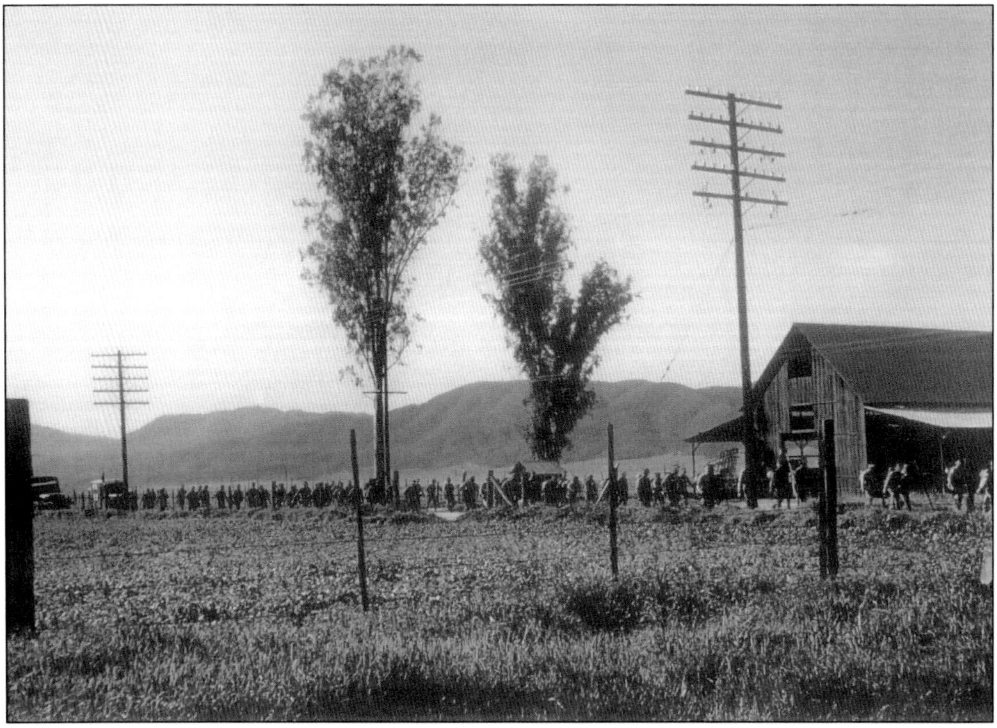

Soldiers Marching North on Highway 395. All north and south inland military traffic traveled on the highway to avoid vulnerability to ship attacks along coastal routes. Many local citizens volunteered for the Civil Air Patrol during World War II, watching the skies for possible attacks. A watch station was set up on Pujol Street. Highway 395 was realigned when Interstate 15 came through. (JR.)

Five

STEPPING TOWARD TODAY

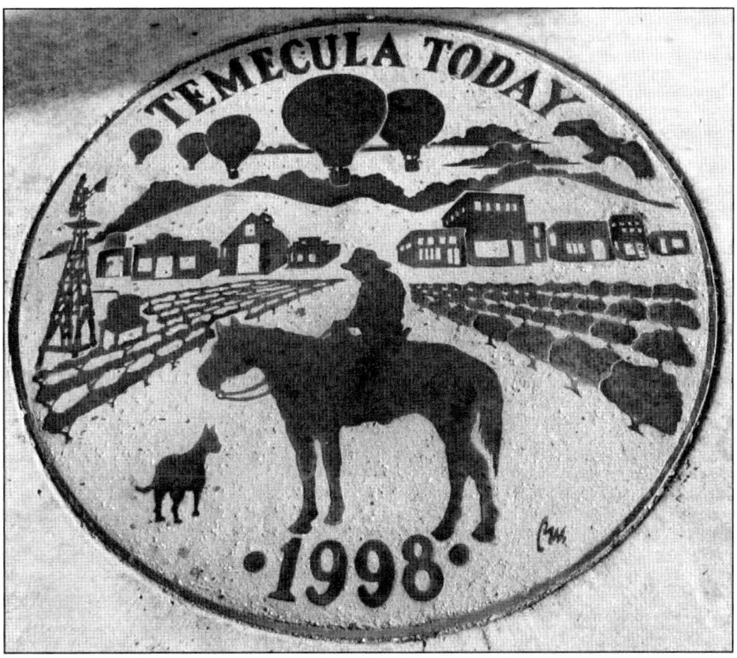

TEMECULA TODAY MEDALLION. John Bianchi, who owned the Frontier Museum on Jefferson Street, called Temecula "the town time forgot." Bumper stickers in the 1980s asked, "Where the hell is Temecula?" The town could not grow until 1964, when the Vail Company sold its 87,500 acres to Kaiser Aetna to build a planned community. Along the way, a few dedicated individuals have tried to preserve vestiges of the past. (BM.)

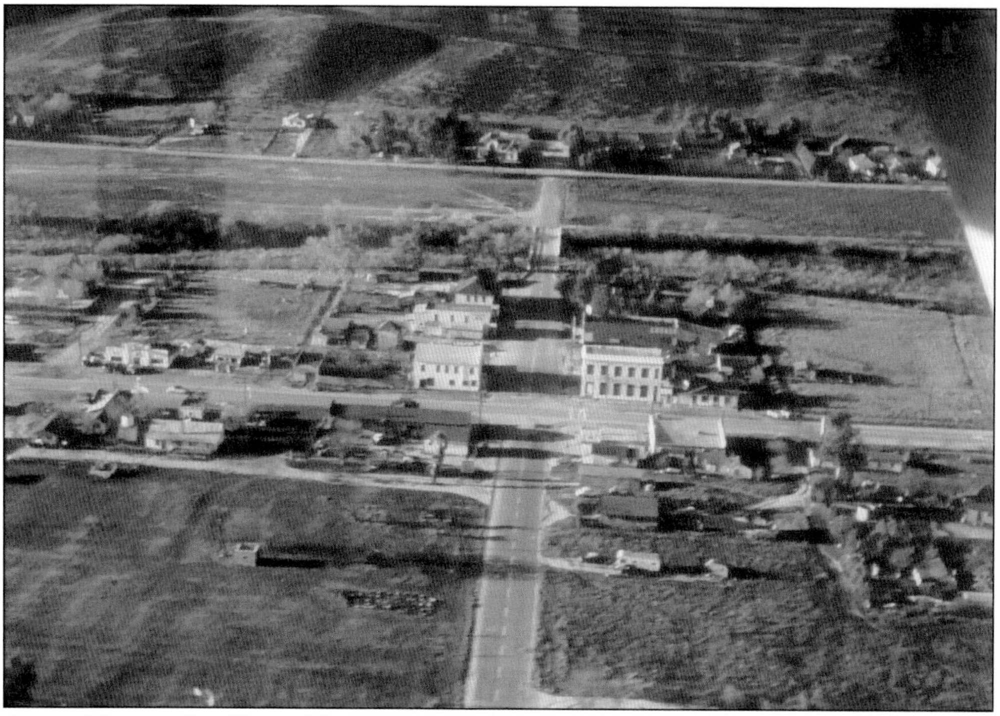

AERIAL VIEW OF OLD TOWN. This is a view looking west from where Interstate 15 is today. The bank, Welty Building, and hotel are some of the most visible structures. The area across the Main Street Bridge is bare, except for the west side of Pujol Street, where the Burnham house is seen. One can imagine a quiet morning as the shadows diminished and the little town awakened. (JR.)

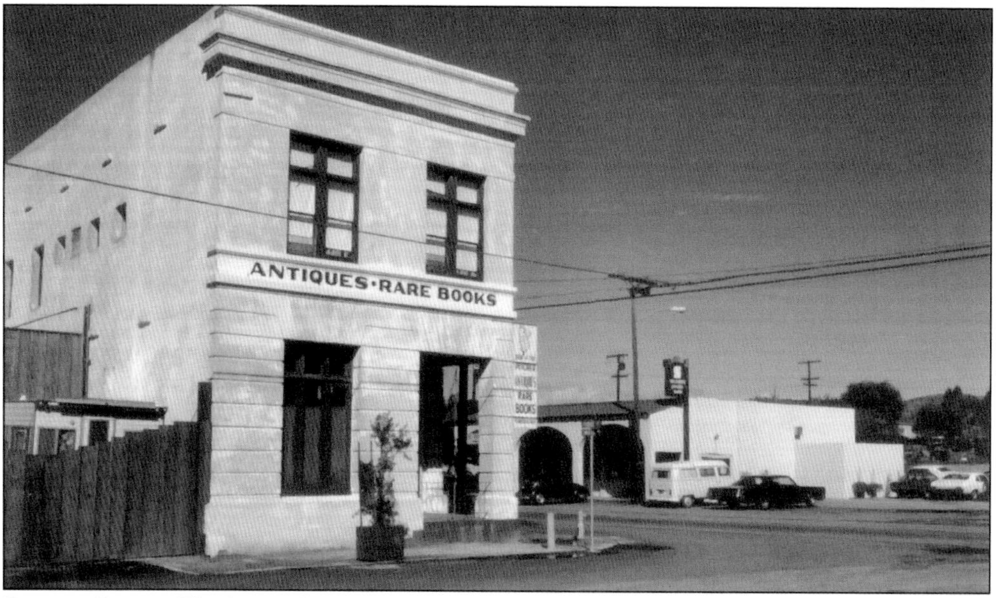

BANK OF BOOKS. The former First National Bank of Temecula opened in 1914 and closed in 1943, when the board of directors liquidated it. For a while, it was an antique store and a bookstore. Since 1978 it has continued as a focal point in Old Town as a Mexican restaurant. Across the street was the Security Bank, at the former location of the Rite Spot Café. (LB.)

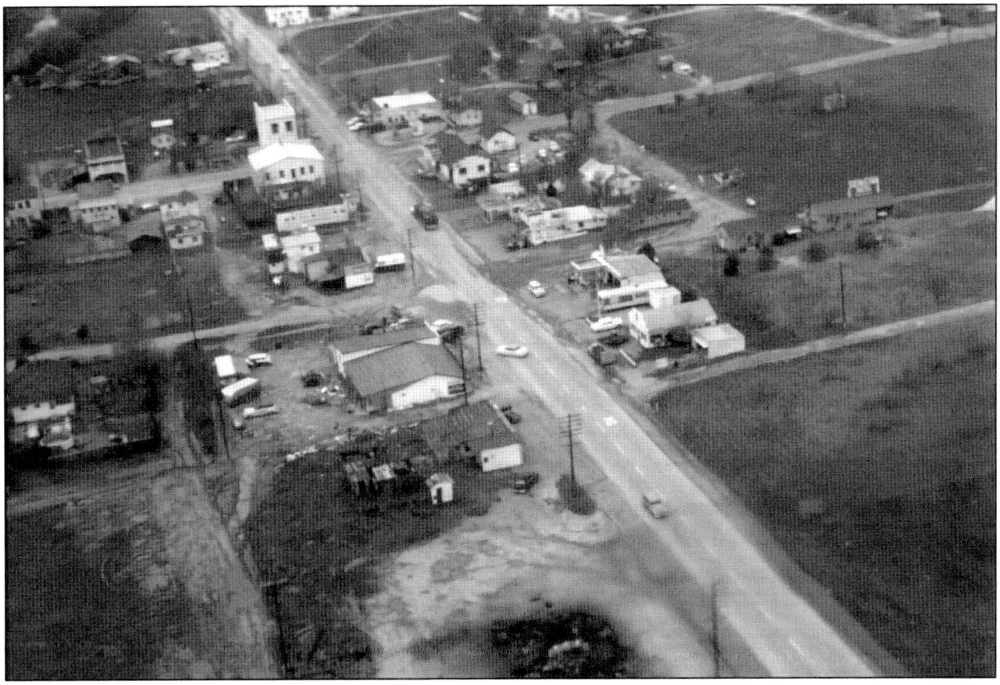

South Front Street, Early 1960s. This shows old Highway 395 looking northward. The Palomar Hotel is at the top, a quarter of the way from the left. The Pujol School is near the top center. There are open fields, five service stations, the Swing Inn Motel, B-H Café, Talley's house, a mercantile store, Anderson's restaurant, and remnants of the burned-out Art Shack in the foreground. (JR.)

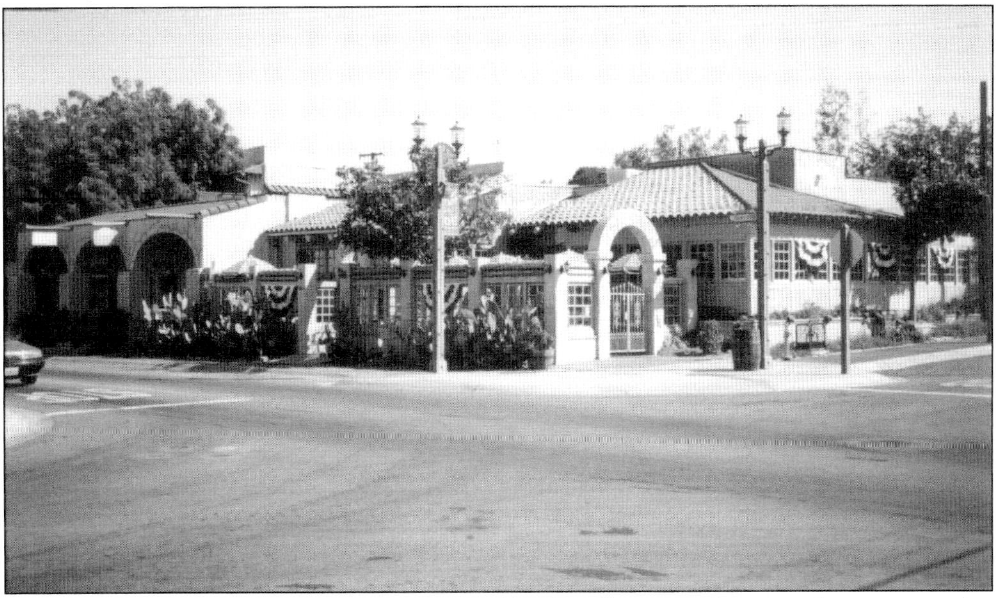

Rosa's Cantina. The Escallier Hotel and Billiard Hall previously sat at the corner and is remembered with a plaque placed by the Temecula Valley Historical Society. The lot stood vacant for a number of years until Mike and Rose Thesing built the cantina in 1991. Now a popular eatery in Old Town, it offers indoor and outdoor dining with views of activities on the street. (LB.)

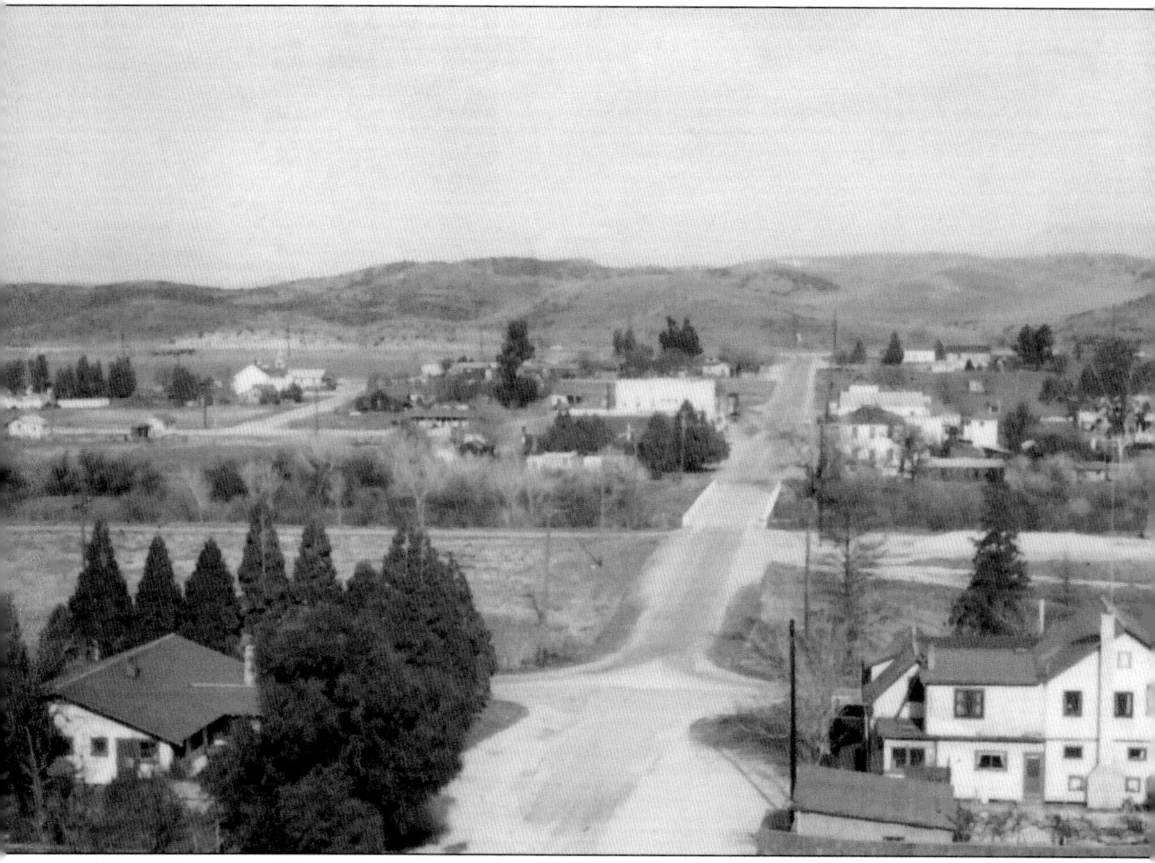

View East from Burnham House. This post-1948 photograph shows the former Albert Nienke house surrounded by trees on the left and the George Burnham house on the right, from west of Pujol Street, looking down Main Street. The Nienke house was later owned by James and Estafena Freeman. According to local lore, the Burnham house was previously the Wildomar Hotel. In the 1890s, it was moved to the present location, rolled from Wildomar on logs. The Pujol School is seen to the left center. Other landmarks are the bank, the Temecula Hotel, and the Welty Building. No evidence remained of the train depot, tracks, turntable, or warehouse along the tracks. In the background are the untouched hills that were later graded to form the Temecula Town Center shopping center and other businesses along Rancho California and Ynez Roads. In the background, cut rocks show the location of the realigned Highway 395, now Interstate 15, which routed traffic away from the center of town. (LB.)

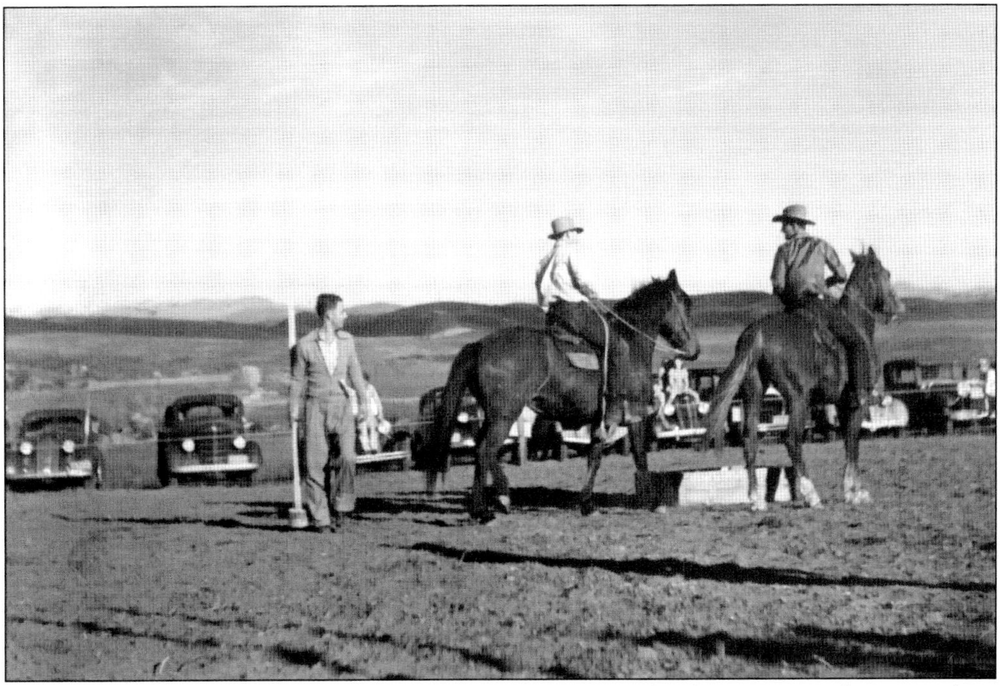

Rodeo Grounds, 1930s. Rodeos were staged near the slaughterhouse on Pujol Street, where Indian Fiestas were previously held and tractor races started decades later. From left to right are Vernon Otto on foot and Al Knott and Ed Yagle on horseback. Before the annual event started, spectators lined up along the sides of the street waiting in anticipation. (JJ.)

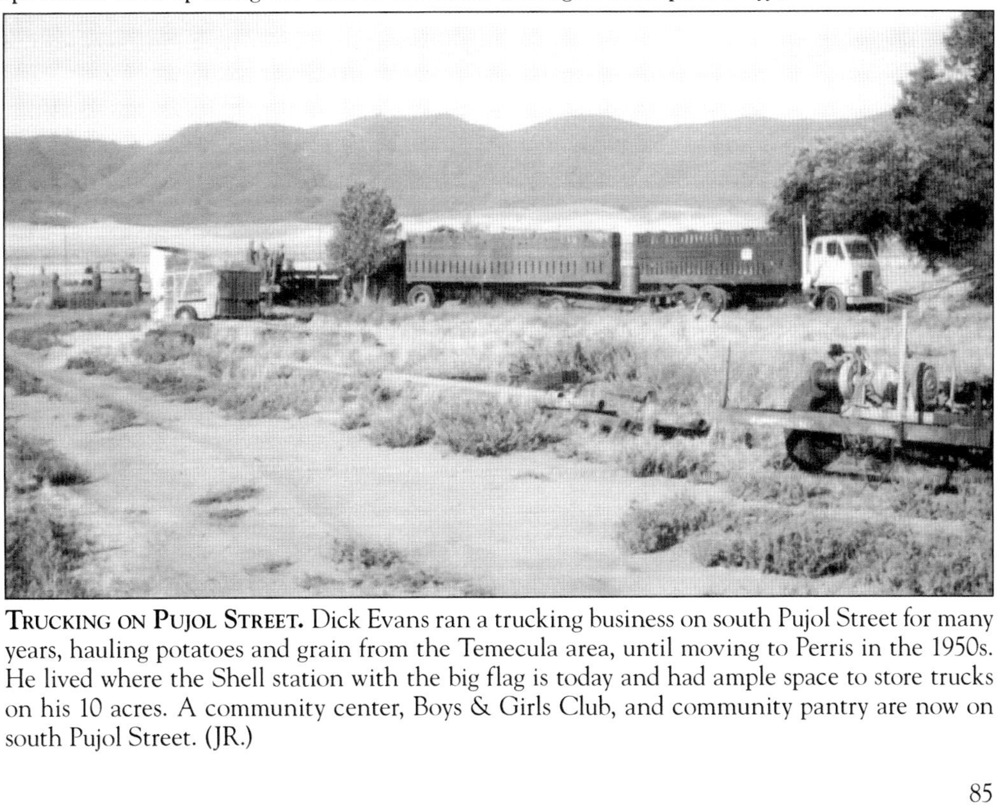

Trucking on Pujol Street. Dick Evans ran a trucking business on south Pujol Street for many years, hauling potatoes and grain from the Temecula area, until moving to Perris in the 1950s. He lived where the Shell station with the big flag is today and had ample space to store trucks on his 10 acres. A community center, Boys & Girls Club, and community pantry are now on south Pujol Street. (JR.)

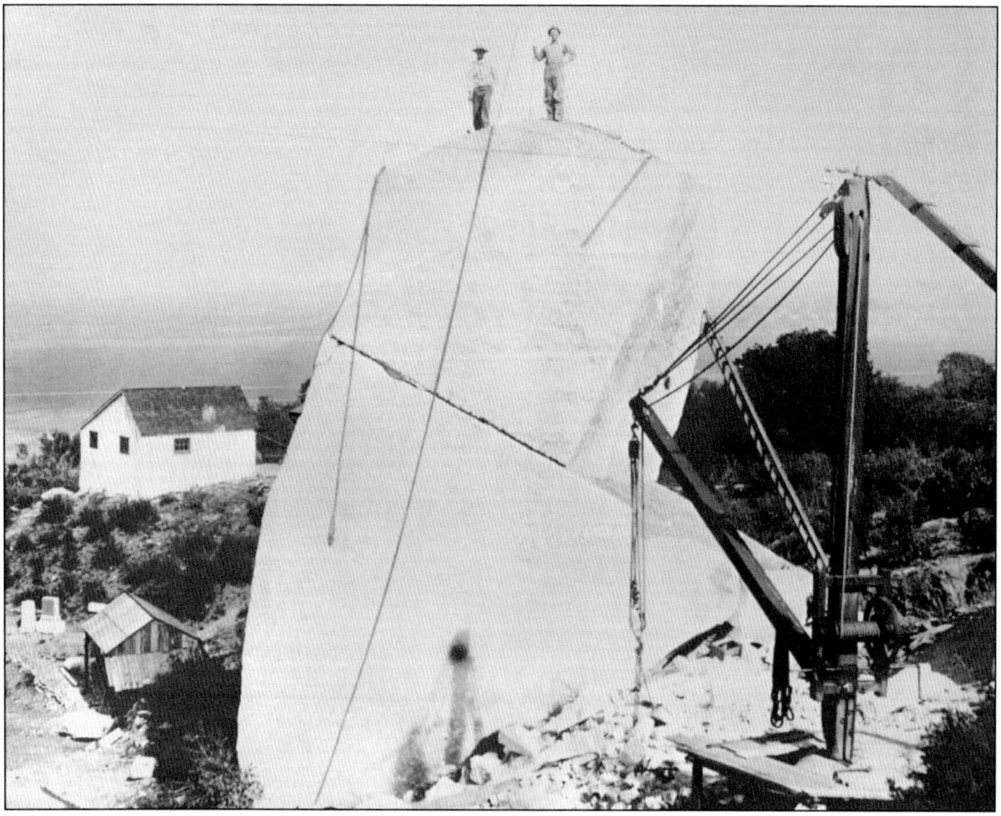

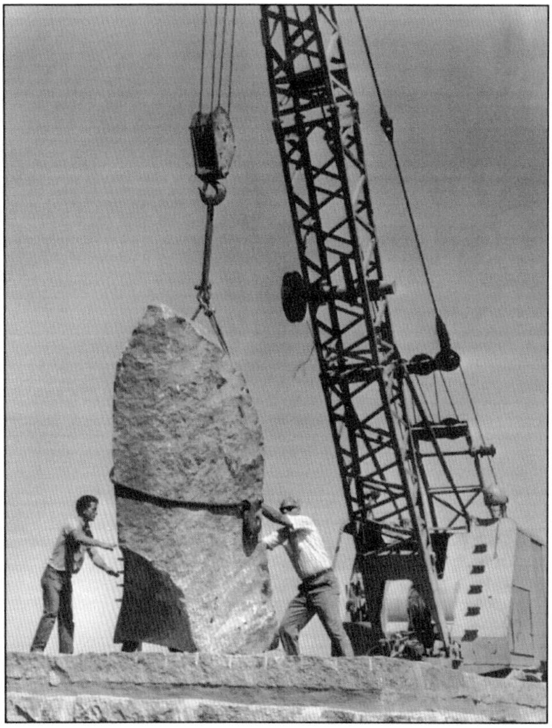

Quarrying Granite. Sam Hicks and Tom Hudson envisioned a monument to commemorate the pioneers who traveled through the Temecula Valley. The Querry family donated granite for the monument from the old Temecula rock quarry on their ranch. The quarry at one time supplied the hitching posts and curbs found throughout Old Town and also supplied granite for gravestones in the Temecula Cemetery. (TVM.)

Positioning the Monument. The "They Passed This Way" monument was dedicated on October 3, 1969, at the corner of Mercedes Street and Moreno Road. It is now known as Sam Hicks Monument Park, named for Temecula's last constable and one of the main supporters for the monument. The Temecula Valley Museum is at the east end of the park and the Chapel of Memories is on the south side. (TVM.)

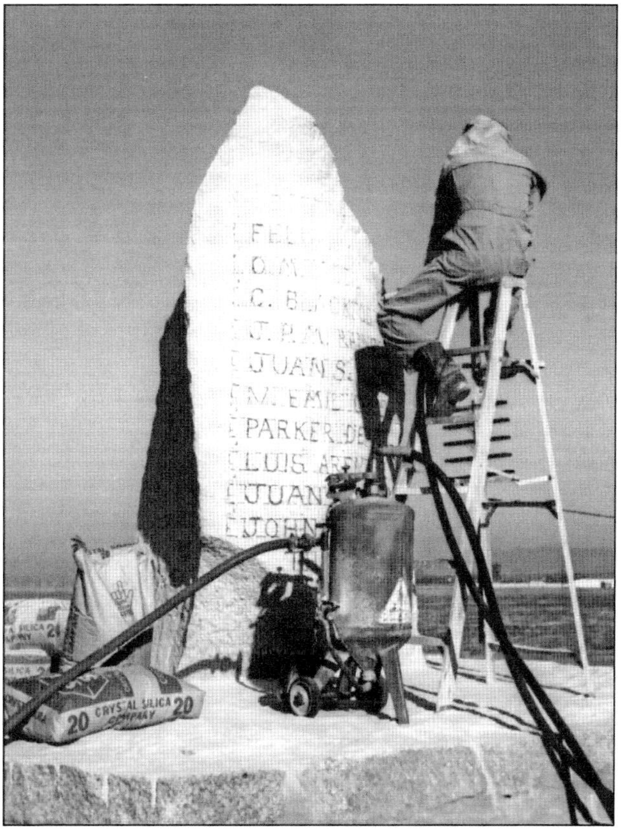

ENGRAVING THE NAMES. Odessa Querry funded the chiseling of the names onto the monument. She had a plaque placed at the base of the monument in memory of her late husband, Frank O. Querry. The monument was dedicated in 1969. Some of the pioneers honored include Parker Dear, Pio Pico, Louis Wolf, Juan Moreno, Nate Harrison, Luis Arena, Ami Golsh, Juan Calac, John Fremont, Pablo Apis, and Cave Couts. (TVM.)

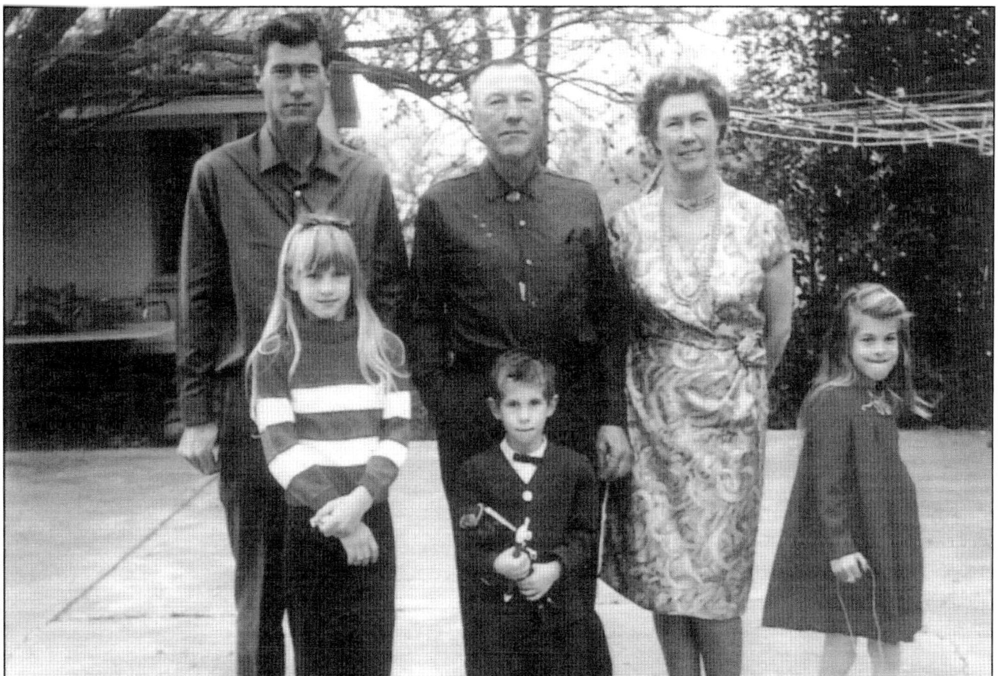

FRANK AND ODESSA QUERRY AND FAMILY. The Querry family lived on their ranch on Pala Road from 1956 to 1996. They were active in Temecula, volunteering their time and resources to the development of the community. Pictured are, from left to right, (second row) Edward, Frank, and Odessa; (front row) DeeDee, David, and Robyn. Edward's wife, Peggy, is not pictured. (EQ.)

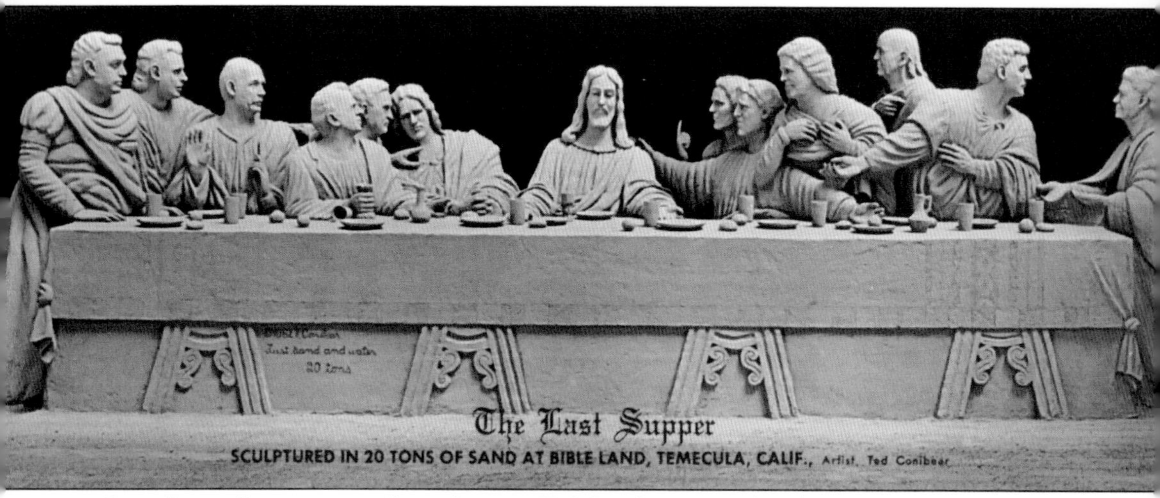

Bible Land Sculpture of Last Supper. Ted Conibear, a sand sculpture artist, produced works of art in public demonstrations around the country. In 1957, his family moved to Temecula. He opened Bible Land near Highway 395, at the present-day location of the Temecula Creek Inn. Conibear asked Temecula residents to pose for the life-sized depiction of the Last Supper. Johnny Munoa was the last model still living at the time this book was compiled. The sculpture was made of 20 tons of sand and water. In 1973, Conibear relocated Bible Land to Yucaipa, California. The free attraction was a favorite stopping point for many along Interstate 10, just as it had been on Highway 395. After Conibear died in 1994, the family decided to destroy the sand sculptures that had been damaged by weather and vandals through the years. Today, photographs of Bible Land are treasured by those who remember the inspirational art. A plaster sculpture of Conibear's "Jesus and the Children" is in the Fallbrook Masonic Cemetery. (TVHS.)

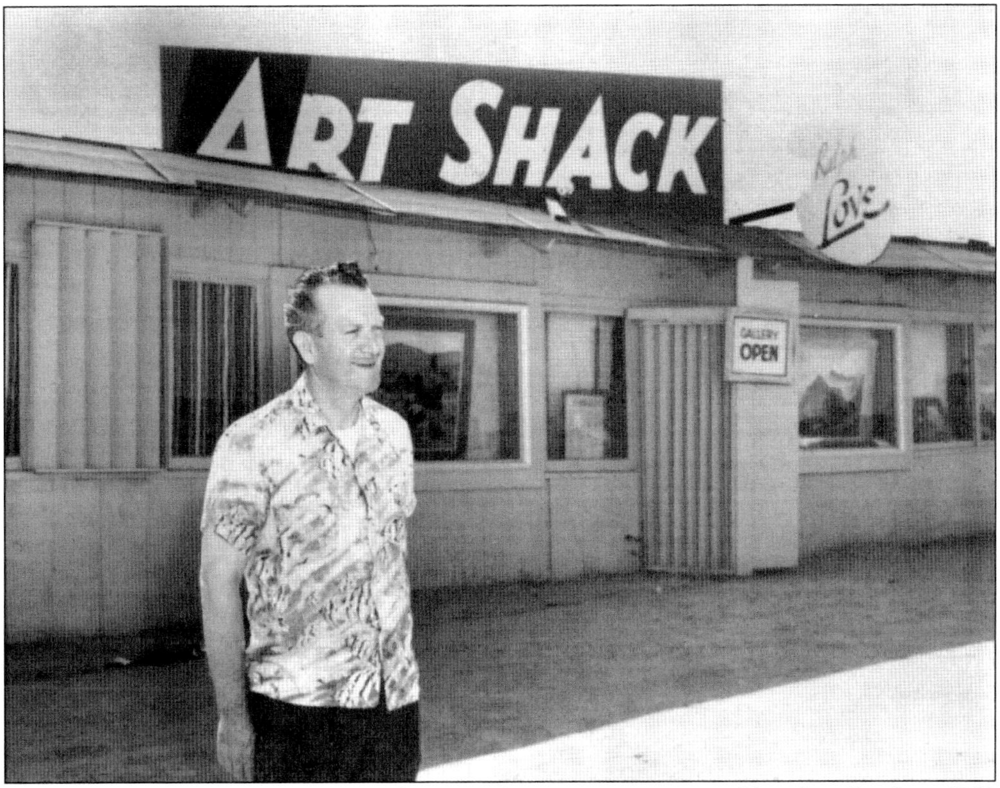

Ralph Love's Art Shack. Temecula's most famous painter opened his Art Shack in 1959 where the Baily's restaurant patio is today. The building, first a library, then a café, and later a secondhand store, was blighted until he brought new life to it. From there, he immortalized scenes of the Temecula Valley, some on canvas and many on the covers of *High Country* magazines. The building burned in 1961. (TVM.)

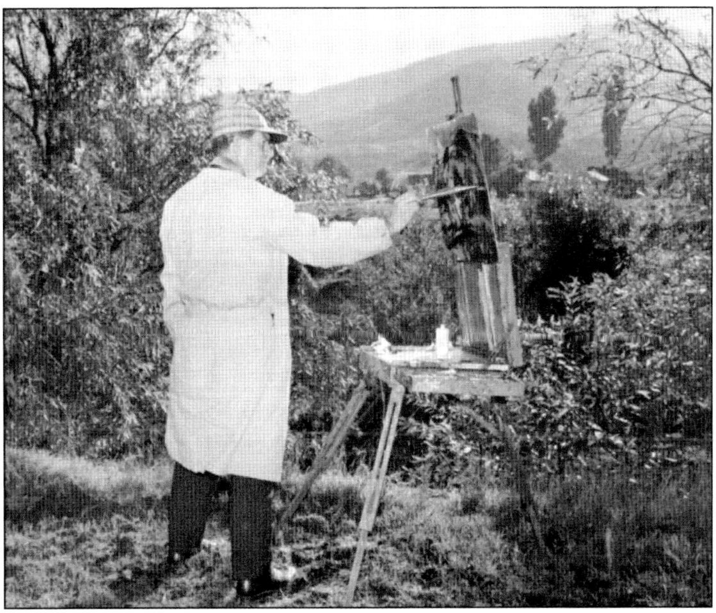

Ralph Love Painting. Love is known for his oil paintings of Western landscapes, deserts, and Temecula Valley. His paintings are highly collectible today. Each year, a plein-air outdoor painting contest is held in conjunction with a street painting contest in memory of this fine artist who settled in a cattle town. The Temecula Valley Historical Society placed a plaque in Baily's courtyard to acknowledge the talented artist. (TVM.)

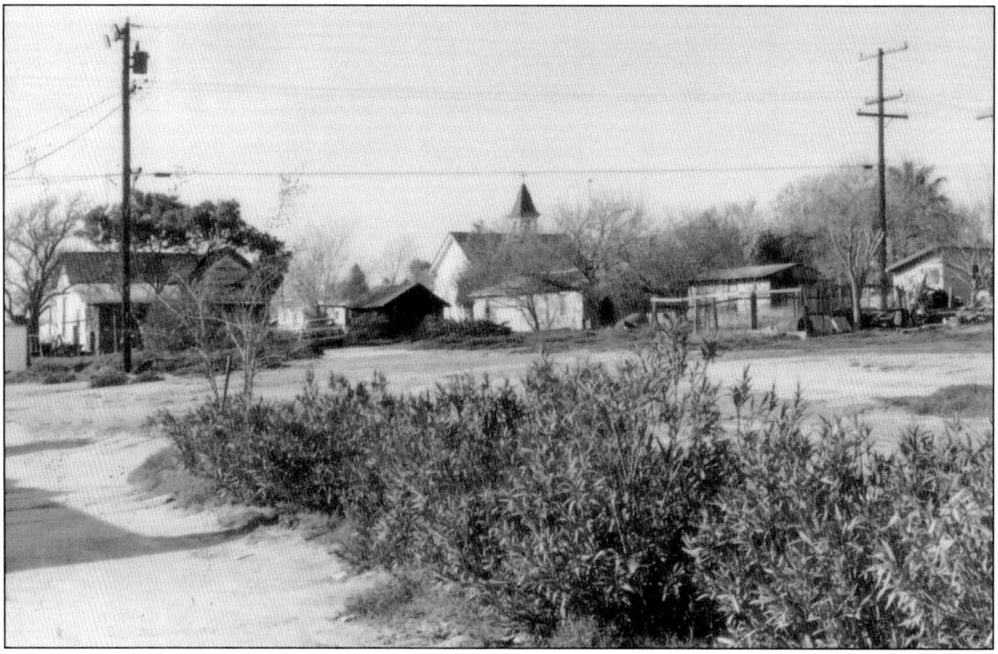

Backyard View in Old Town. This shows the corner of Fifth and Front Streets looking north between Mercedes and Front Streets in 1974. There were no sidewalks, and the streets were not paved. Weeds grew in vacant lots between houses; hodgepodge buildings and lean-tos had no fences. It still looked like a cowboy town. Code enforcement began with cityhood in 1989. (TVHS.)

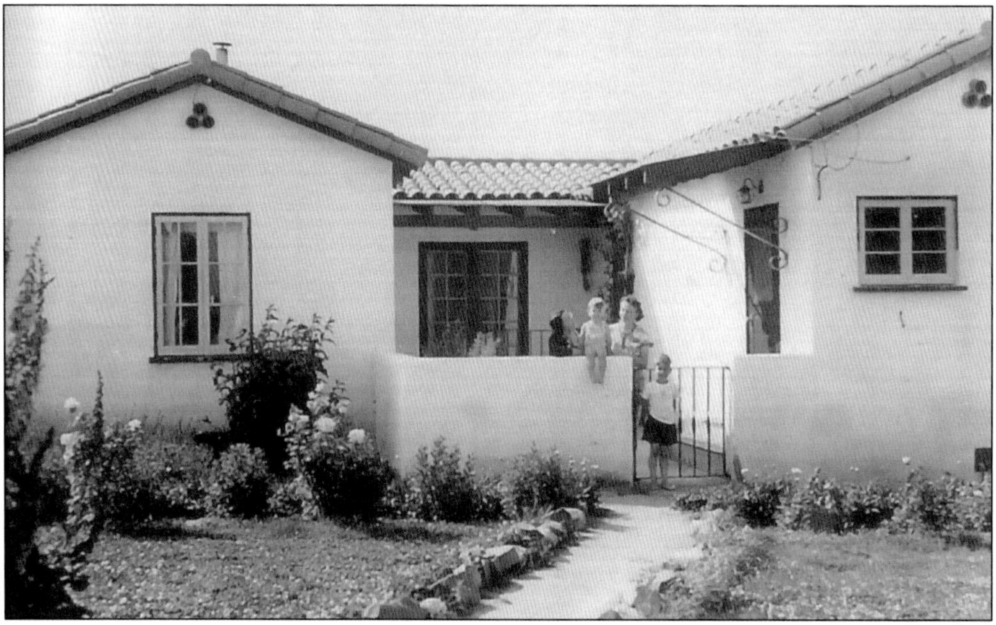

House on Pujol Street, 1940. At one time, all the merchants and prosperous people lived on Pujol Street north of Main Street, including Nienkes, McConvilles, Burnhams, Friedemanns, Barnetts, and Ottos. Living close to Sixth Street was considered better. Migrant workers lived on the south end of Pujol near the slaughterhouse, where the air carried a less-than-pleasant aroma. This house is still standing. (LB.)

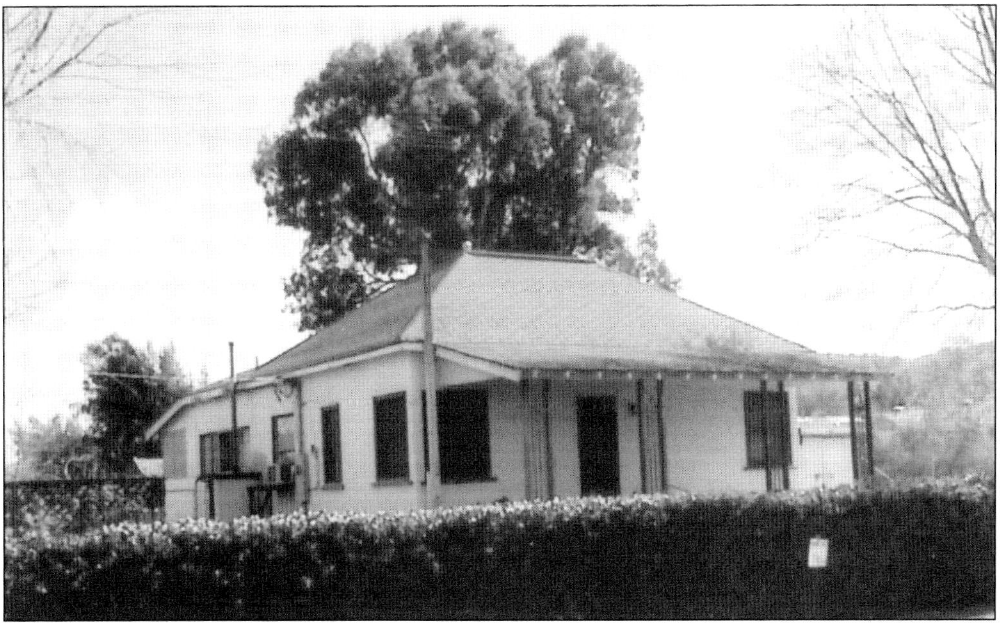

TALLEY HOUSE. This home sat near the Murrieta Creek on Third Street, where the Warehouse at Creekside is today. Jack Talley served as a border patrol agent, starting in Chula Vista in 1929 and becoming the officer in charge of the Temecula Station in 1939. He retired in 1954. Mary Talley worked at the Temecula Market. (DF.)

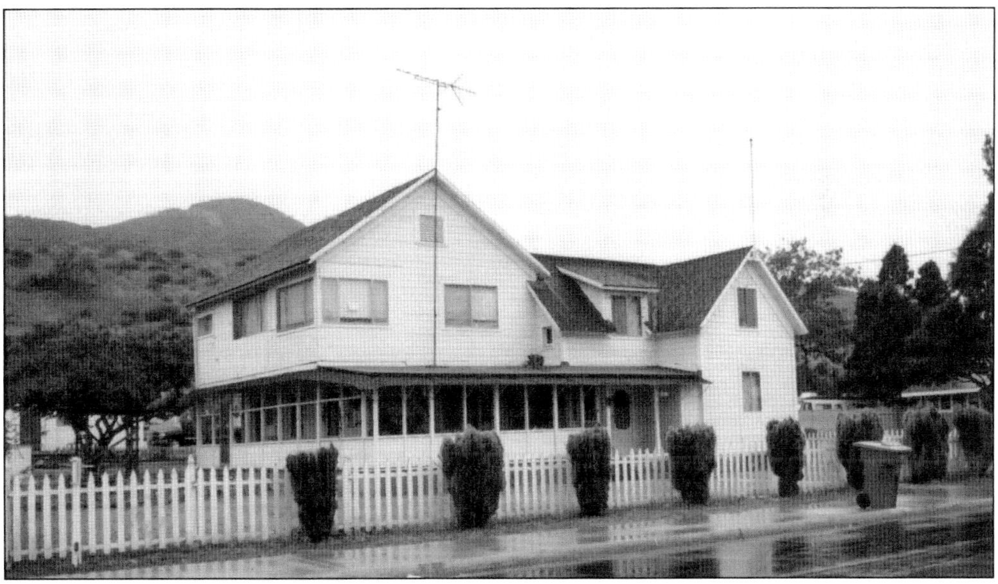

BURNHAM HOUSE. This, the largest home on Pujol Street, demonstrated the financial success of the Burnham family. Before moving into this house on the southwest corner of Main and Pujol Streets, the family lived on Main Street at a site now occupied by the Temecula Civic Center. This home is visible in the movie *Three Word Brand*. George Burnham purchased the mercantile store on Main Street from Philip Pohlman. (DF.)

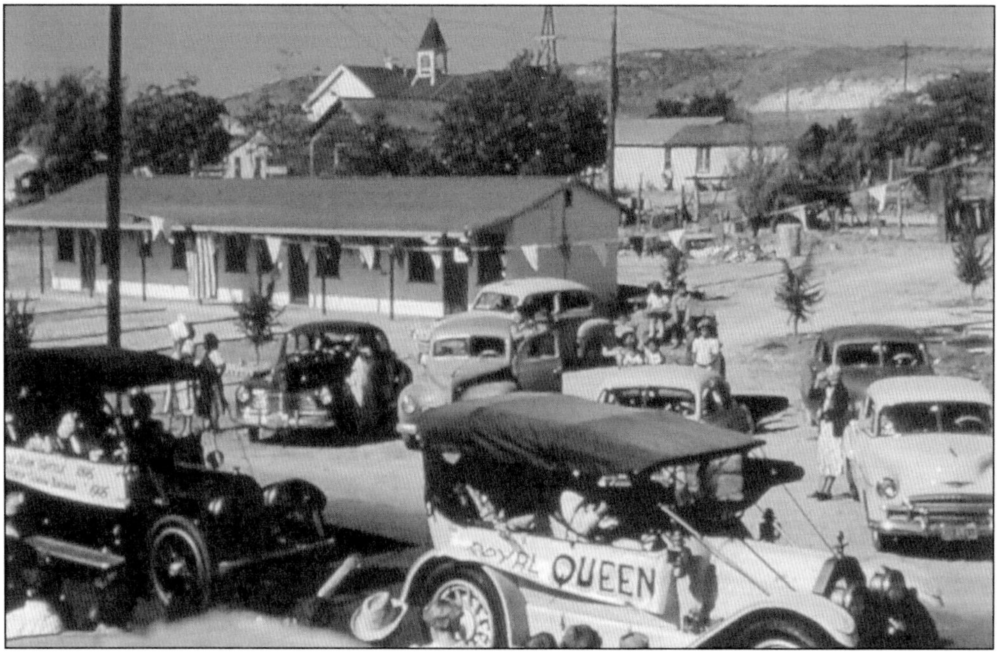

CALIFORNIA CENTENNIAL PARADE, 1950. Temecula hosted a parade to celebrate 100 years of statehood in 1950, as did many towns in California. The procession on Front Street passed a former motel that had been converted into a commercial building. It was located where the Rancon Plaza Building is today. Prior to 1950, Highway 395 went down Front Street and was the only paved street in Old Town. (DB.)

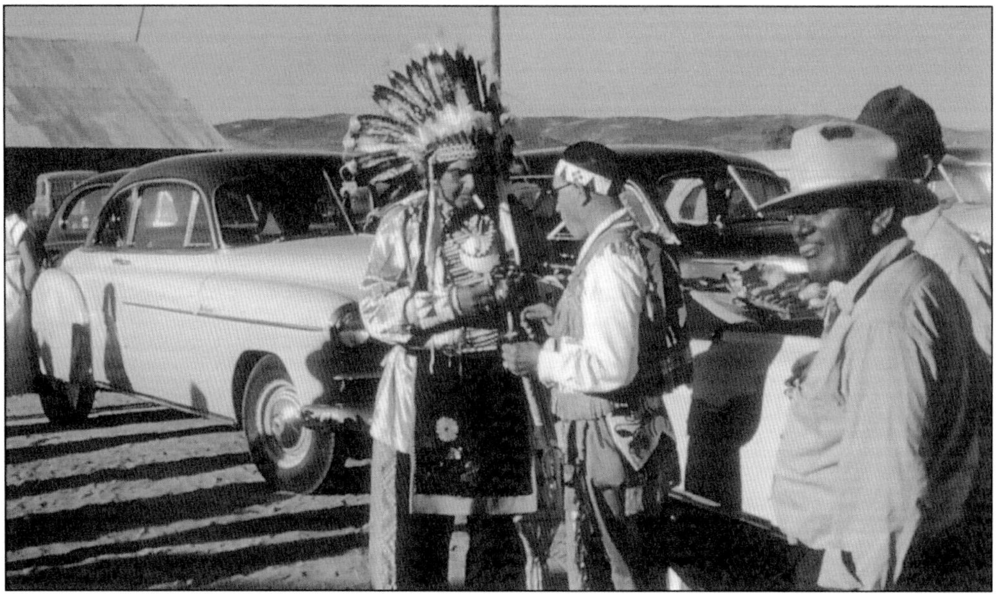

SILENT DAWN. Two years after the California Centennial, another parade ended at the Vail Ranch headquarters for the unveiling of a plaque to commemorate the signing of the Temecula Treaty. At this celebration of the signing of a treaty that was never honored by the US government, Silent Dawn (pictured at left), also known as US Army colonel Ted Davis, an Apache, spoke about the injustice done to Native American people. (DB.)

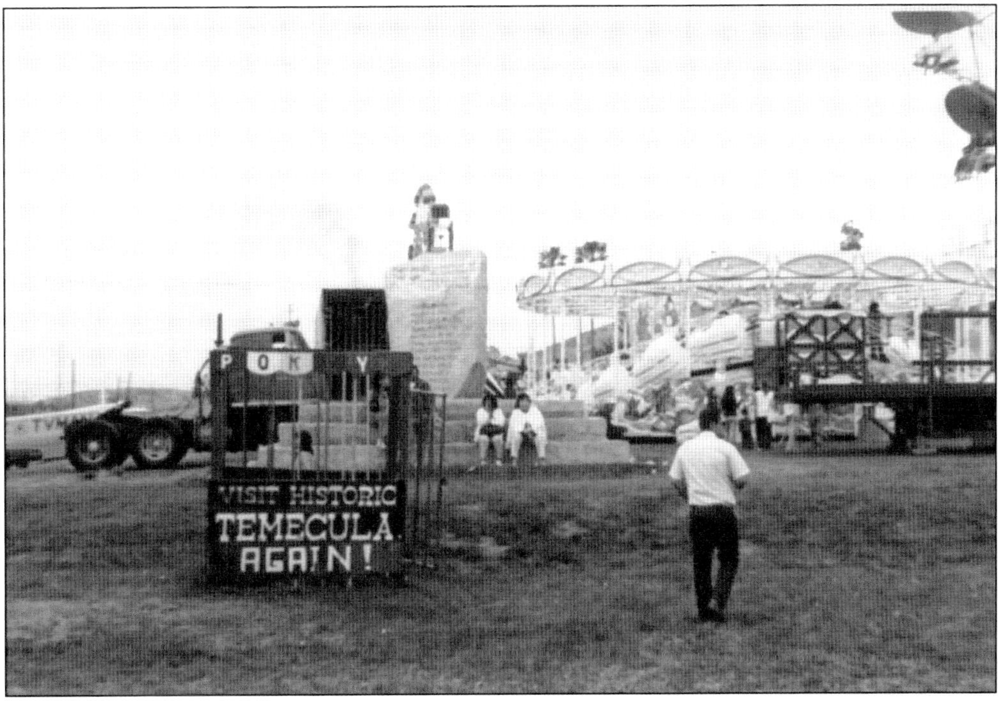

CARNIVAL AT SAM HICKS MONUMENT PARK. The Temecula Town Association started in 1969 and promoted Old Town as a shopping and touring destination. Frontier Days started in 1968 as entertaining community gatherings. Sam Hicks came to Temecula to work for author Erle Stanley Gardner and stayed and raised his family here. He encouraged the 1890s historical theme for Old Town. (TVM.)

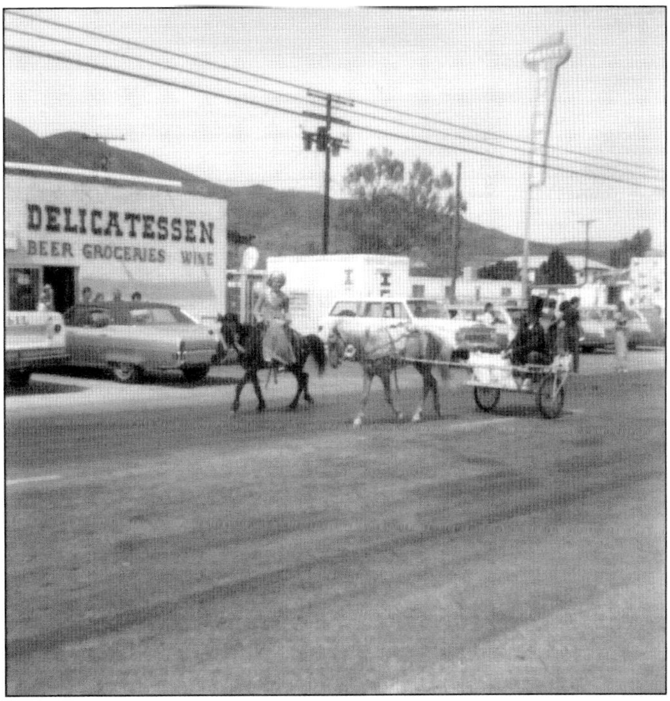

PARADE ON FRONT STREET. The icebox still sits at that location next to the Country Porch antique store on Third and Front Streets. The store was the only market in town until Rancho Market opened in the 1960s and Stater Brothers and Safeway opened in 1981. After the Long Branch Saloon closed, bikers sat in front of M&M Market and drank beer. It was later a delicatessen. (JJ.)

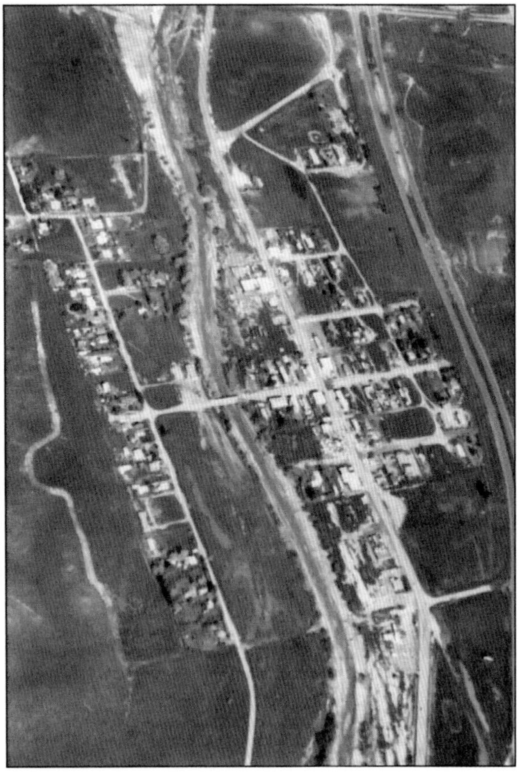

High above Old Town. This aerial view shows Murrieta Creek and the layout of the streets. It shows the divided highway bypassing town. There are more homes on the east side of town. Front Street was realigned by this time. The river looks clean, a task done by farmers to prevent flooding. (TVM.)

Snow on Front Street. This early-1960s photograph shows a rare snowfall covering Front Street. The Swing Inn Café and the parked cars are covered with a thin layer of snow. Richfield's service station is seen north of the café. By 1950, Highway 395 bypassed Front Street. The tall signs were erected to attract motorists into town from the highway. (TVM.)

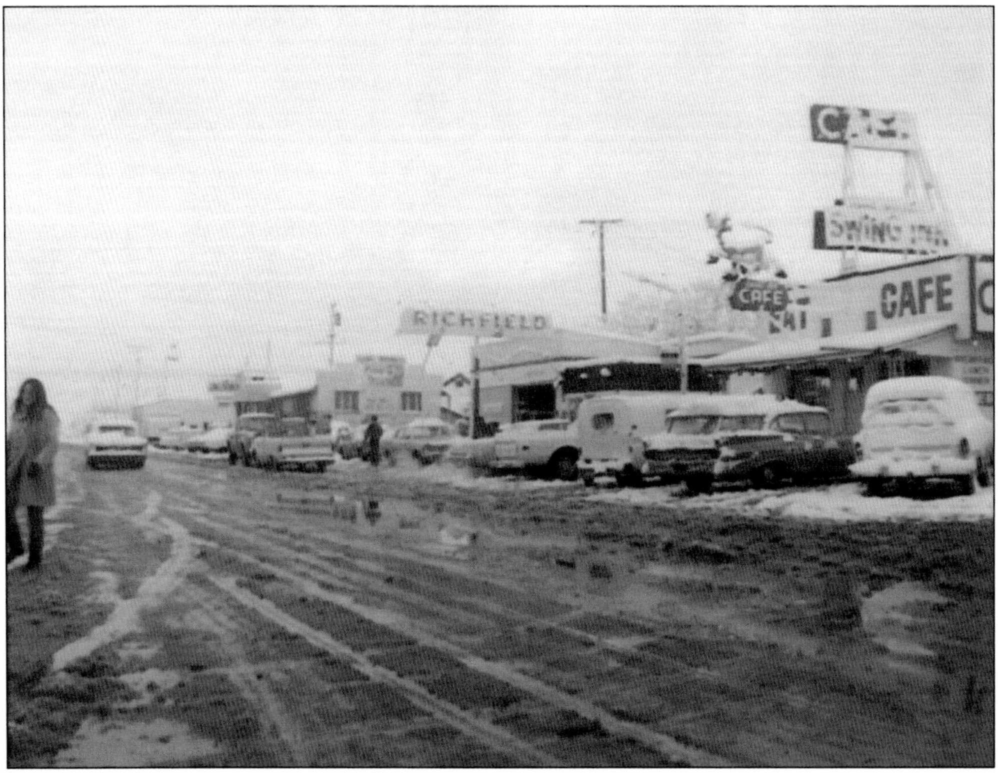

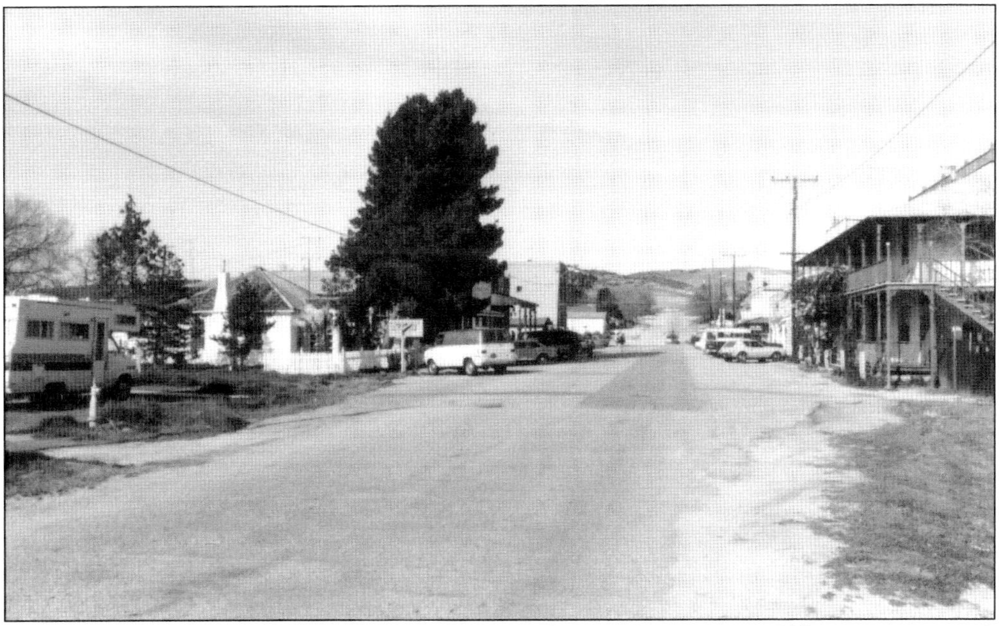

LOOKING EAST ON MAIN STREET, 1974. Until the mid-1980s, few streets in Old Town were paved, there were no sidewalks, and it was a quiet town with little traffic, "a town time forgot." A few notable modern changes were the porch to the upper story of the hotel, the white picket fence around Ole Larson's house, telephone poles, power lines, and angle parking. (TVHS.)

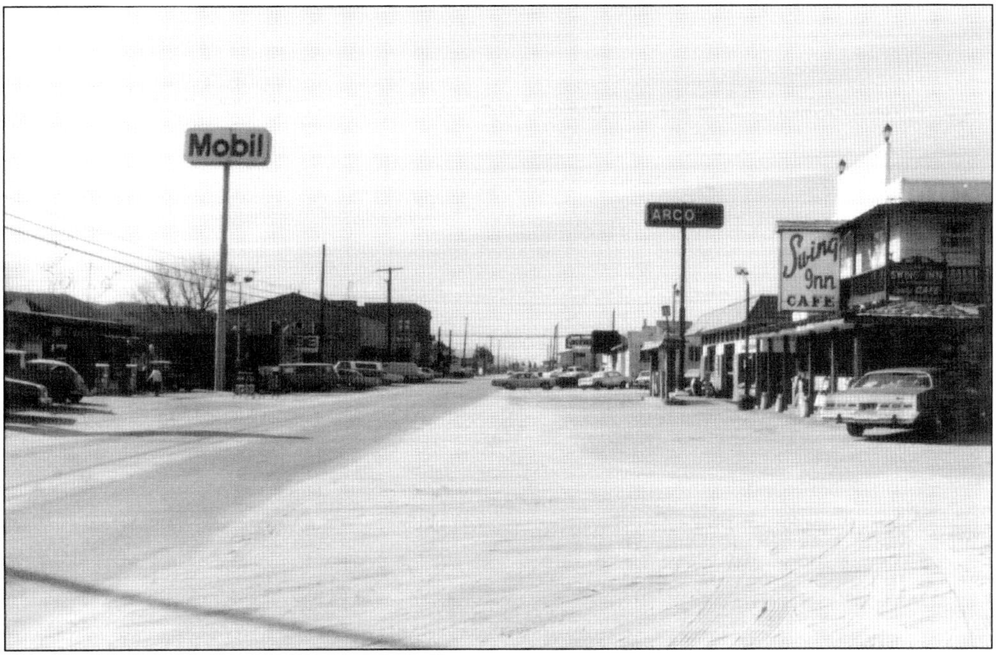

LOOKING NORTH ON FRONT STREET, 1974. Front Street was paved, but all the others were dirt. The two visible gasoline stations featured high signs to draw traffic into town from the highway. There was not a moving car on the street. After Tommy Hotchkiss bought the Andersons Café and named it the Swing Inn, they changed the facade and started the movement toward an 1890s Western theme for Old Town. (TVHS.)

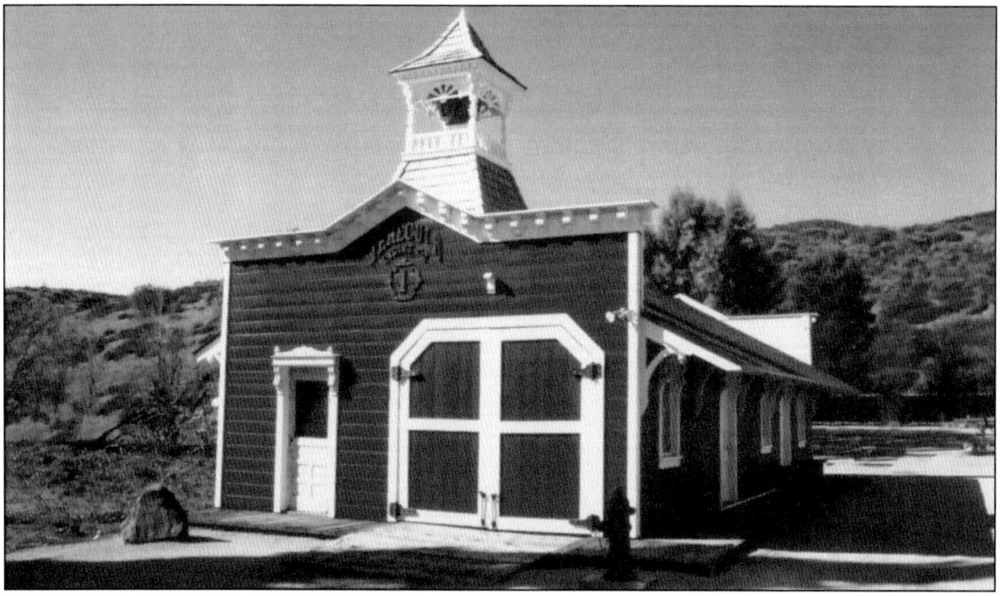

Never was a Firehouse. Howard Raish moved to Temecula in the late 1960s. He purchased the old McConville place on Pujol Street and built what he called the "Temecula Cultural Center" as a tourist attraction to view from the street. He built this structure in 1980 to represent a 1900-era firehouse. Raish was one of the key promoters for keeping the Old Western theme for Old Town. (LB.)

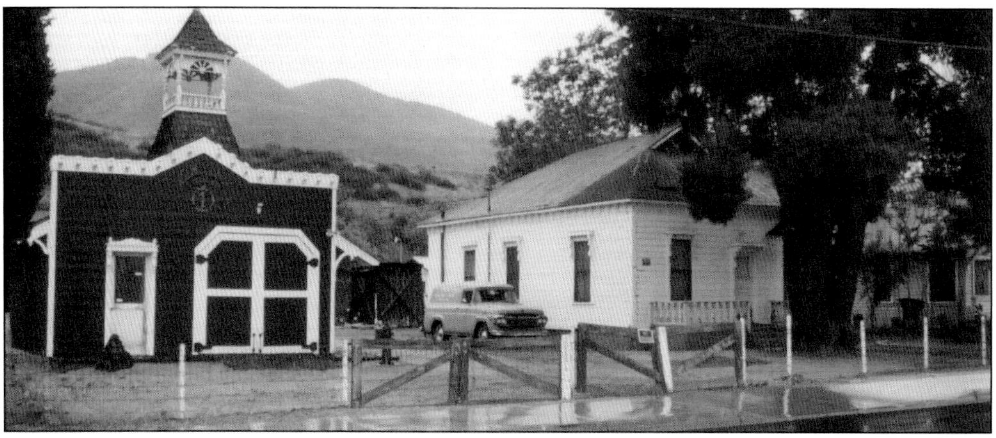

McConville Property. The house was built when the railroad came in and was one of the first homes on Pujol Street. The house is one of the few in town with a basement, which was constructed from local granite. Hugh McConville married Laura Welty. McConville owned the livery stable located at the site of today's Bank Restaurant. He was a prominent businessman, a deputy sheriff, and a civic leader. (LB.)

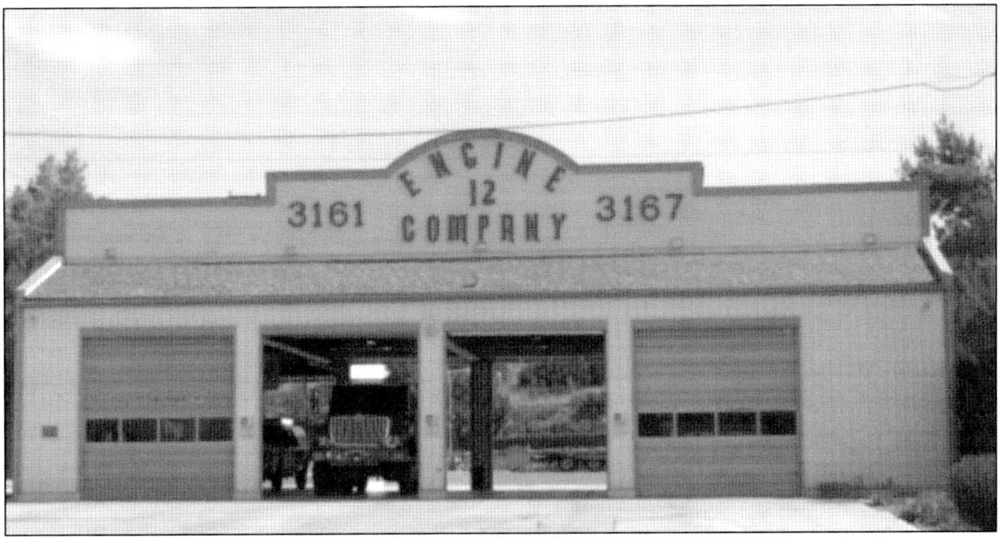

TEMECULA FIRE STATION. This station, still in use, was built in 1975 on Mercedes Street, near the Sam Hicks Monument Park. It was the first station constructed in California with combined funding by three agencies. Those agencies were the developer Kaiser Aetna, the State of California, and the County of Riverside. The Rancho California Volunteer Fire Department formed in 1969. (LB.)

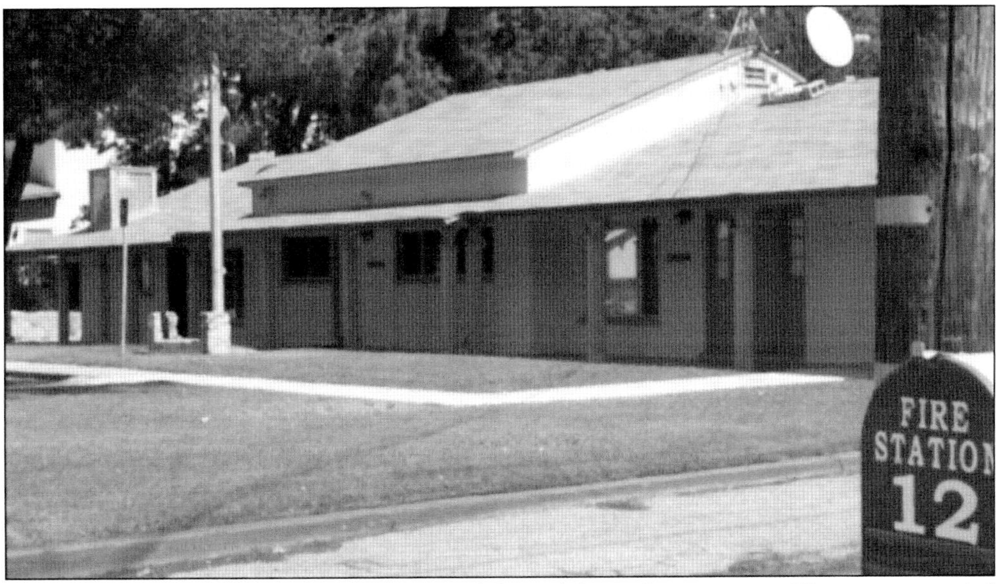

FORESTRY STATION. The Temecula division of the California Department of Forestry responded to calls or Teletype messages from Rainbow to Lake Elsinore and east to Aguanga. The station housed fire apparatus and had living areas for the crew and the chief's family. The Lowerys were the last family to live there. Before this building was built in 1952 a standby fire truck was kept at random sites in the valley. (LB.)

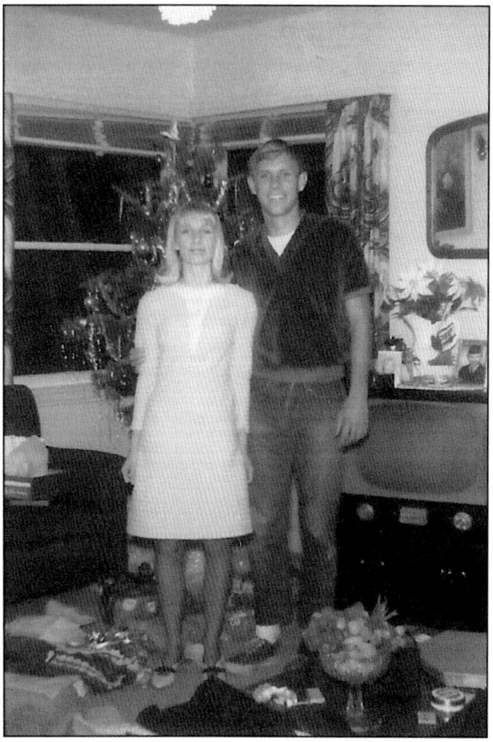

Patricia and Mike Talley. Mike excelled in school and athletics. He attended the Temecula Union School, graduating from eighth grade in 1960. He was an Army officer and tank commander during the Vietnam War and received the Silver Star for his valor. As a civilian, he was an expert craftsman, gunsmith, and fisherman. Patricia served many years as manager of the Lake Elsinore Public Cemetery. (TG.)

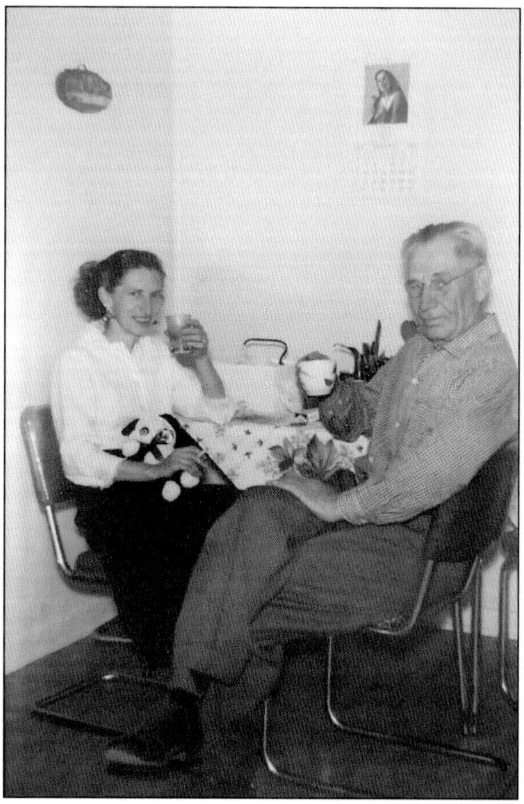

Mary and Jack Talley. The Talleys enjoyed breakfast together in their typical Old Town Temecula house in the 1950s. Jack was born in Gonzales, Texas, in 1896 and served in World War I. He was stationed at the newly formed US Border Patrol station in Temecula in 1946. He was mild-mannered and respected in the community. He died in Fallbrook, California, in 1968 and was buried in the Temecula Cemetery. (TG.)

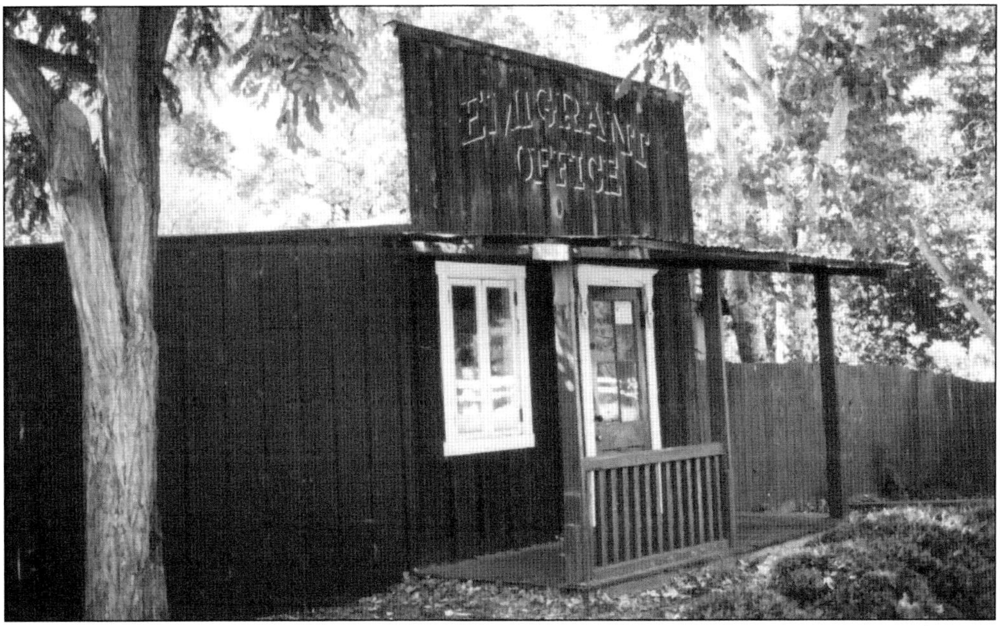

EMIGRATION OFFICE, 1974. This was the US Border Patrol station for many years. It is on the east side of the Main Street Bridge, next to the Temecula Hotel. After World War II, border patrol agents constructed it with old lumber for use as an office. A broken-down bus was used for a jail. Artist Roy Morrisey later used it as a studio. (TVHS.)

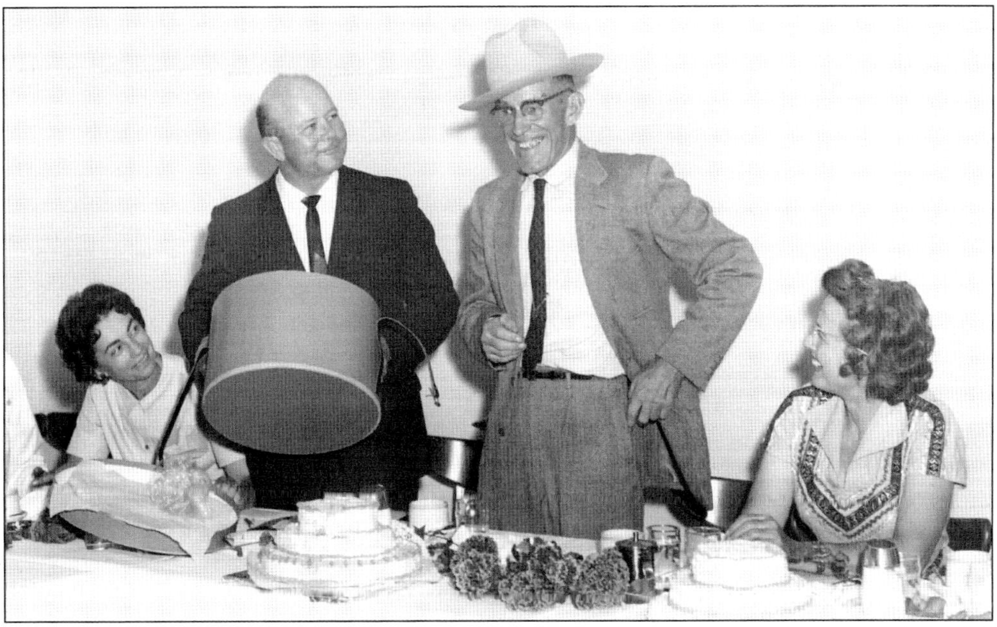

DICK RAMSAY'S RETIREMENT PARTY. Ramsay retired in 1965 after 21 years of service with the US Border Patrol. He was involved with the community, leading the Temecula 4-H Club for many years. The participants in 4-H had agricultural projects involving growing livestock and showing them at the Riverside County Fair in Hemet. His wife, Margaret, is at right; the other people are not identified. (TVHS.)

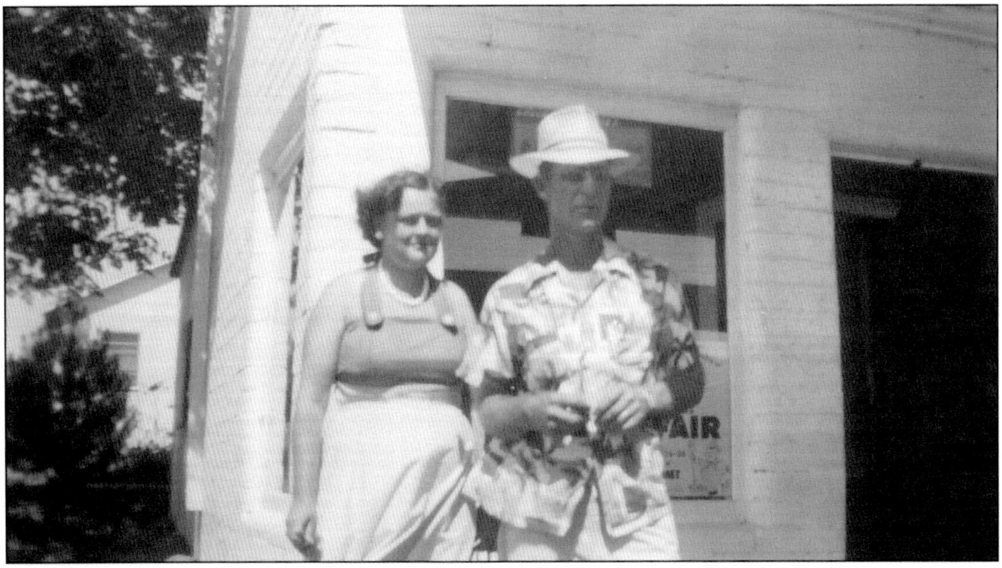

VERNON AND ELIZABETH OTTO. The Ottos and Nienkes, who were relatives, built several houses on Pujol Street. The Ottos did whatever they could to make ends meet in the 1940s and 1950s, like most of the residents of Old Town. Besides doing construction, they owned a gasoline station. Vernon drove a school bus and did janitorial work for the school. Elizabeth was postmaster and helped at the station. (JJ.)

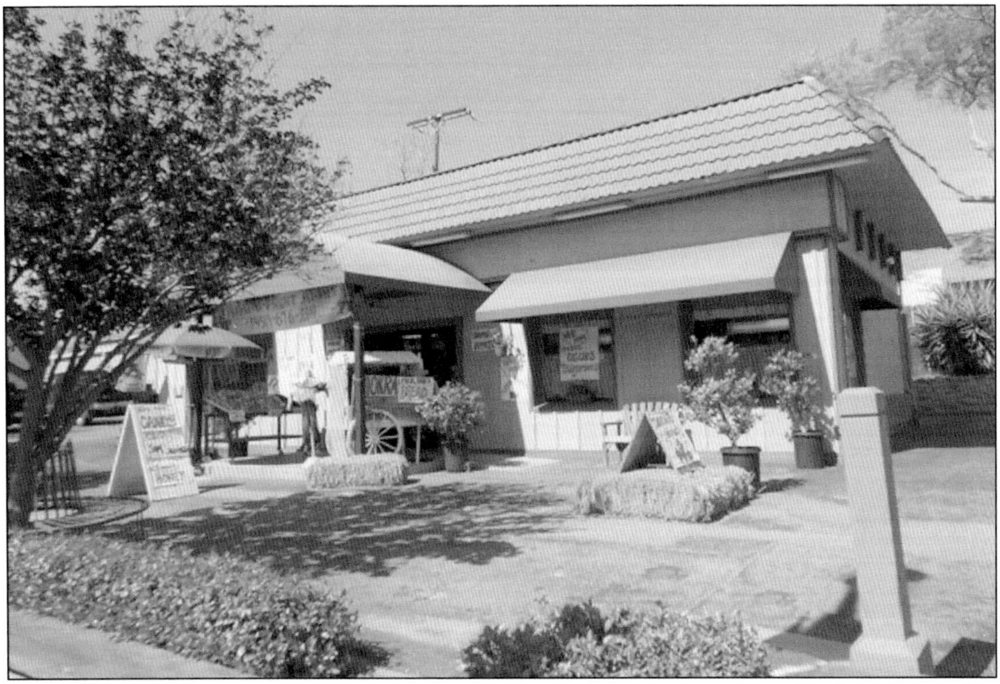

FORMER ARCO STATION. After a long time of serving motorists along the inland roadways, this former gasoline station was a location for the Temecula Valley Museum. When the museum moved to a new place, Helga Berger opened the Chocolate Florist there, selling flowers and fudge. Now, Randy and Becky Bevel offer their produce there, bringing it back to town after their produce stand burned in south Temecula in the 1990s. (RF.)

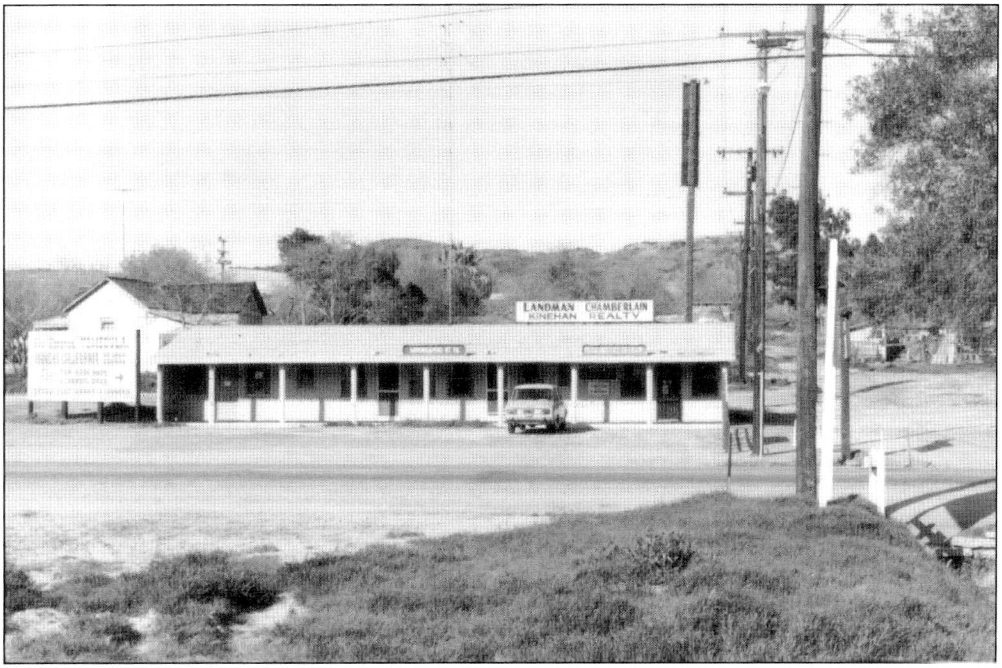

OLD MOTEL BUILDING, 1974. This former motor inn was on the east side of Front Street. The large billboard advertised the Temecula Chamber of Commerce on the left side of the building, and the sign over the door on the right identifies the location of the Kinehan Chamberlain Realty. The old motel as well as the real estate office was razed in 1980 for the construction of Rancon Plaza. (TVHS.)

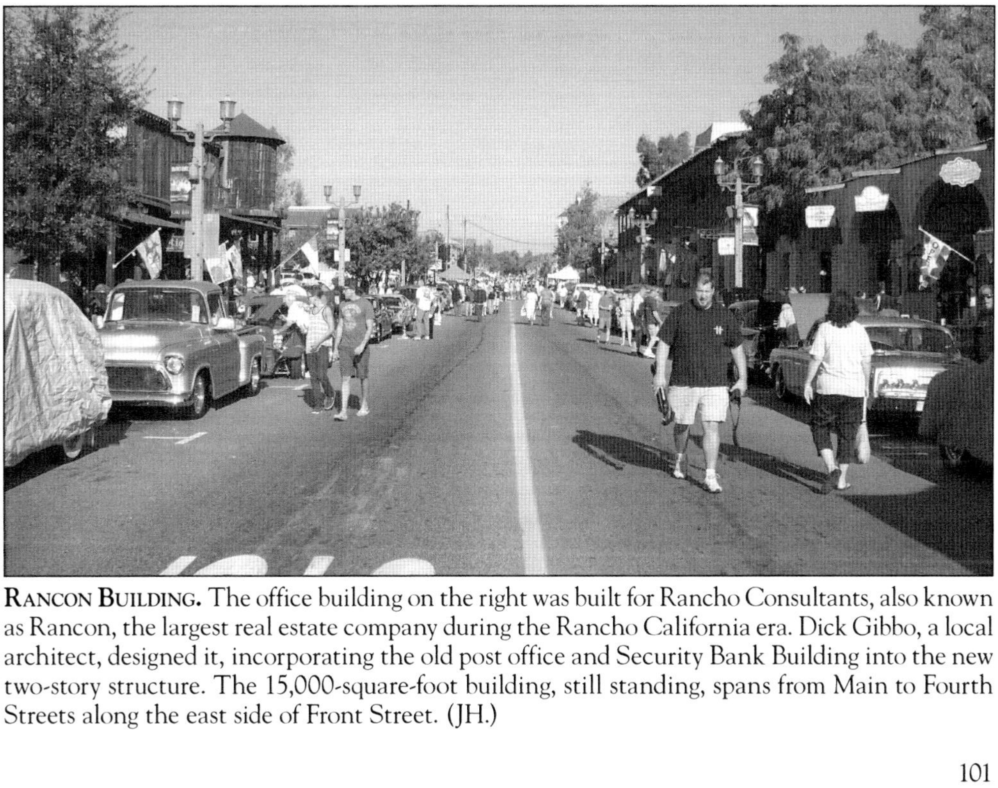

RANCON BUILDING. The office building on the right was built for Rancho Consultants, also known as Rancon, the largest real estate company during the Rancho California era. Dick Gibbo, a local architect, designed it, incorporating the old post office and Security Bank Building into the new two-story structure. The 15,000-square-foot building, still standing, spans from Main to Fourth Streets along the east side of Front Street. (JH.)

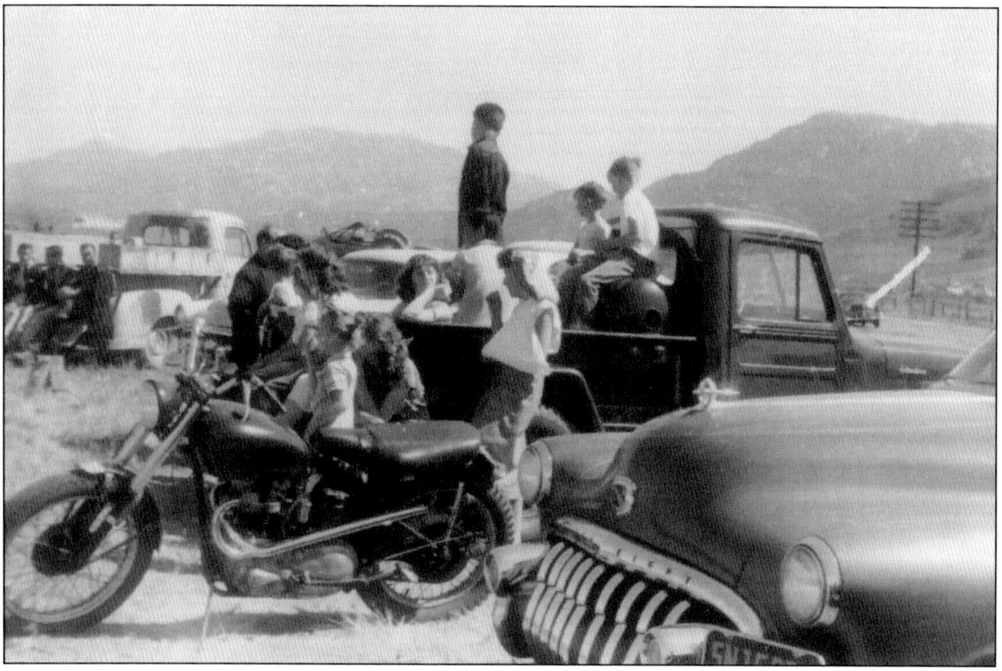

GO-KART RACES. In the tradition of Temecula sports and competition, interest shifted through the years from fiestas and rodeos to motorized racing. In the 1940s and 1950s, racing was popular, starting in the same location as the fiestas of years before. This shows part of the crowd watching a go-kart race. In the absence of bleacher seats, people stood or watched from the backs of pickup trucks. (JJ.)

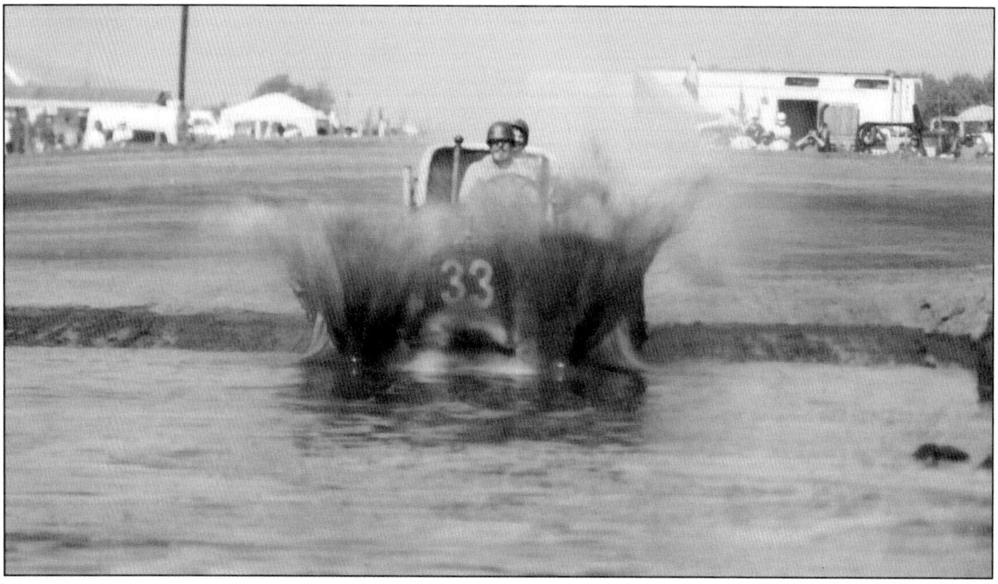

TEMECULA TRACTOR RACE. Temecula celebrated its agricultural roots when tractor races started in 1977. Founders Bob Morris and Tommy Hotchkiss provided entertainment with comic routines on their old tractors as they raced in and out of Murrieta Creek south of Old Town. As the Great Temecula Tractor Race gained popularity, people came in from all over Southern California to watch. The event moved to the north end of Diaz Road. (RM.)

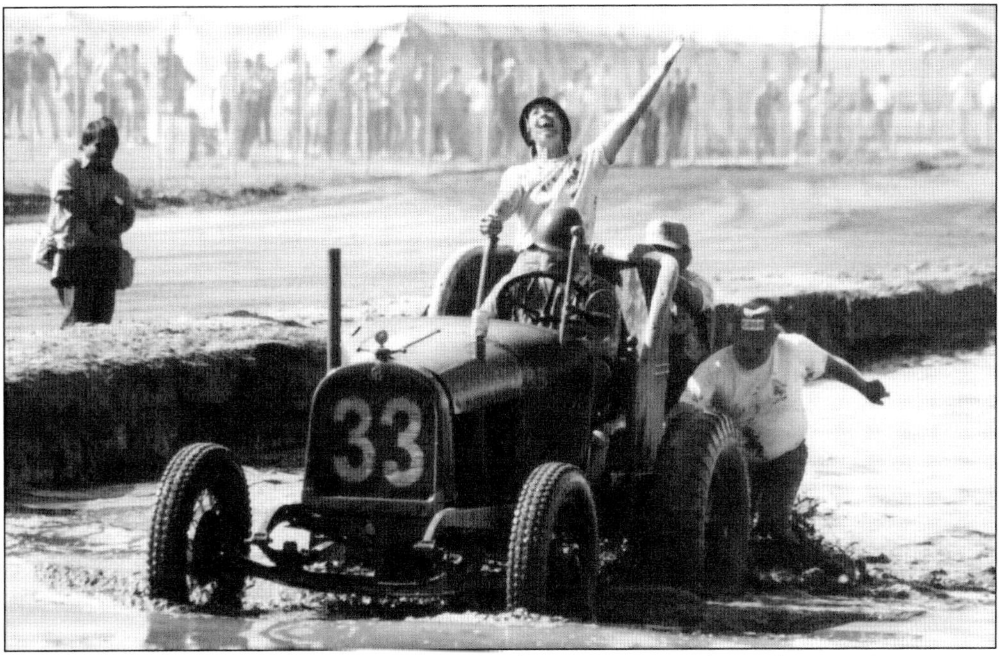

Victory Cheer. Belinda Morris, daughter of Bob Morris, gave a cheer after winning a messy, muddy round in a tractor race. Grandstands were built at the Diaz Road location and vendors sold wares. Local service clubs hosted booths and served everything from Indian tacos to ice cream. The whole community looked forward to the annual fall event. Mud surfing was another one of the competitive events. (RM.)

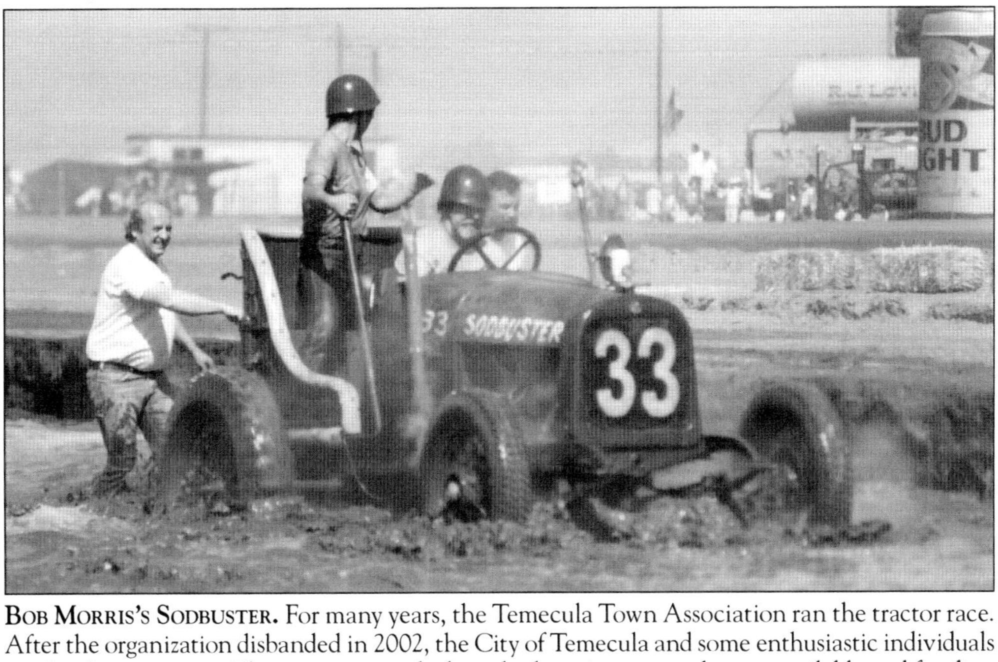

Bob Morris's Sodbuster. For many years, the Temecula Town Association ran the tractor race. After the organization disbanded in 2002, the City of Temecula and some enthusiastic individuals tried to keep it going. The event stopped when the location was no longer available and funding ran out. Tommy Hotchkiss's tractor, Sharecropper, and some of the original signs from the event are on display at the Little Temecula History Center. (RM.)

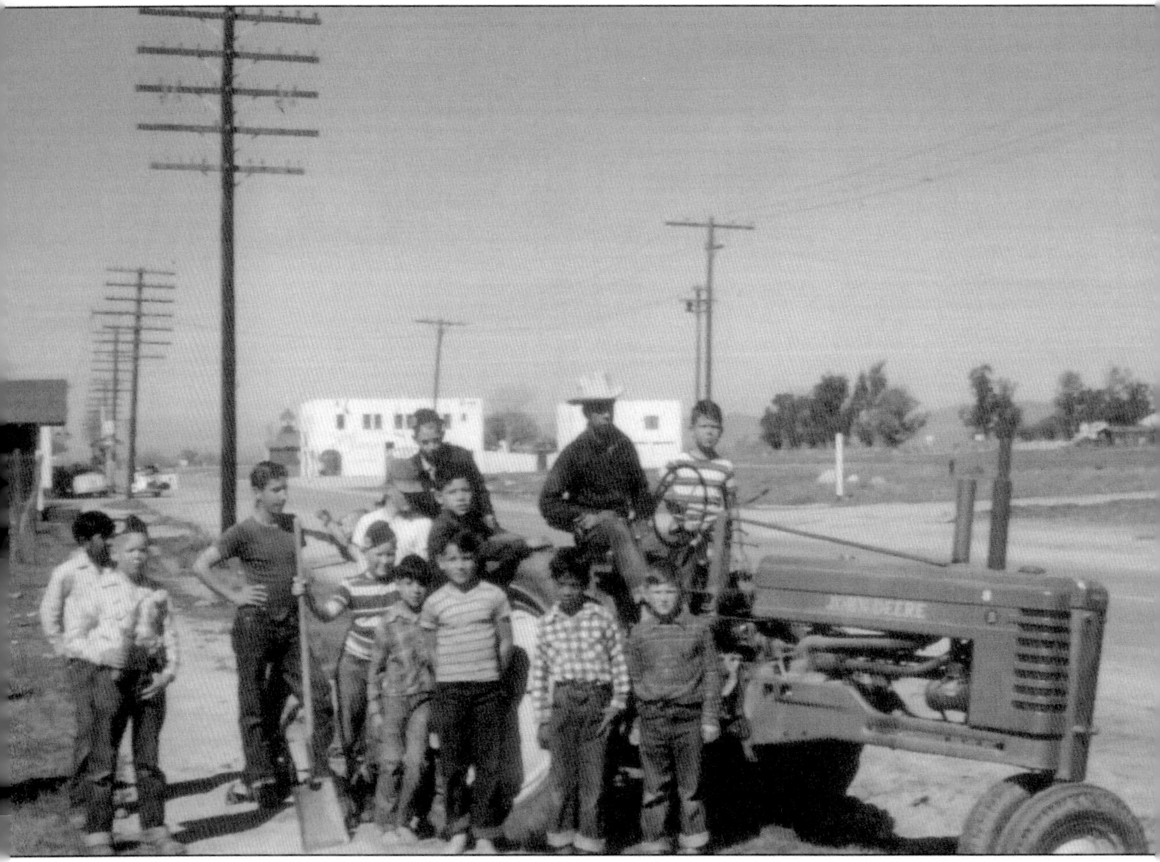

4-H MEMBERS IN TEMECULA, 1940S. While ranching dominated the area, the youth were groomed for future careers in agriculture. Families represented in the photograph include McEihinneys, Barnetts, Guenthers, Borels, Knotts, and Kitches. They were working on a 4-H project in Old Town, as indicated by their hats and shovels. They were across the street from the old motor inn shown on page 101. (DB.)

Six

Building with the Past in View

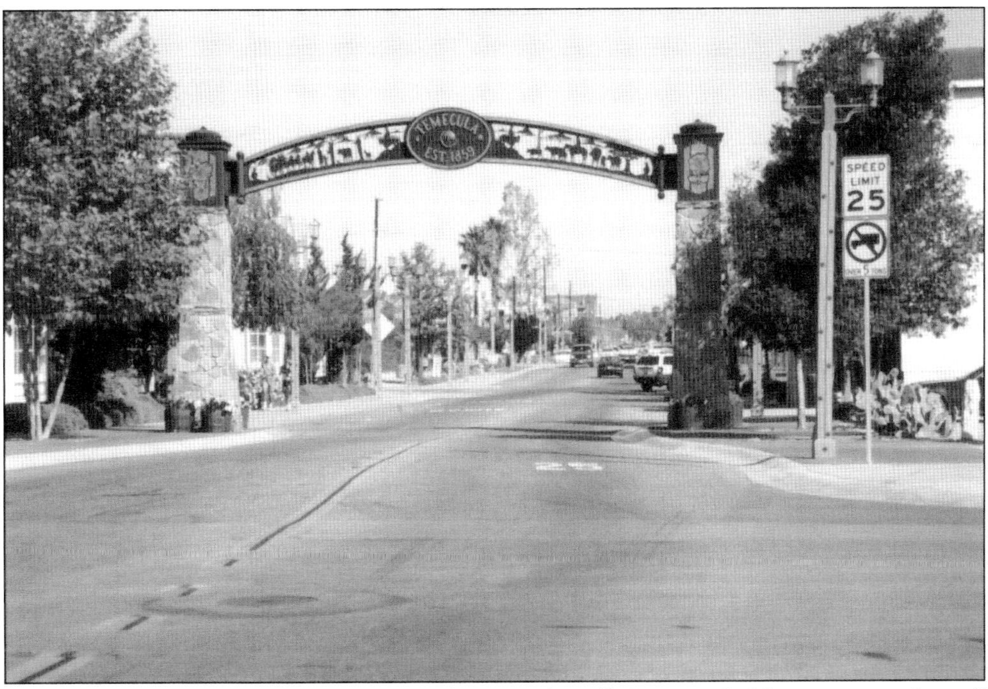

Arch at South End of Front Street. John Bianchi called Temecula "the town time forgot." Change was inevitable, but Temecula has not forgotten the old times. As modern conveniences merge with the 1890s motif, groups like the Old Town Review Board and others watch to ensure the historic past is not forgotten in this small segment of town between the two arches designed by Bob Morris. (LB.)

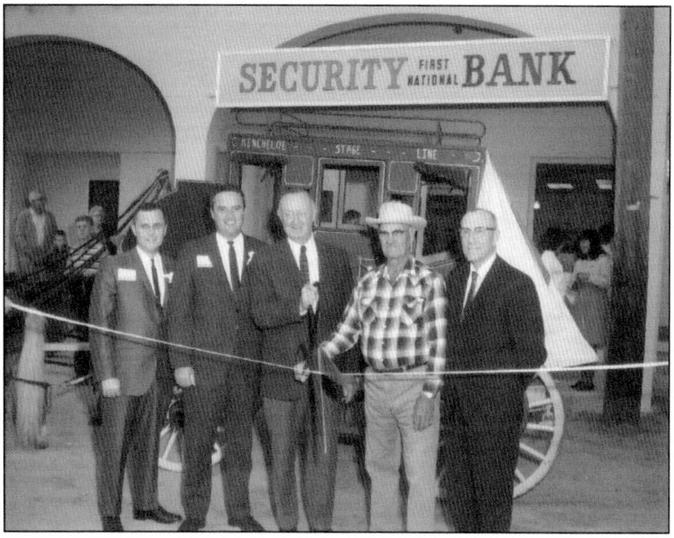

SECURITY BANK OPENING, 1965. A newspaper article announced "a new chapter in Temecula history" began with the bank's grand opening. From left to right are bank manager Peter VanVechten, regular vice president Lorenz Victor, senior vice president William Cottle, Carl Swanguen of Temecula, and bank director Irwin Farrar. The stagecoach in the background kept with the Old West theme of Old Town. (MK/LZ.)

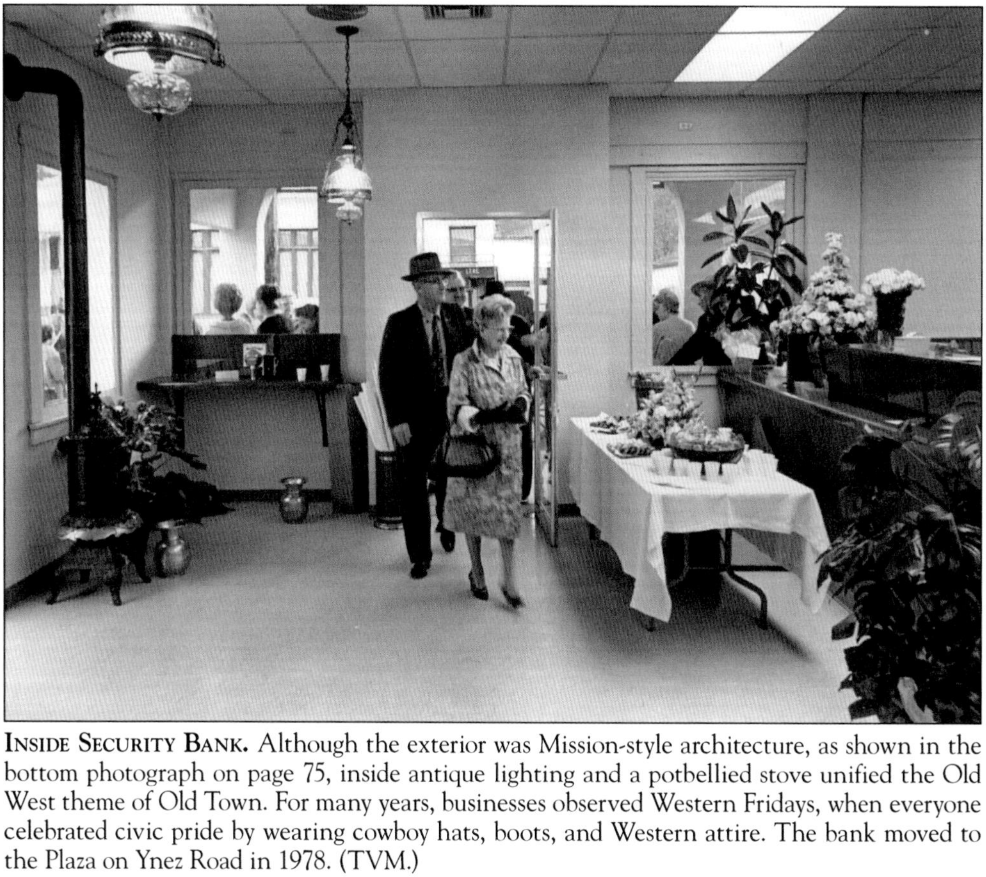

INSIDE SECURITY BANK. Although the exterior was Mission-style architecture, as shown in the bottom photograph on page 75, inside antique lighting and a potbellied stove unified the Old West theme of Old Town. For many years, businesses observed Western Fridays, when everyone celebrated civic pride by wearing cowboy hats, boots, and Western attire. The bank moved to the Plaza on Ynez Road in 1978. (TVM.)

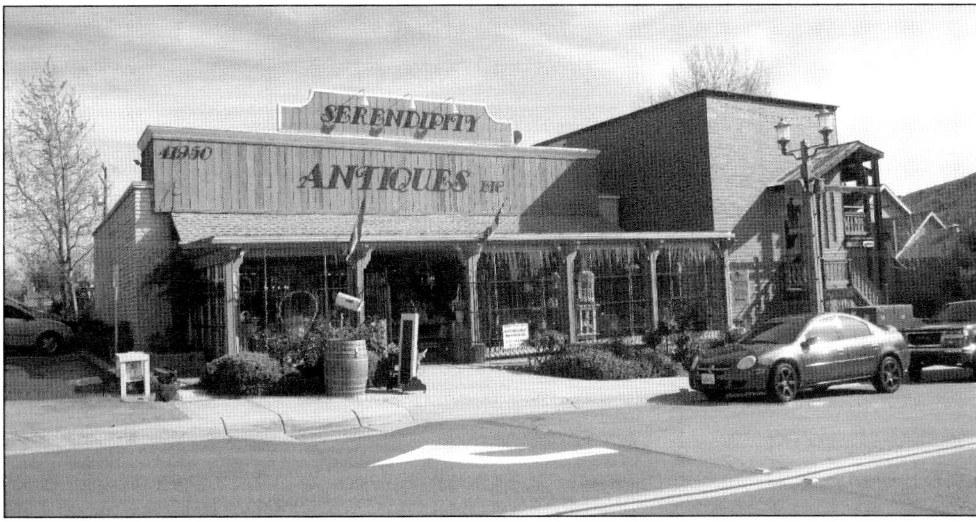

SERENDIPITY ANTIQUES ETC. This store on Main Street near the new Temecula Civic Center was the Sears Catalog store, run by Dick and Pat Birdsall and Dick's mother, Laura May "Sis" Herron, who were involved with the Temecula Town Association. Pat was a member of the first city council. It was also the home for the Temecula Valley Museum for a while. In 1994, Walter and Helga Berger purchased the building. (BM.)

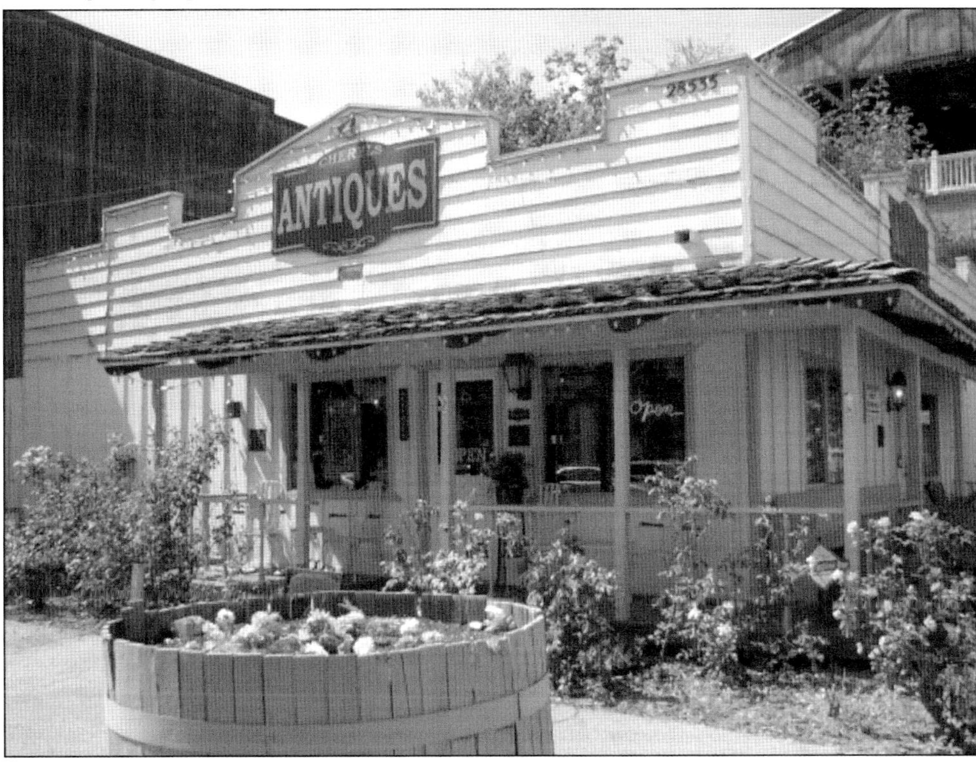

KNOTT HOUSE ANTIQUE STORE. The two large Penfold Buildings dwarf the little one-story house today. In the 1990s, the former home of Al and Freda Knott was a Victorian tearoom. It is now an antique store. The Knott families of Temecula and Murrieta were not related to the Knott family who started the Berry Farm attraction in Orange County. (LB.)

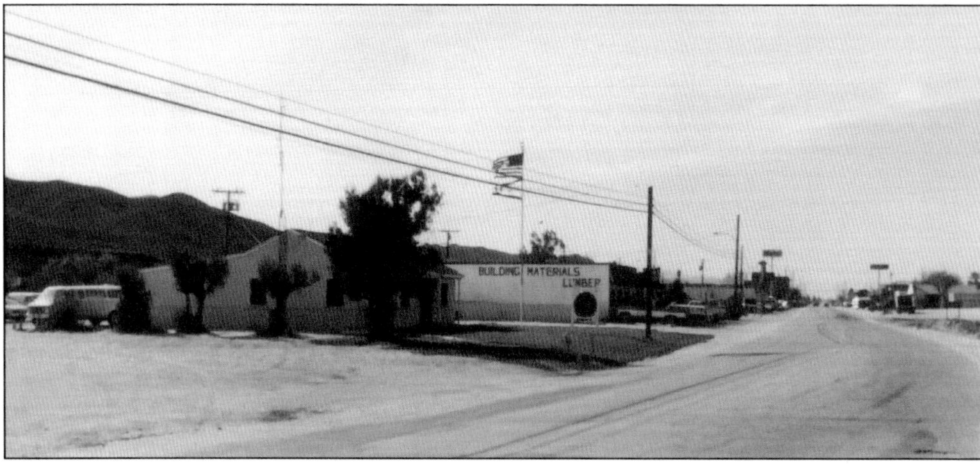

Temecula Lumberyard, 1974. As the building boom started in the 1970s, the lumberyard and hardware store enjoyed a brisk business. This was a replacement lumberyard after the first one, owned by Al Nienke, burned down on the west side of Murrieta Creek. This business also burned, as seen in the photograph below. (TVHS.)

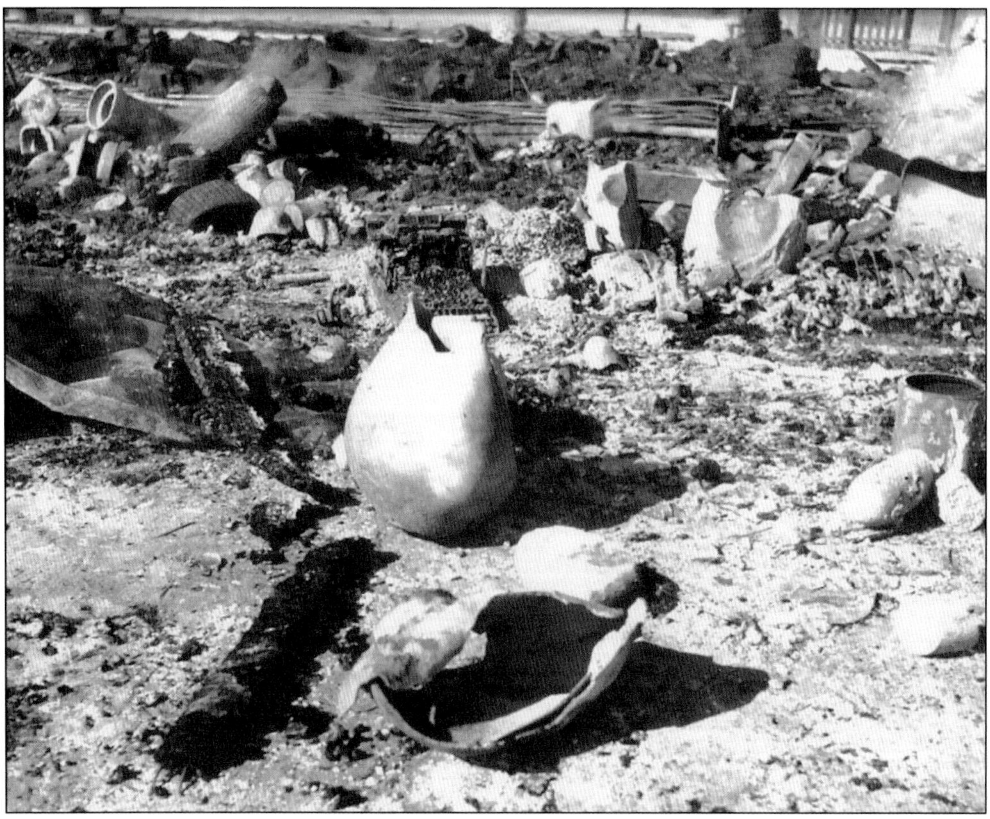

Indian Pots in Burned Lumberyard. As each building is demolished and each old-timer passes, information about Old Town's past is lost. Native American *ollas*, *metates*, and *manos* peek from the ashes as reminders of the original village and people of Old Town. Defective wiring started this fire on Front Street after midnight on September 4, 1956. State forestry stations responded from Elsinore, Perris, and San Jacinto. (SL.)

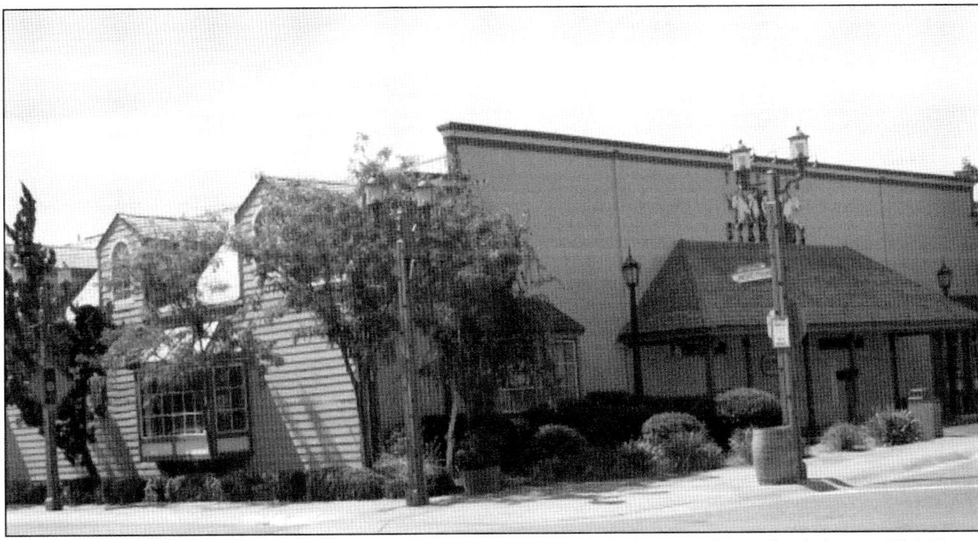

The Stampede. Lloyd Mullins opened the Stampede in 1995. It rivals nightclubs in Old Town and Pechanga as an entertainment destination where a historic Western theme permeates. Line dancing and Country Western music entices patrons to don their cowboy duds and get onto the dance floor. The business has also been used as a church. Nearby Dan's Feed and Seed is a longtime business where horsemen buy hay and supplies. (LB.)

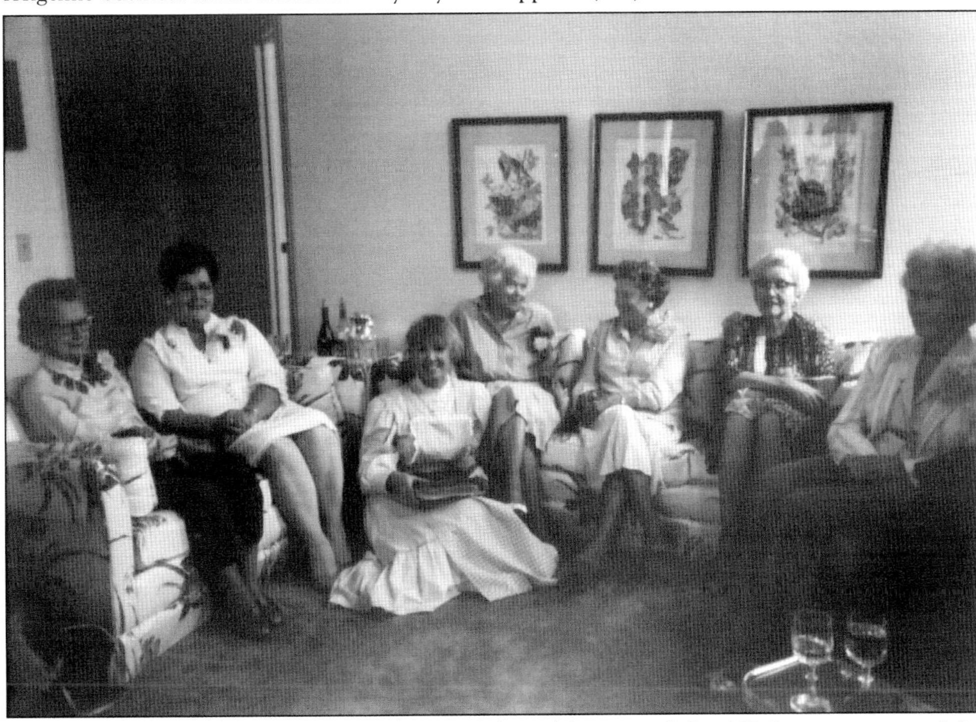

Temecula Sweethearts. In 1989, as part of the celebration of the 130th anniversary of the Temecula Post Office, these women were honored as longtime residents of Temecula. They are, from left to right, Margaret Ramsay, Nathaline Liefer, Peggy Querry, Leverne Parker, Marion Roripaugh, Mildred Tobin, and Odessa Querry. Also honored, but not in the photograph, were Mary Talley, Nellie Escallier, Dorothy Hotchkiss, and Annie Santa Maria. (EQ.)

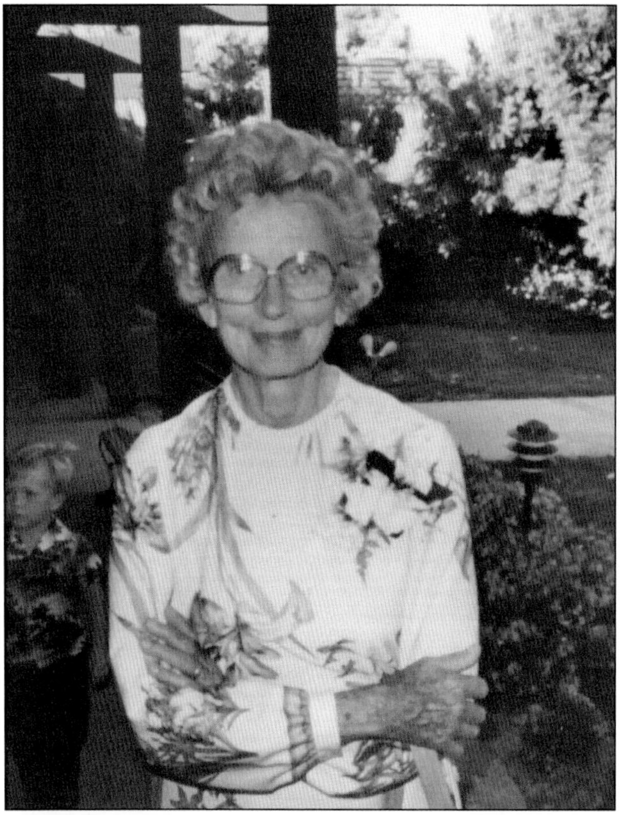

Margaret Roripaugh Ramsay. Margaret was the great-granddaughter of Eli Barnett, an early businessman in Temecula. She lived in the Temecula Valley all her life and married Dick Ramsay, shown in the bottom photograph on page 99. She opened the first antique shop in Temecula, called the Hitching Post, which featured a trademark hitching post in front of her store. She was a strong advocate for keeping Old Town historical. (EQ.)

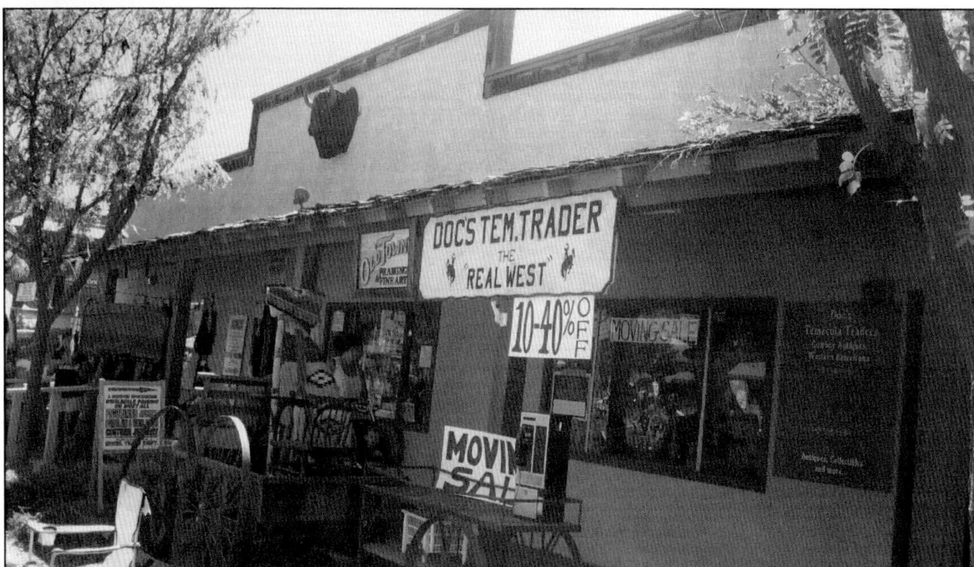

Doc's Temecula Trader. For many years, "Doc" Laine operated an antique store on Front Street near the Welty Building. He offered everything from Native American blankets and baskets to old military hardware and art. He regaled tourists and residents with Temecula lore until he passed away in 2011. An associate custom framer took over the store and moved it to Butterfield Square, calling it Old Town Framing and Fine Art. (RF.)

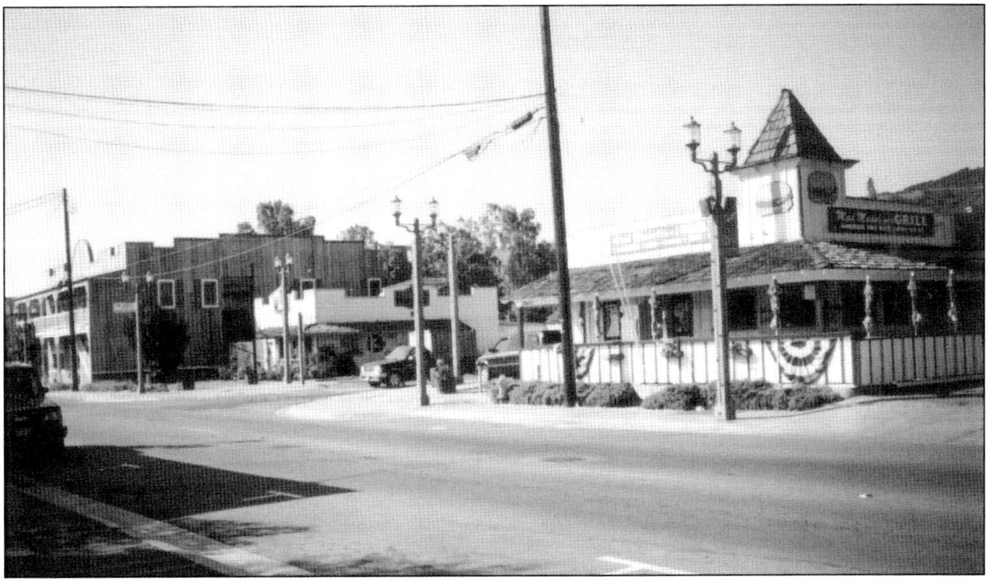

Mad Madeline's. This restaurant was constructed by Rancon in the late 1970s across the street from the former Knott home. The Temecula Creek Plaza was designed as a new center in the 1890s theme. Also in the plaza is the 4,000-square-foot Hardy Building, completed in 1980. Tesoro Winery has a tasting room and gift shop downstairs, and Destination Temecula has an upper-story office. (LB.)

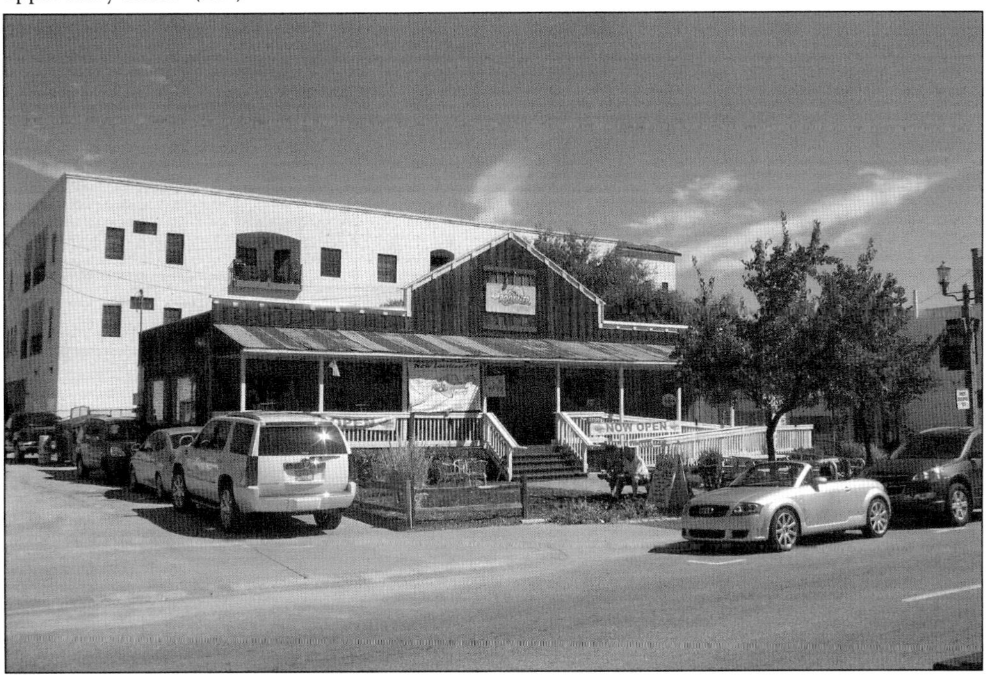

Old Town Root Beer Company. This building was made from a double-wide mobile home with a facade and tin roof to fit in with Old Town's Western theme. Until a surge of construction in the new millennium, many of the businesses in Old Town were of similar composition, some of which were moved from the dismantled Camp Haun. This was a thrift store, a wine bar, and delicatessen before its present use. (LB.)

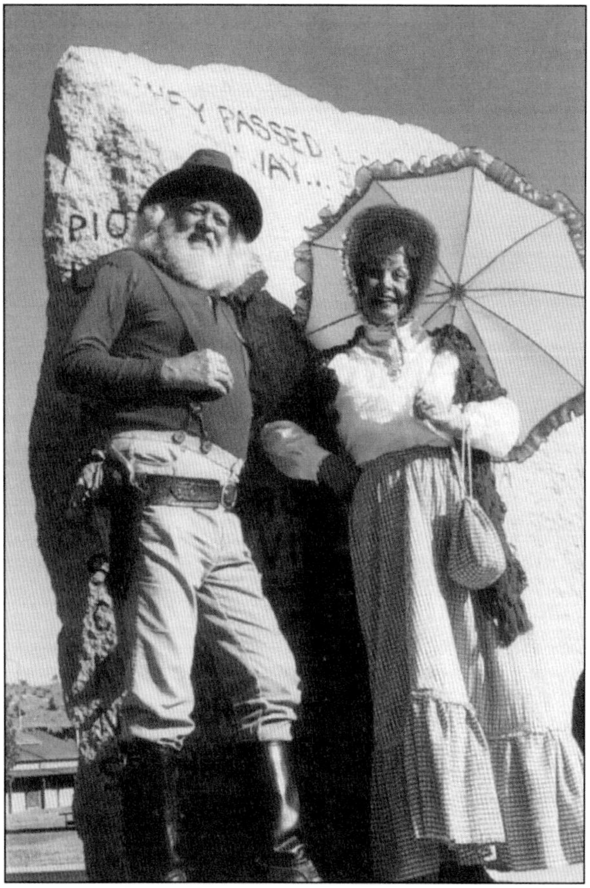

Bob and Bea Taylor. The Taylors served as Old Town greeters in the 1980s and 1990s, making visitors feel welcome and entertained in Old Town. Bob, at a tall six feet, four inches, was hard to miss on Old Town streets. He dressed as a California prospector, and Bea wore a bonnet and carried a parasol. They interacted with tourists and told stories about Temecula history, always spiced with humor. (BT.)

Temecula Valley Museum. John Bianchi built a frontier museum in what is now the Army-Navy store on Jefferson in 1982. He closed it in 1985 and sold his artifacts to private collectors and the Gene Autry Western Heritage Museum, and some became the basis for the Temecula Valley Museum collection. This museum opened in Sam Hicks Monument Park in 1999. A Senior Activity Center is next door. (LB.)

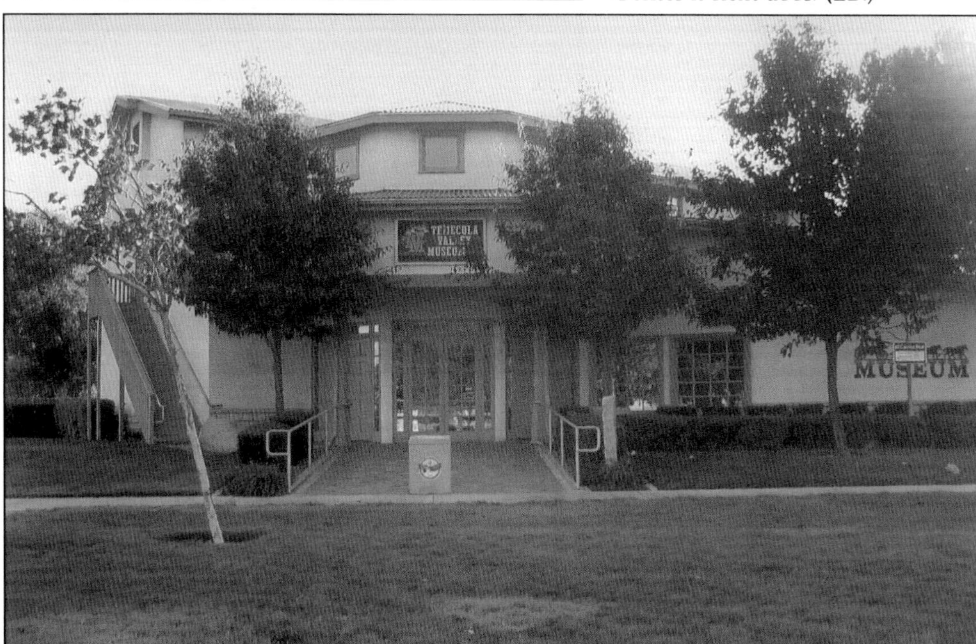

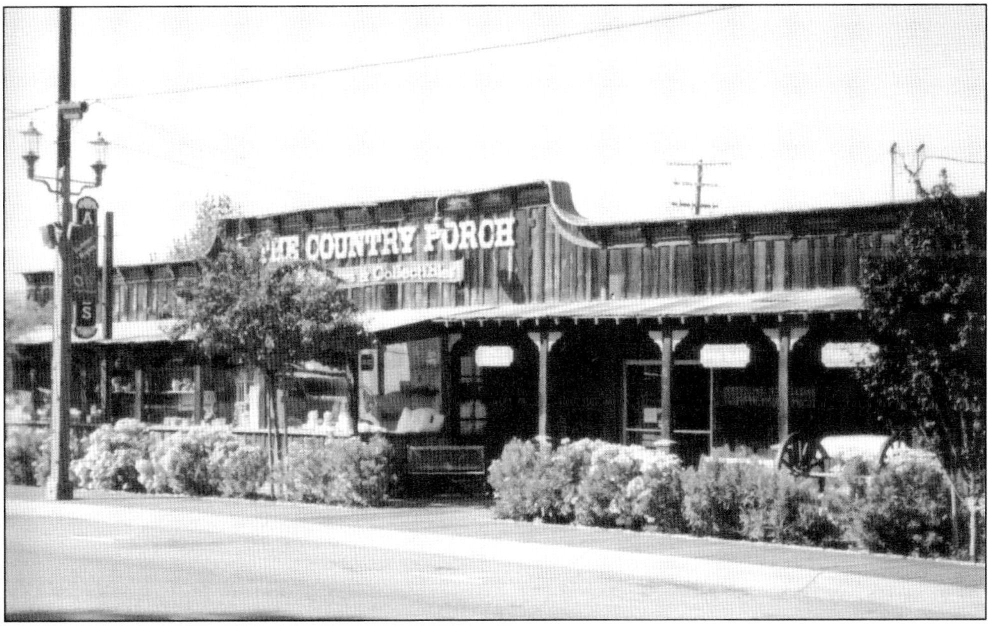

TEMECULA MARKET. Friedemanns opened a meat market at this location, and it later was a small grocery store, the only market in town after the Burnham Store closed. The former market became Country Porch Antiques, and the building was razed in 2012. (LB.)

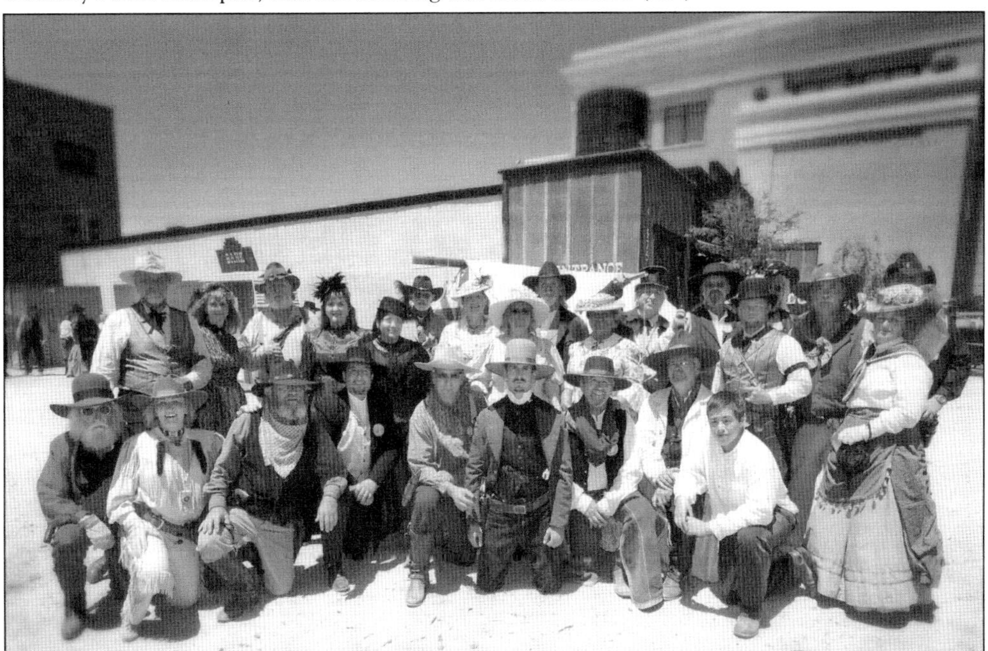

OLD TOWN TEMECULA GUNFIGHTERS. The Old Town Temecula Gunfighters started in Temecula in 1989. They perform skits monthly in Old Town to help keep the spirit of the Old West alive and to entertain the locals and tourists. The Old Town Temecula Gunfighters dress in 1880s clothing and host Western Days, an annual event in Old Town, with other reenactor groups from Southern California. They promote gun safety and raise money for various groups. (SE.)

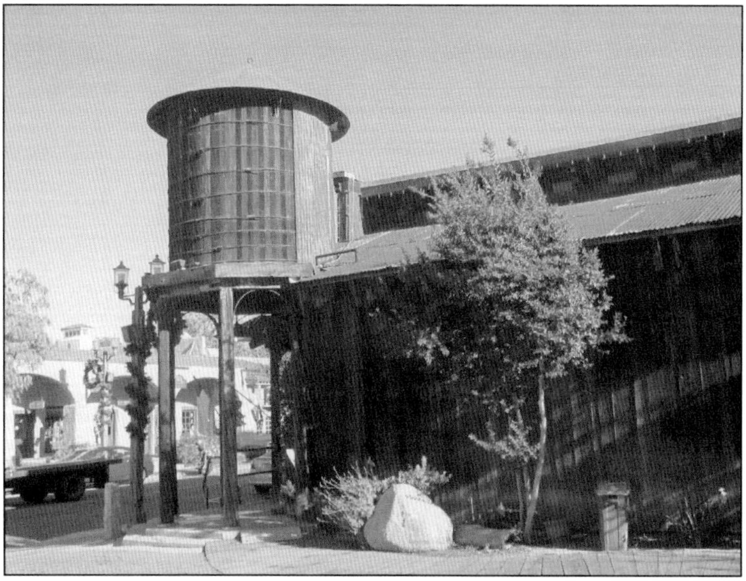

Water Tank on Front Street. In the 1970s and 1980s, Old Town became the palette of artist Bob Morris and his imprint is everywhere. This shows Morris's reconstruction of the buildings north of the bank, including details like the water tank, which is also seen in the photograph at the top of page 53. (JH.)

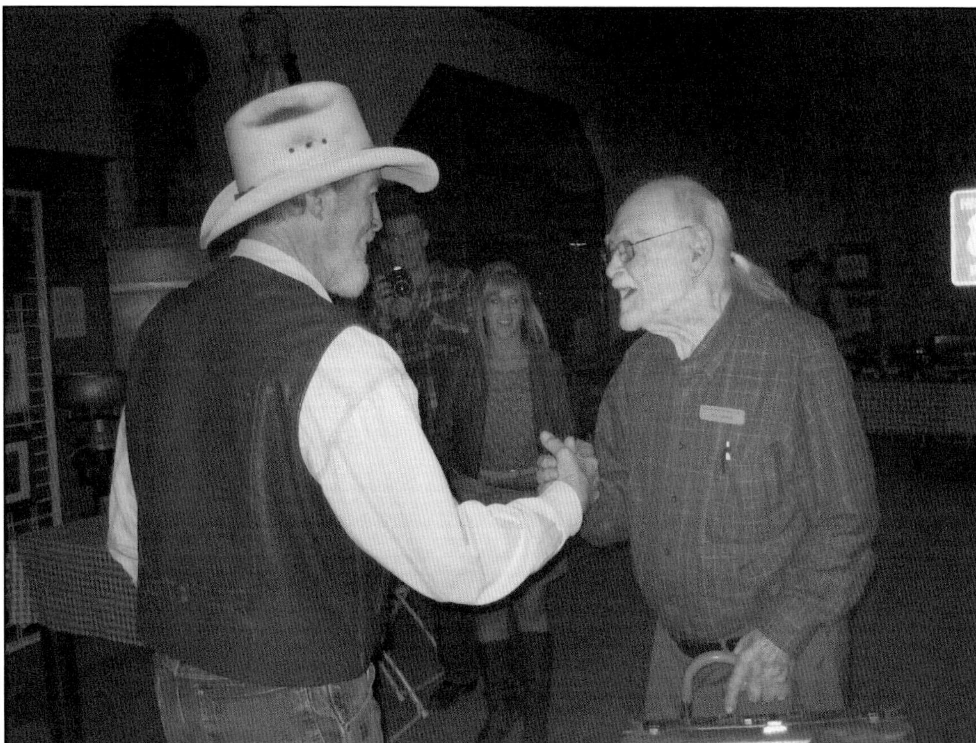

Bob Morris and Bill Harker, 2010. The Vail Ranch Restoration Association applauds these two men who have greatly influenced the saving of the historic Old Town. Bill, shown on the right, served as treasurer of the historical society well into his 90s, helped to start the Balloon and Wine Festival, served on the Old Town Review Board, and owned *Rancho News*. His chronicling of the historic past always includes a humorous and memorable quip. (RF.)

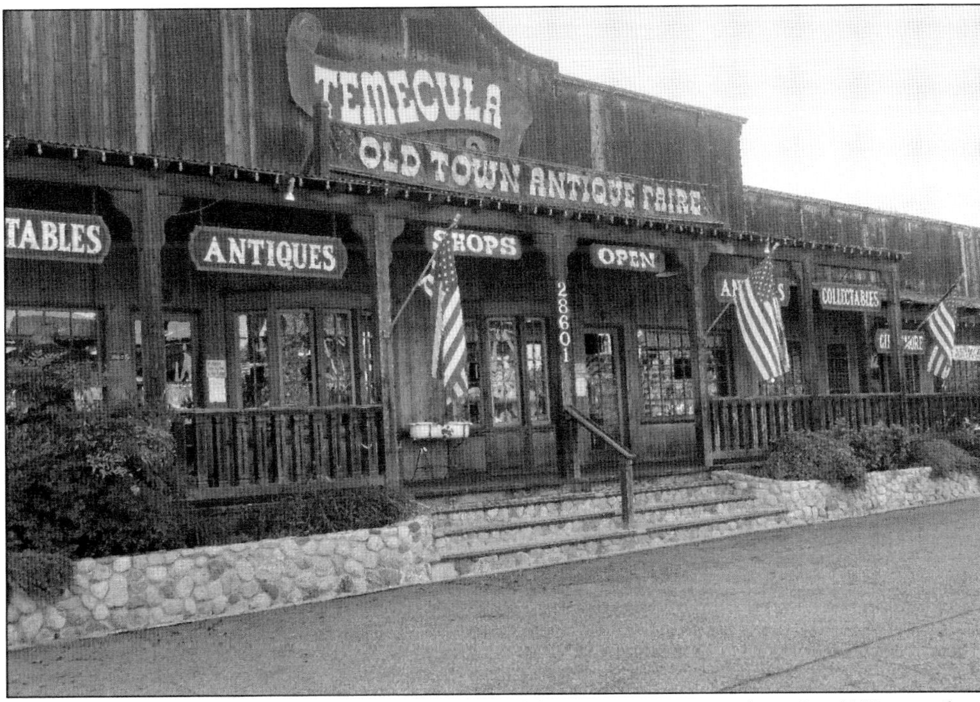

TEMECULA OLD TOWN ANTIQUE FAIRE. This building was constructed in the 1970s north of the bank. It is one of the many antique venues that draw tourists to Temecula. Café Daniel is located at the south end of the building where weary shoppers rest their feet. A long porch with several entrances invites customers to check the wares of several antique vendors with booths inside. (BM.)

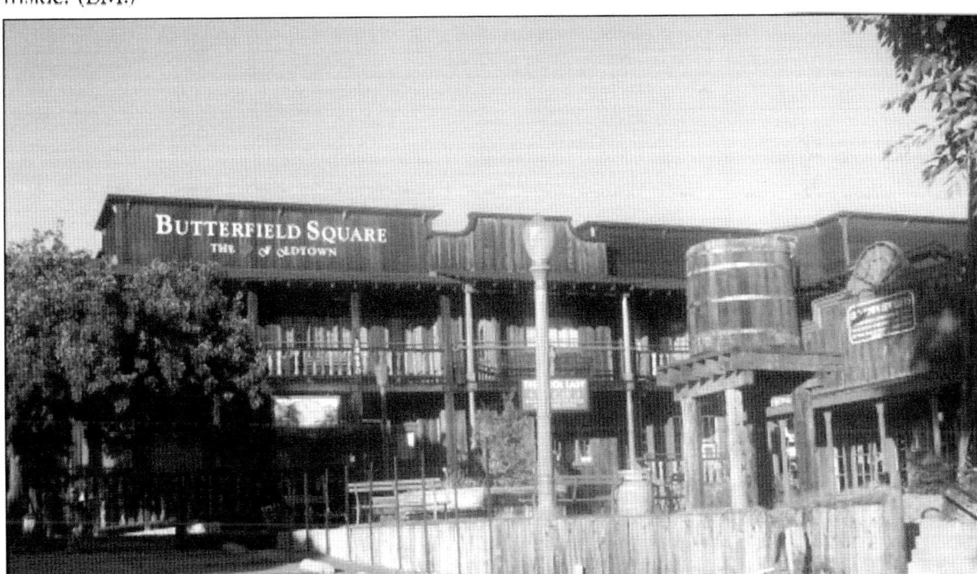

BUTTERFIELD SQUARE. While many saw this as a desolate ruin where a 76 Station and old motel once sat, Bob Morris saw a prime location to build his first architectural project in Temecula. From materials collected from an old Vail barn and elsewhere, he designed the unique Western center with wood-plank sidewalks and porches and a windmill. It opened for business in 1980. (LB.)

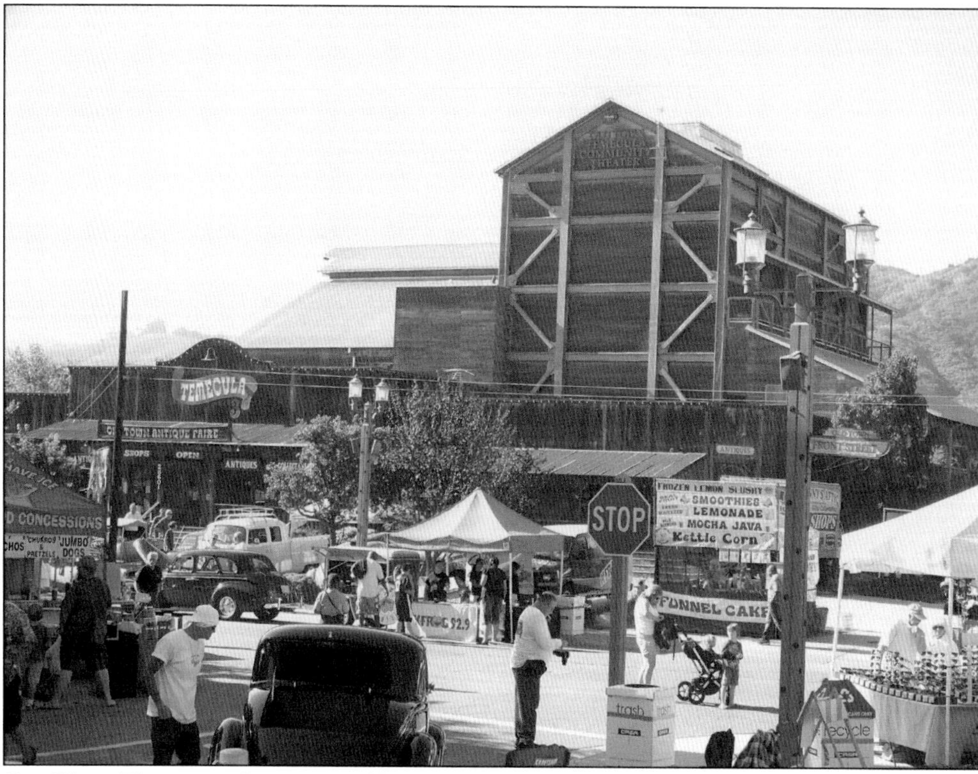

Old Town Temecula Community Theater. Jeannie Burns envisioned a permanent performing arts center for Temecula but did not live to see what her estate eventually helped to fund. She started the Temecula Players in 1977, and they performed in a warehouse on Ynez Road where the audience sat in plastic patio chairs. It was a far cry from the $11-million theater auditorium that opened in 2005 with 358 seats and an orchestra pit. (JH.)

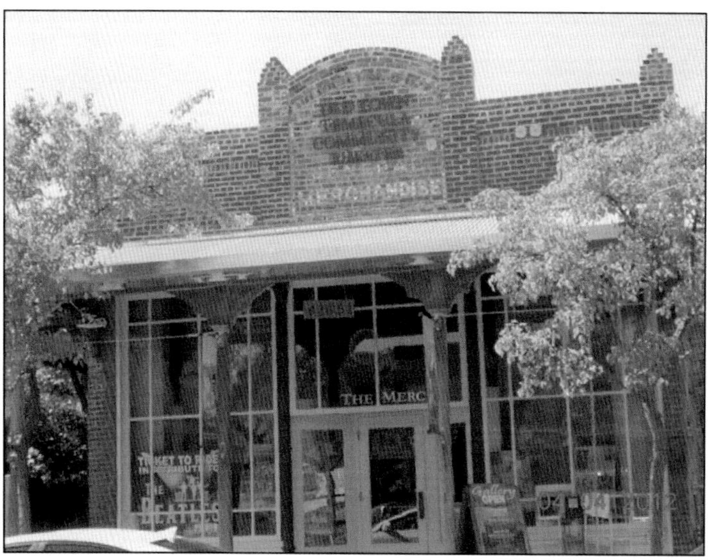

Temecula Mercantile Building, 1964. The community theater, shown in the photograph above, is behind the old mercantile store that was retrofitted and is now used as a ticket office, small performance venue, and an art gallery. This was once a center of community commerce as well as an antique store. (DB.)

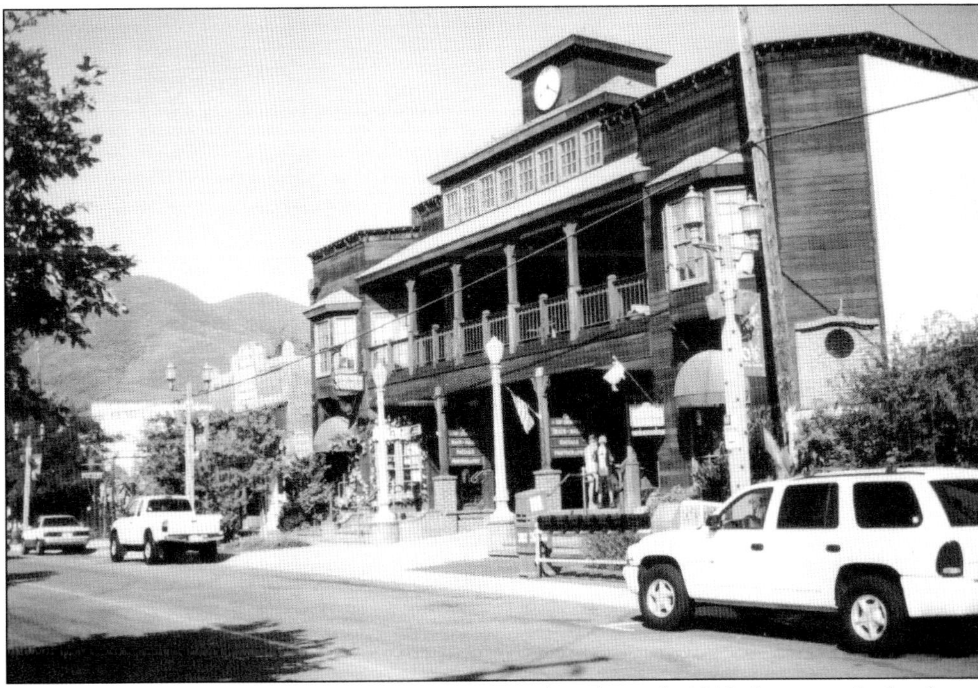

CLOCK TOWER BUILDING. This building, constructed in the early 1990s between the bank and mercantile store, formerly had a gallery and small concert venue upstairs. It now has several suites leased by different businesses. It is notable for its drive-through design and a bronze Morris art piece embedded in the driveway. (LB.)

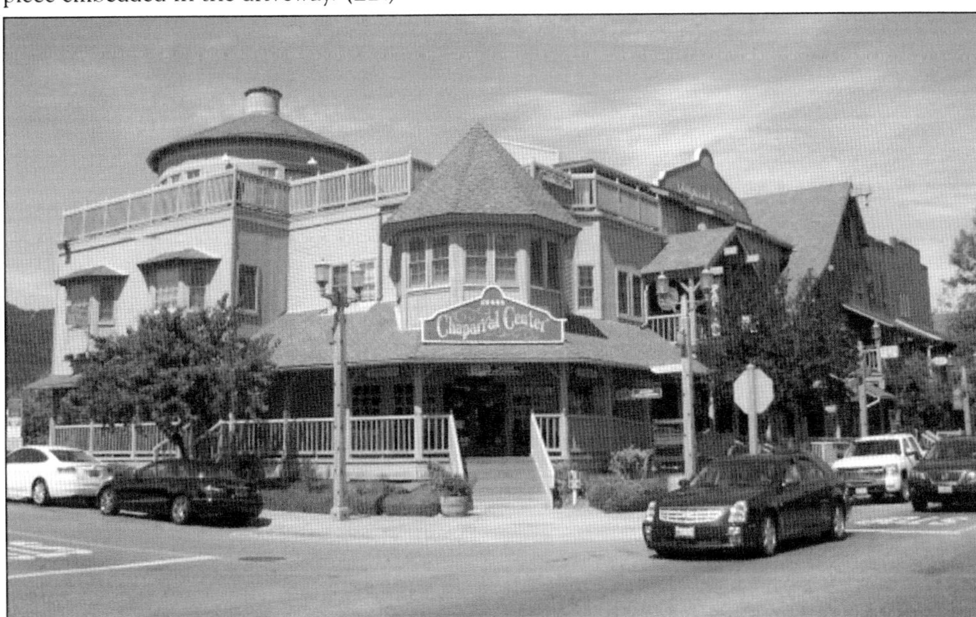

CHAPARRAL CENTER. When it was constructed in 1986 on the corner of Sixth and Front Streets, it was the first three-story built in Old Town, a distinction for two decades. Retail shops were on the first floor with business offices on the second and third levels. Lydia's Salon upstairs was owned by the wife of Karel Lindemanns, one of the first city councilmen. (BM.)

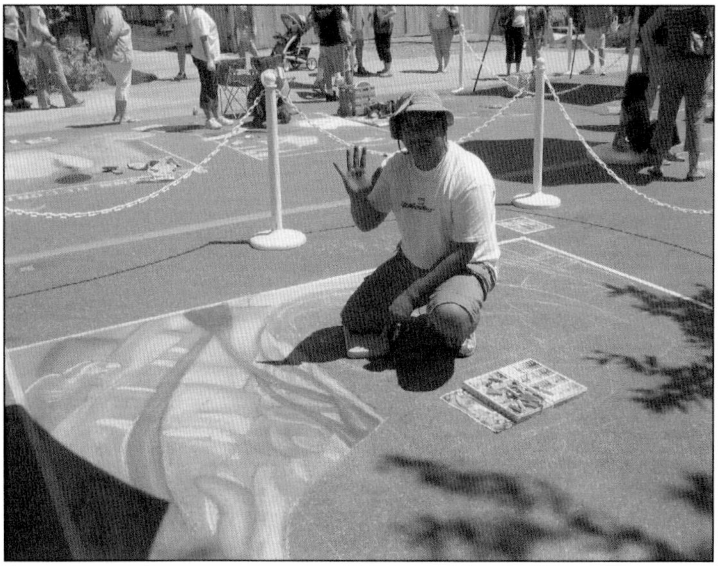

Street Painting Festival. Since the annual event began in 2001, the streets of Temecula are ornamented by vibrantly colored chalk art. Over 80 artists bend over hot asphalt for two days competing for awards. Children are given chalk and a small square of pavement to participate alongside accomplished artists. This photograph shows award-winning artist Jesus Gutierrez. (JG.)

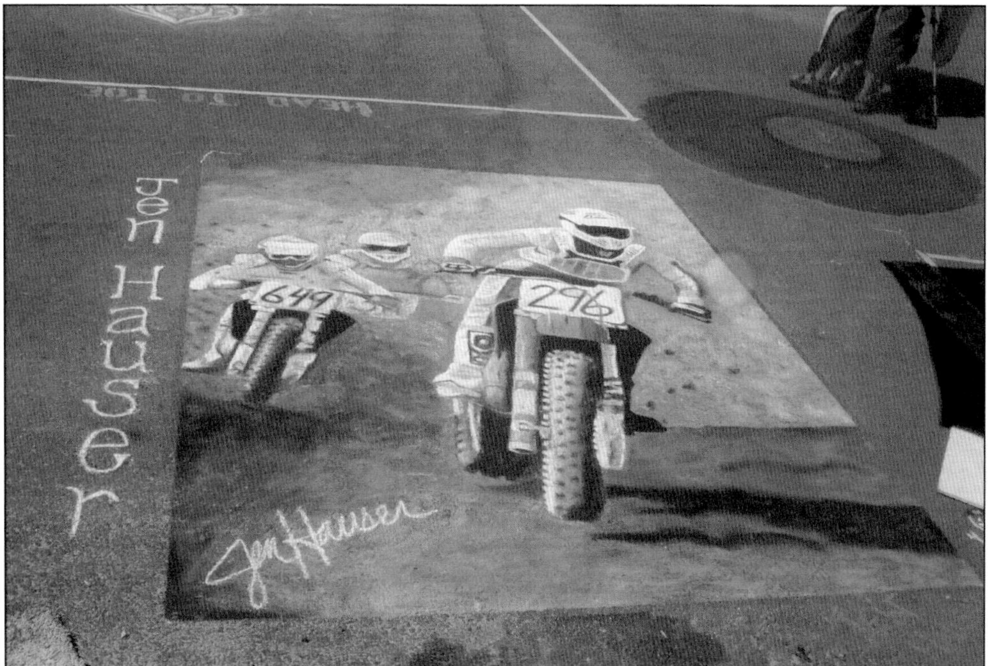

Chalk Painting to Honor Gene Knott. In this chalk painting duplicated from a photograph, Jennifer Hauser gave a tribute to Eugene Knott, a descendant of a pioneer family, remembering his love of sports and the outdoors. The attached dedication said: "Gene Knott is what Temecula history is all about; he loved this city. He will always be in people's hearts." (JK.)

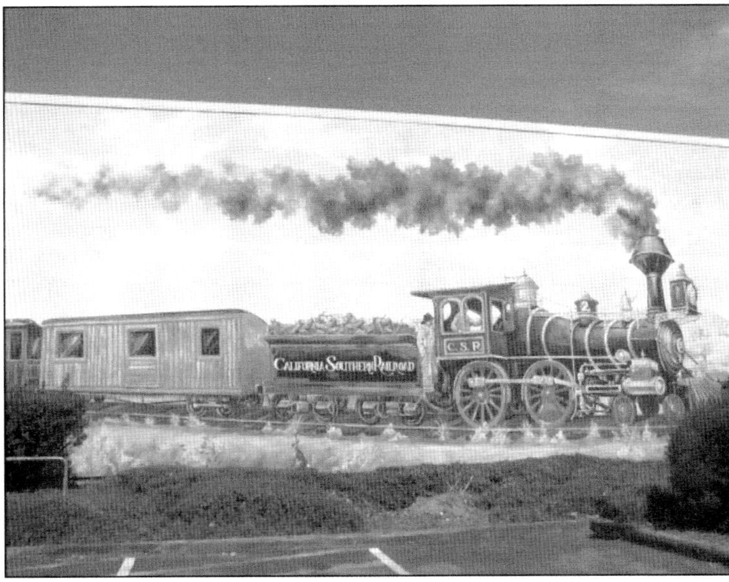

Stage Stop Mural. The Temecula Stage Stop (the Greyhound bus depot) is on the corner of Front and Sixth Streets. A 450-foot-long mural by Robin Golden in the parking lot behind it depicts Temecula's history from stagecoaches to trains and on through the balloon and wine era. On Saturday mornings, crowds come for the farmer's market in the parking lot. (LB.)

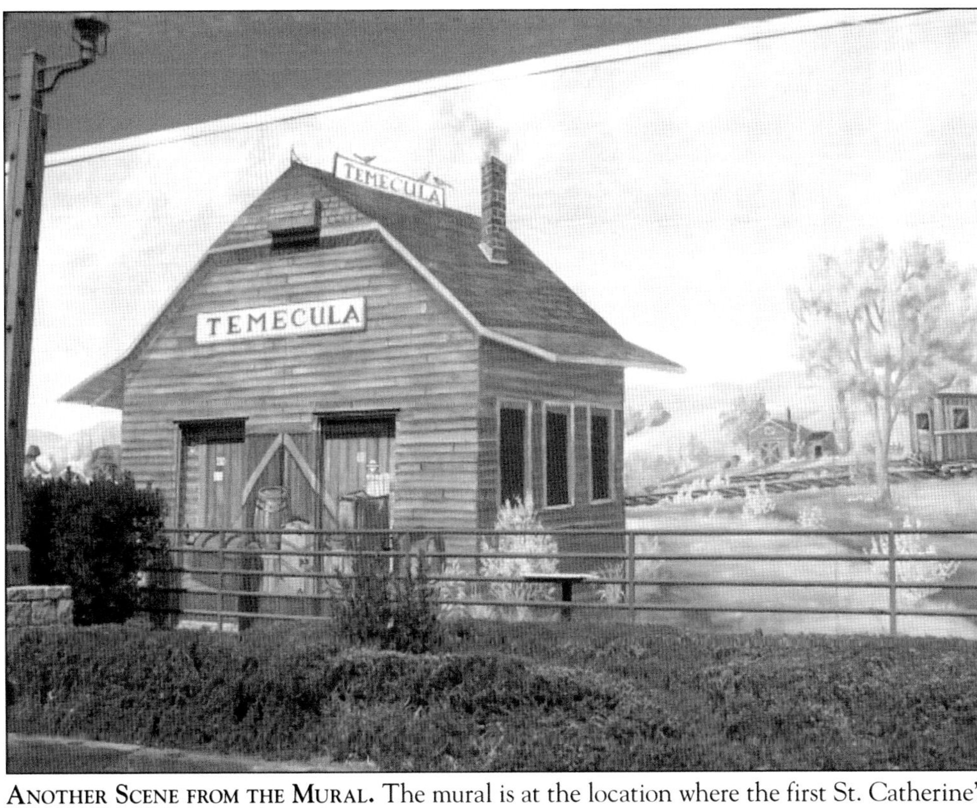

Another Scene from the Mural. The mural is at the location where the first St. Catherine's Church sat. A depiction of the Balloon and Wine Festival, once held in Old Town, is presently obscured. The festival started in 1984 and attracts over 40,000 visitors. Car shows like the annual Rod Run attract up to 65,000 car enthusiasts using Old Town as their background since the early 1980s. (LB.)

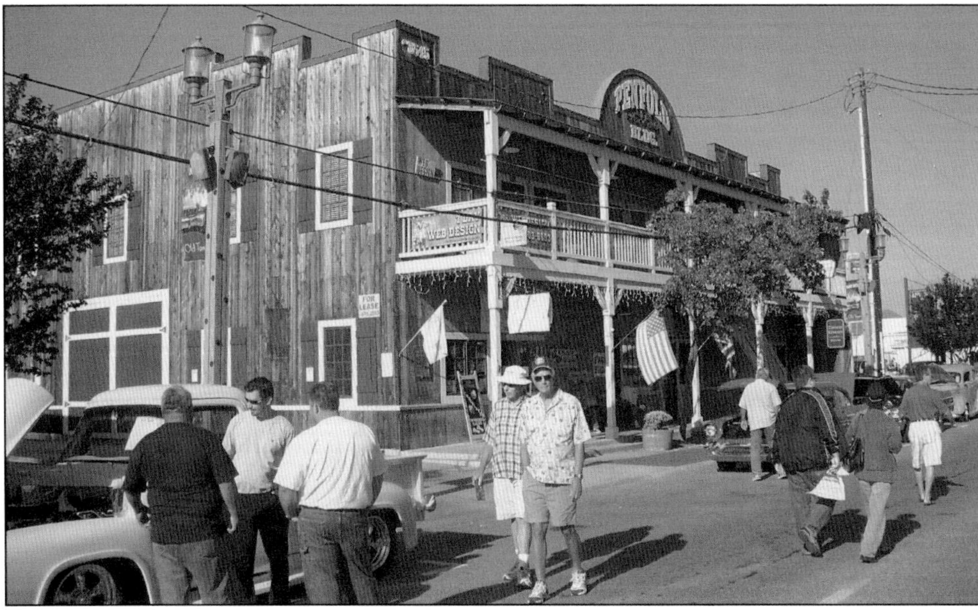

Penfold Building No. 1. Ladd Penfold built the two-story, 11,000-square-foot building on the former site of Al Knott's Garage in 2002. The structure with its wooden facade is in keeping with the 1890s Old West motif adopted by the Temecula Town Association in 1977. The Knott garage is shown in the bottom image on page 70. This photograph was taken during the fall 2011 Rod Run. (JH.)

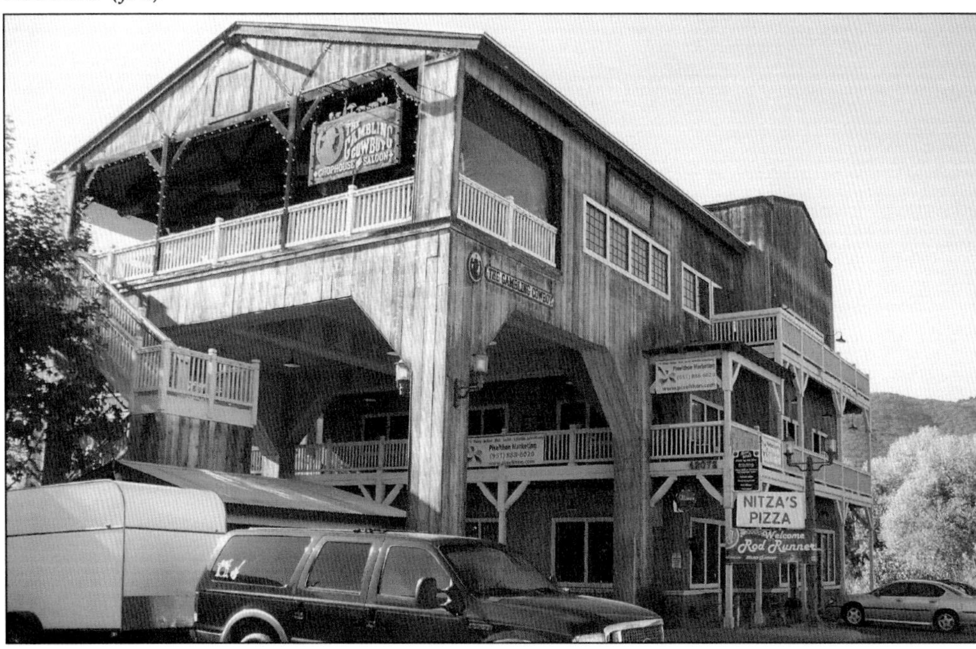

Penfold Building No. 2. In 2005, Penfold built a second structure, a three-story, 23,000-square-foot building, behind the first. The first level leases for retail shops and the second level to business offices. An elevator to the third floor goes to an upscale steakhouse restaurant, with a 16-by-40-foot porch offering a good view of the historic town. The Penfolds also own the Penfold restaurant and formerly owned the KRTM radio station. (JH.)

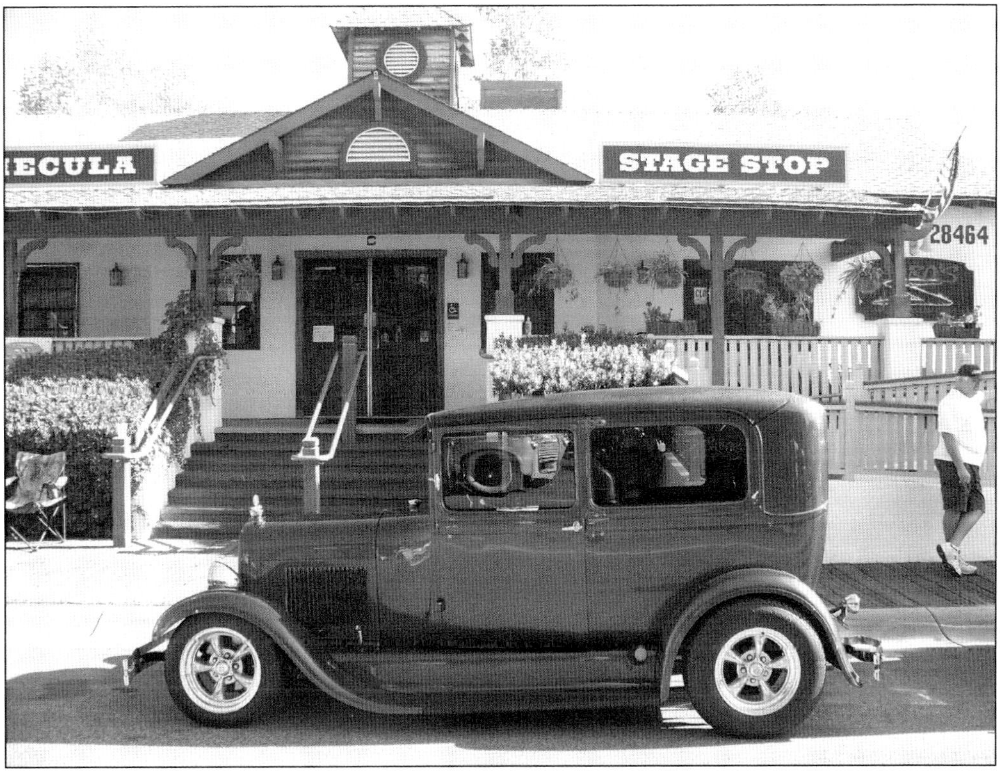

The Temecula Stage Stop. This bus station was designed to represent the old Temecula Train Depot. The Temecula Old Town Review Board and the Temecula Planning Commission give approval for each structure and sign in Old Town to keep the historic district theme. Sorro's restaurant is the current tenant, following McDonald's and Sweet Lumpys. Other businesses are a camera shop and Ed Dool's beer garden at the north end of the building. (JH.)

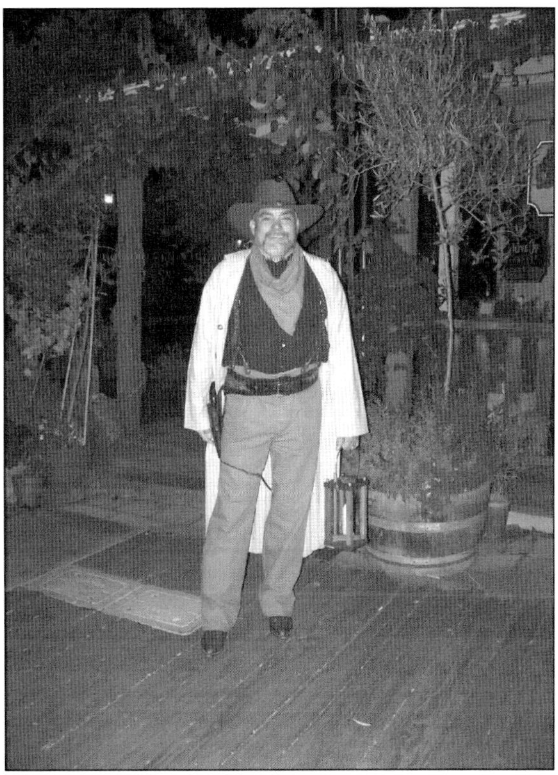

Walking Tours. There are several ways to see Old Town on foot. One is with Dale Garcia, pictured, on one of his Candlelight Tours that start at the Palomar Hotel on Saturday evenings. The Temecula Valley Museum also gives occasional walking tours. Old Town merchants offer free self-guided walking tour brochures produced by the Temecula Valley Historical Society. On weekend evenings in the summer, carriage rides are available. (LB.)

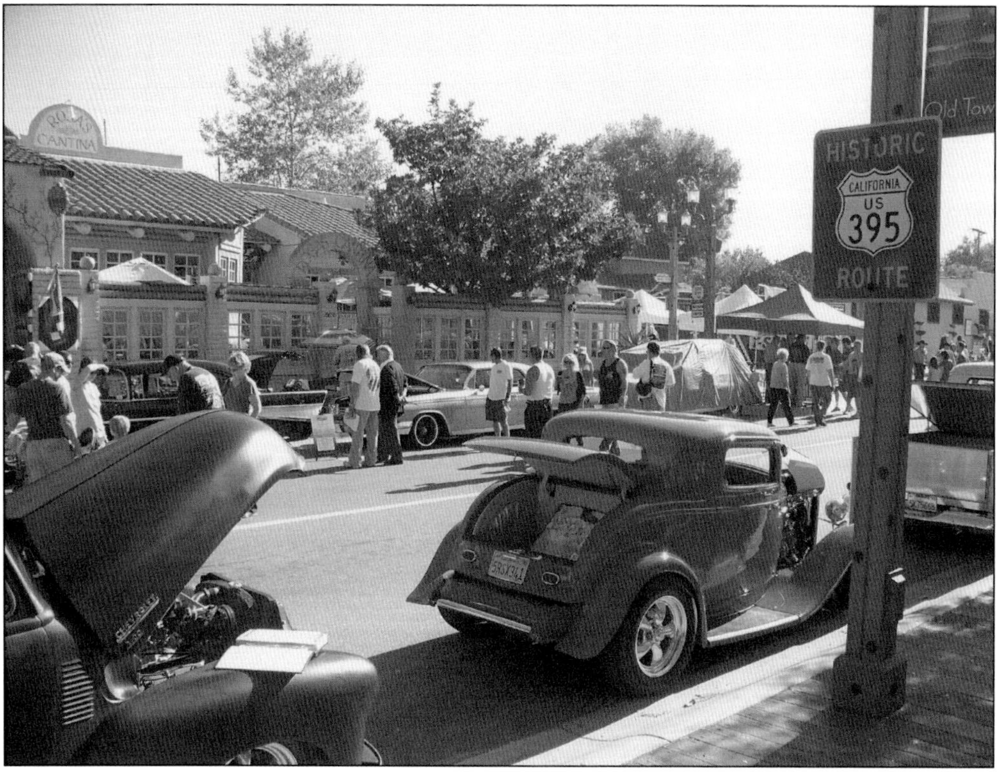

HIGHWAY 395. The sign shown in front of Rosa's Cantina is there because of a concerted effort by the Historic Route 395 Association, founded in 2010, and the Temecula Valley Historical Society after the State of California designated the original US Highway 395 a historic route from San Diego to Oregon. By the end of 2011, over 100 signs had been installed, including signs on Front Street. (JH.)

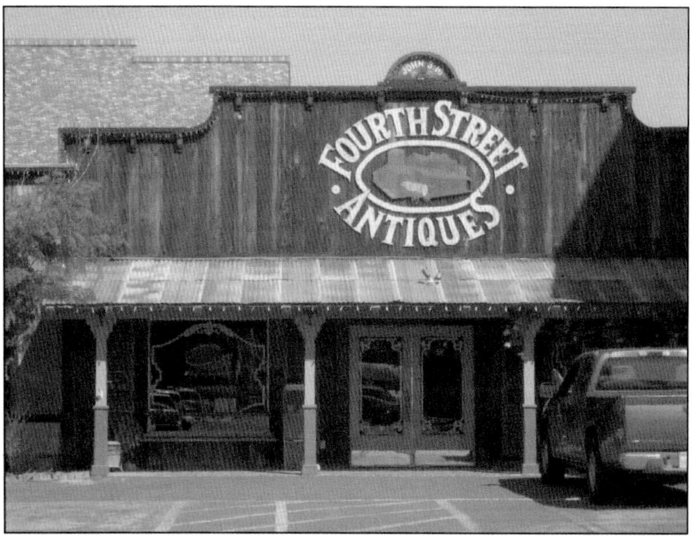

FOURTH STREET ANTIQUES. The tin roof and historic facade blend the former Napa automobile parts business, built in 1970, with Old Town architecture. The white Burke Building next door, completed in 2007, is Classical Revival style similar to a turn-of-the-century bank. The professional office has a grand wood staircase, marble floors, and a two-story mural featuring local history in the lobby. (LB.)

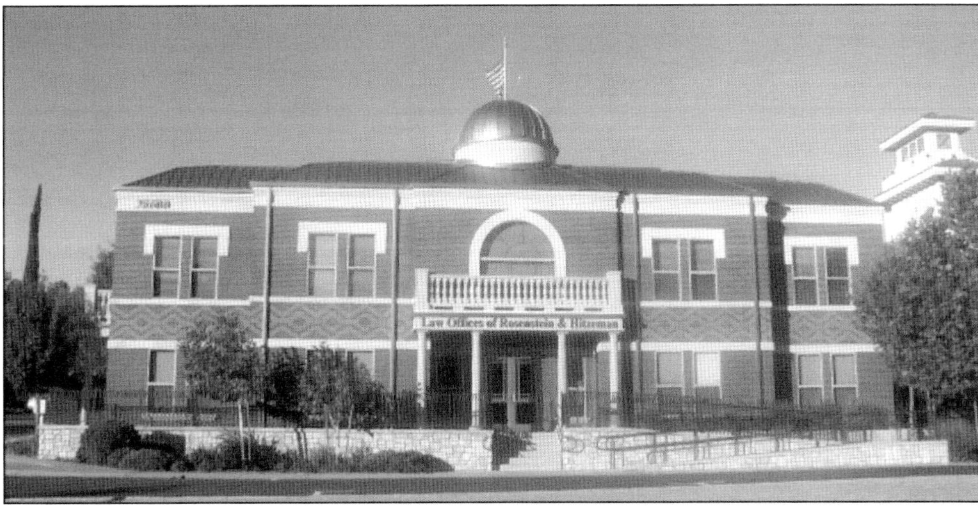

PENNY DOME BUILDING. Built in 2005, the Penny Dome Building is a two-story structure reminiscent of an 1850s brick facade courthouse. Located at the corner of Fourth and Mercedes Streets, the law offices of Rosenstein & Hitzeman currently occupy the building. It was constructed by Stuart Seidner, General Contractor, Inc. (LB.)

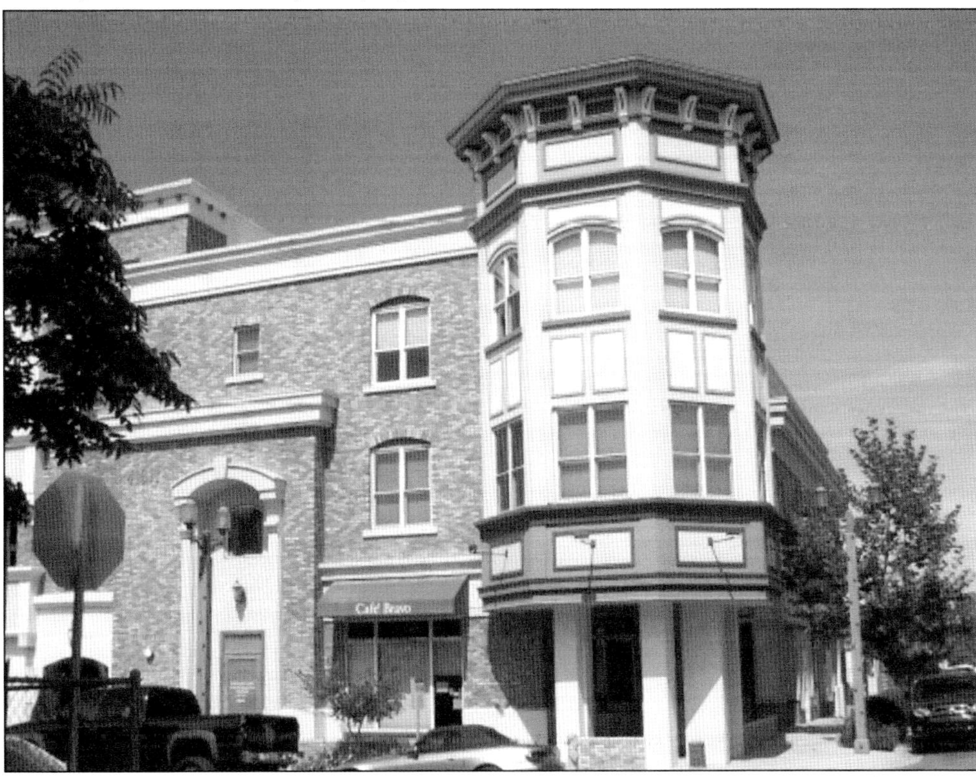

DALTON BUILDING. The Dalton I, a three-story building on the corner of Fifth and Mercedes Streets, has a 19th-century San Francisco facade. Café Bravo was the first retail business to occupy the corner on the first level, with businesses on each level. Now Robin's Nest—a coffee, lunch, and catering business—is in the former Café Bravo space. Dalton II is adjacent, providing storefront businesses and apartments. (JH.)

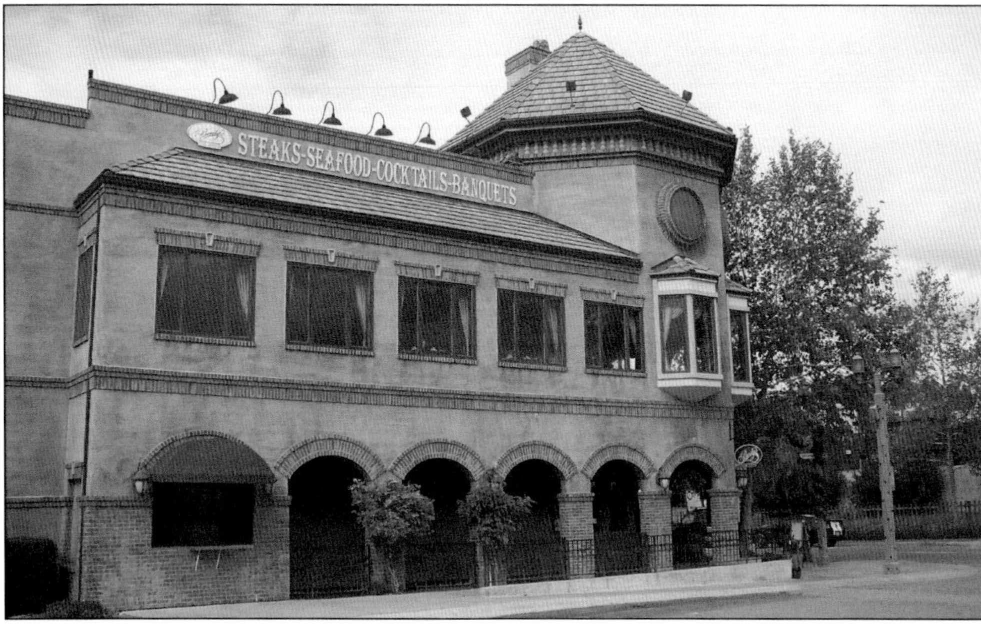

FRONT STREET BAR & GRILL. In October 2004, Chris and Kim Baily opened two restaurants in this two-story building at the corner of Front and Second Streets. The first-floor Front Street Bar & Grill offers casual indoor or patio dining. On the second floor, Baily's is an upscale restaurant. This building was the first in a construction trend of multistory themed buildings in the historic district. (LB.)

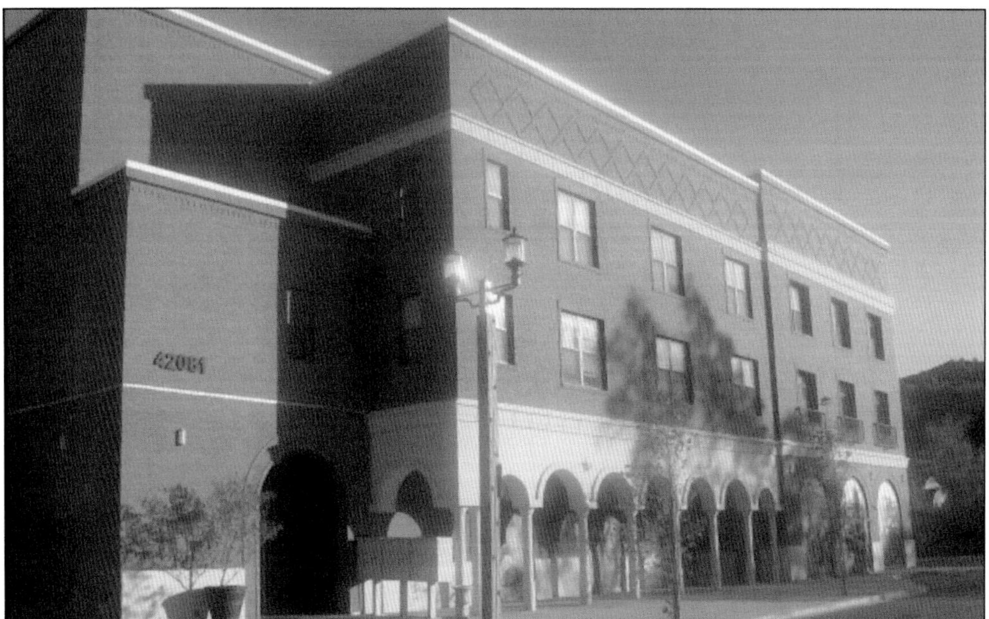

WAREHOUSE AT CREEKSIDE. Another Dalton development is the Warehouse at Creekside on Third Street. The three-story, 60,000-square-foot, brick building was completed in 2009. The building was partially financed with redevelopment funding and provides 32 affordable apartments. The first level was designated as restaurant space. At the time of this writing, it is still empty. (LB.)

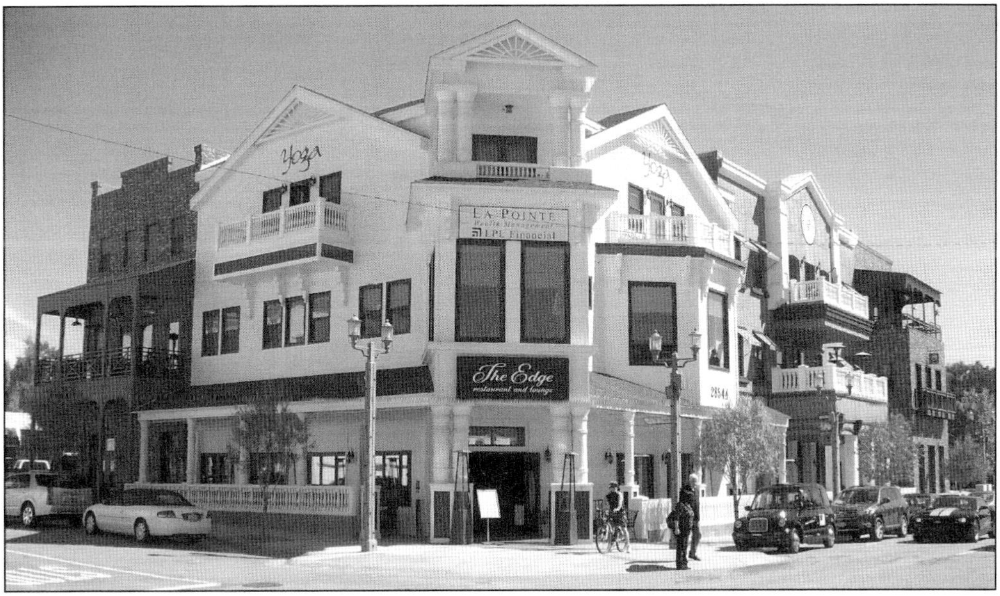

THE EDGE. The Old Town Center Building at the corner of Fifth and Front Street was completed in 2009. The three-story building features six facades representing 19th-century styles. With 29,502 square feet of space, the first floor provides for retail and an upscale restaurant, The Edge. The upper floors are professional office suites, some include private balconies. The Collective, a consortium of winemakers, has a business in this building. (JH.)

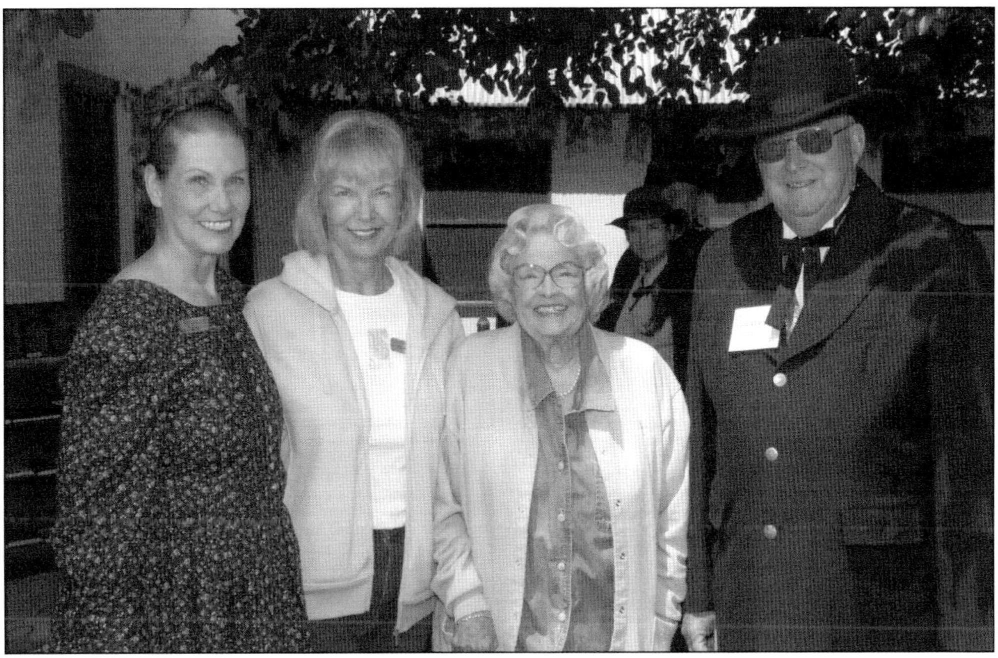

PRESIDENTS OF TEMECULA VALLEY HISTORICAL SOCIETY. The Historical Society headed by John Bianchi lasted from about 1977 to 1985. The Temecula Valley Historical Society formed in 2000. The first four presidents were, from left to right, Charolette Fox, Barbara Tobin, Eve Craig, and Jimmy Moore. They were followed by Bonnie Martland. The society helps to ensure the preservation of historical structures and presents information to the community. (RF.)

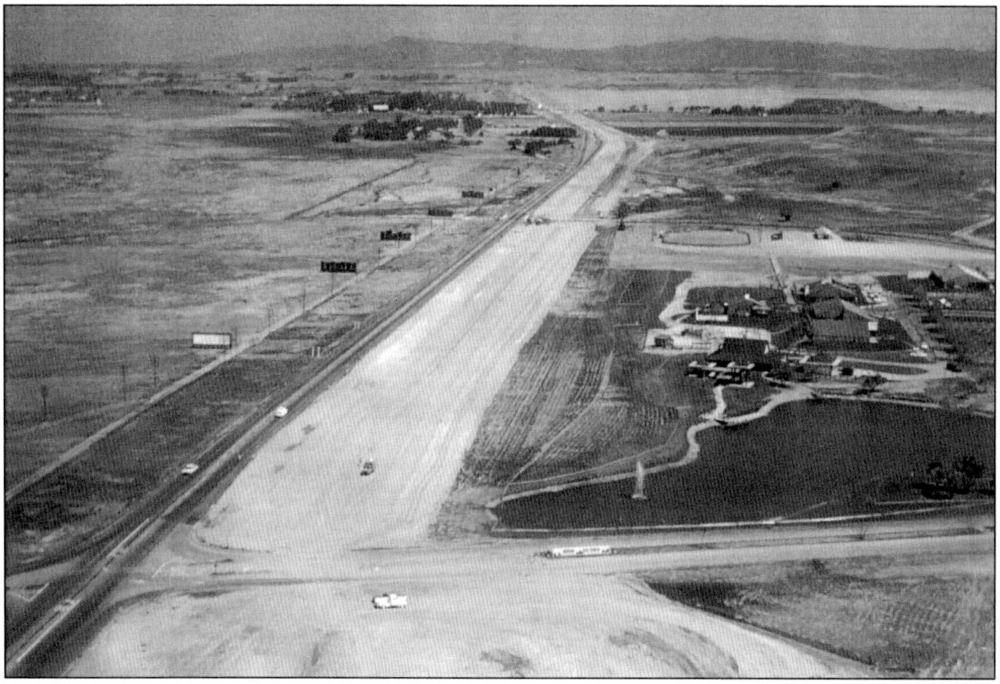

Construction of Interstate 15. Interstate 15 and Interstate 15 East replaced US Highway 395 by 1980. With the opening of the interstate highway, traffic increased in Temecula. During the housing booms of the 1980s and 1990s, people moved to the country with good freeway access to jobs in Los Angeles, Orange, and San Diego Counties. The Plaza is the development seen on the right. (JR.)

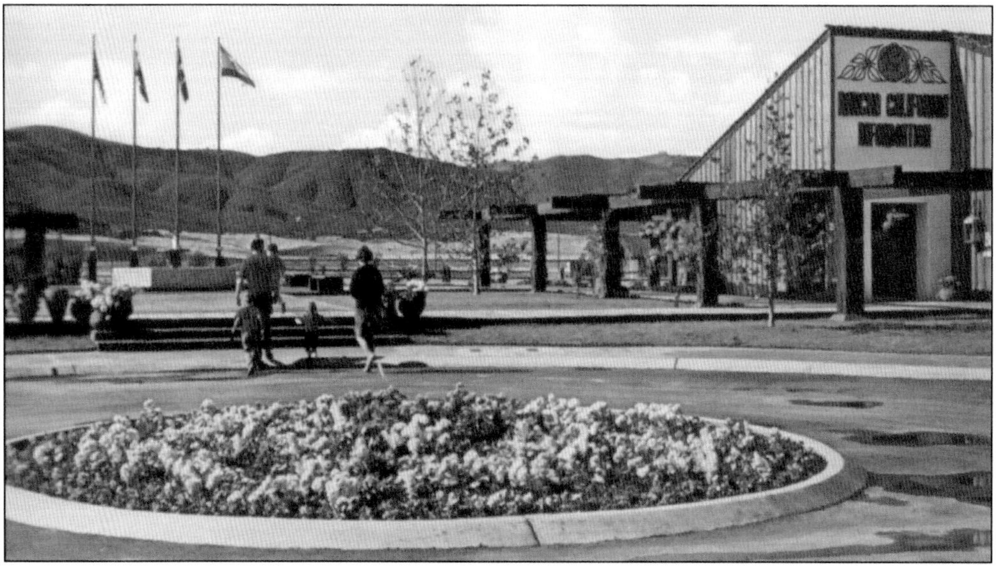

The Rancho California Plaza. The Plaza was built at the corner of Rancho California and Ynez Roads in 1967 to serve the first 1,500 households built in Rancho California. Some of the first businesses were a Richfield service station, motel, Rancho Market, Rancho Pharmacy, and Homestead restaurant. It expanded with a postal annex, a beauty salon, and a storefront public library. (TVHS.)

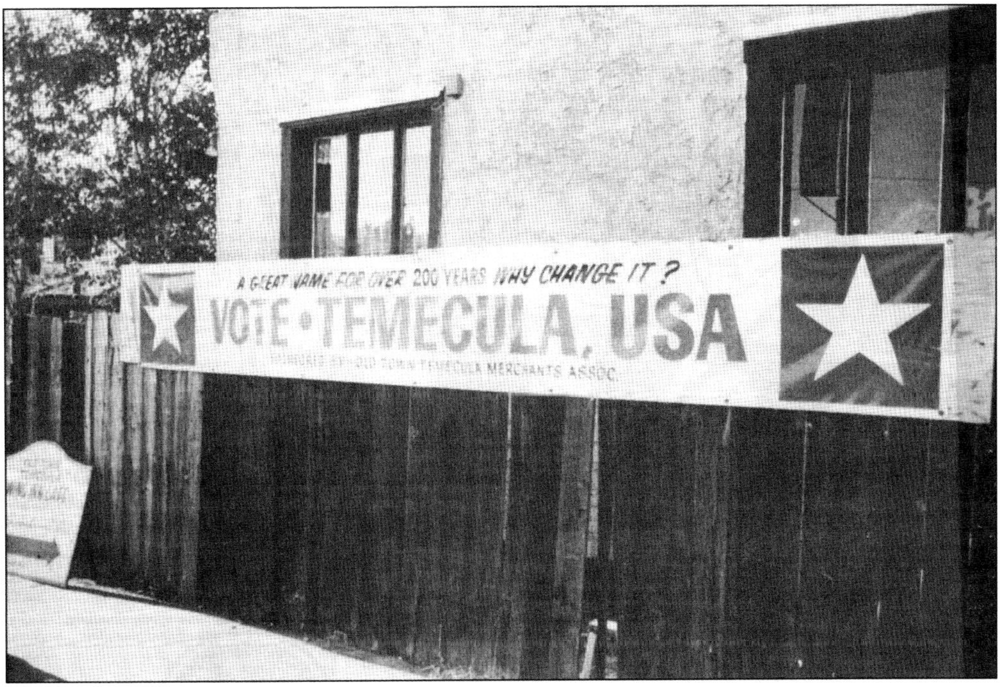

Temecula Cityhood. In 1989, the residents of Temecula voted in favor of cityhood and for the historical name, instead of Kaiser Aetna's Rancho California or the suggested Rancho Temecula or Temecula Valley. The members of the first city council were Ron Parks, Pat Birdsall, Sal Munoz, Karel Lindemanns, and Peg Moore. Parks served as the first mayor. The city has benefited from the strength and longevity of good leadership. (TVM.)

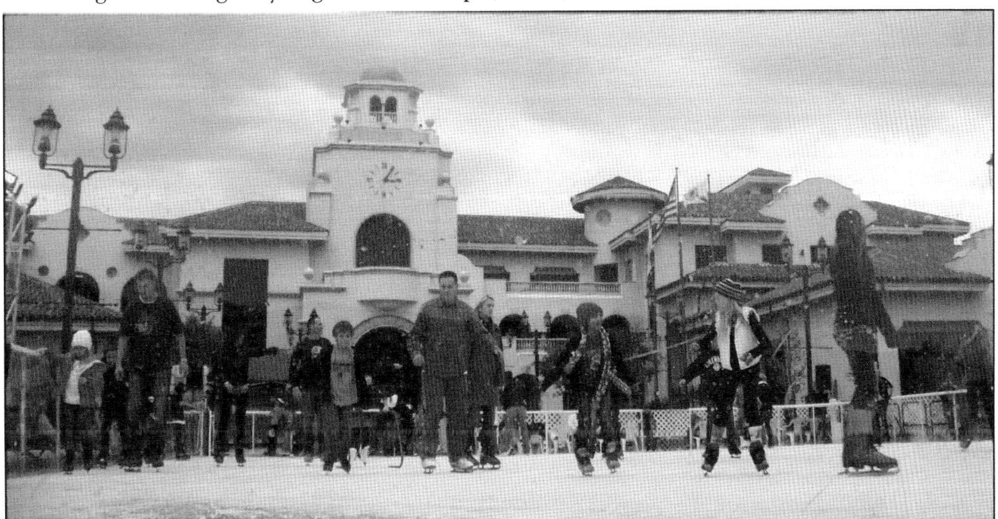

Civic Center. The Temecula Civic Center is a three-story stucco building with Mission-style architecture, a clock tower, and a red tile roof. The 95,500-square-foot structure is located at the east end of Main Street. It provides a conference center and parking garage and space for a police substation and the Temecula Valley Convention & Visitors Bureau. An ice-skating rink during the Christmas season adds holiday cheer. (JH.)